# Performance
# Measurement

**Harry P. Hatry**

*with a chapter by*
*Joseph S. Wholey*

# Performance Measurement

## Getting Results

THE URBAN INSTITUTE PRESS
Washington, D.C.

**THE URBAN INSTITUTE PRESS**
2100 M Street, N.W.
Washington, D.C. 20037

Library of Congress Cataloging in Publication Data.

Performance Measurement: Getting Results/Harry P. Hatry.

Includes bibliographical references and index.

1. Benchmarking (Management).   2. Performance—Evaluation.   I. Title.

HD62.15.H38
658.4'013—dc21

1999

99-41582
CIP

ISBN 0-87766-692-X (paper, alk. paper)

Printed in the United States of America

Distributed in North America by
University Press of America
4720 Boston Way
Lanham, MD 20706

THE URBAN INSTITUTE is a nonprofit policy research and educational organization established in Washington, D.C., in 1968. Its staff investigates the social and economic problems confronting the nation and public and private means to alleviate them. The Institute disseminates significant findings of its research through the publications program of its Press. The goals of the Institute are to sharpen thinking about societal problems and efforts to solve them, improve government decisions and performance, and increase citizen awareness of important policy choices.

Through work that ranges from broad conceptual studies to administrative and technical assistance, Institute researchers contribute to the stock of knowledge available to guide decisionmaking in the public interest.

Conclusions or opinions expressed in Institute publications are those of the authors and do not necessarily reflect the views of staff members, officers or trustees of the Institute, advisory groups, or any organizations that provide financial support to the Institute.

# DILBERT    Scott Adams

DILBERT reprinted by permission of United Feature Syndicate, Inc.

# Contents

## Part I: Introduction

## Part II: The Performance Measurement Process

## Part III: Analysis and Use of Performance Information

## Part IV: Other Performance Measurement Issues

## Part V: Summary

# Exhibits

# Preface

The origin of the performance measurement principles in this book dates back to the 1960s, if not the 1950s, when the RAND Corporation of Santa Monica, California, introduced what it called *systems analysis* (also called *cost-effectiveness analysis*) into its work for the Department of Defense. RAND undertook major studies, particularly for the Air Force, comparing the costs and effectiveness of different future weapons systems. Charles Hitch, who led that effort, subsequently became comptroller of the Defense Department under Secretary Robert McNamara.

At the Defense Department, Hitch introduced these cost and effectiveness concepts into planning, and the agency installed a technically sophisticated staff to perform the analysis required.

This initiative led to the development of program budgeting and what became known as Planning-Programming-Budgeting Systems (PPBS), pioneered in the Defense Department and then introduced into nondefense federal agency planning by President Lyndon Johnson in the late 1960s.

State and local governments also began experimenting with the techniques, but it quickly became clear that the analytical requirements of program budgeting, PPBS, and systems analysis generally were much more difficult to apply in the nondefense sector, where many different categories of customers were directly served and made their presence felt.

At about the same time, what became known as *program evaluation* began to spread widely in government—particularly the nondefense agencies of the federal government—encouraged by the new quantitative movement spurred on by PPBS. The U.S. General Accounting Office, under Elmer Staats, applied an analogous idea, that of program results auditing, which in countries such as Canada and the United Kingdom became known as *value-for-money* auditing. Unlike systems analysis and cost-effectiveness analysis, which are basically prospective analysis procedures, program evaluation and value-for-money auditing analysis primarily look backwards (but their eventual application is to help produce better decisions about the future).

The Urban Institute, shortly after its beginning in 1968, began to work in both program budgeting and program evaluation at the federal, state, and local levels. Its evaluation work was led by Joseph Wholey, the author of chapter 13. He has been one of the promulgators of *evaluability assessment*—a technique to be used before intensive evaluation work begins in order to ensure that the program selected for such examination can usefully be evaluated.

As the Urban Institute began working with state and local governments in an attempt to apply cost-effectiveness and systems analysis to their programs and services, it quickly became apparent that *state and local agencies had little information on the quality and outcomes of their services.* While some agencies routinely collected data on service outcomes (such as crime rates, traffic accident rates, health statistics, and education test scores), even these data were not typically used in a very systematic way to evaluate services. Over the next two decades, the Institute worked with state and local agencies to identify procedures that agencies could use to track the outcomes and quality of specific services—always with a citizen-customer focus. Such procedures later became known collectively as *outcome-focused performance measurement systems*, to be used as part of program and agency performance monitoring.

The Institute tested and promulgated the use of relatively new techniques, such as surveys of customers and trained observer ratings, finding them to be reasonably practical for state and local agencies.

Interest in the 1970s was low, with only a very small number of cities, such as Charlotte, North Carolina, Dayton, Ohio, and Sunnyvale, California, undertaking regular performance measurement. Meanwhile, a customer and service quality orientation received considerable emphasis in *In Search of Excellence* (Thomas J. Peters and Robert H. Waterman, 1982) and the work of W. Edwards Deming (such as *Out of the Crisis*, 1982)—both focusing initially on the private sector and eventually seeping into the public sector. A later book, *Reinventing Government*, by David Osborne and Ted Gaebler (1992), had considerable influence on federal, state, and local governments, giving particular emphasis to performance measurement and managing-for-results activities.

A major milestone occurred when, with bipartisan support, Congress passed and the executive branch passed and signed into law the Government Performance and Results Act of 1993 (P.L. 103–62). This forced all federal agencies and their major programs to begin to take performance measurement seriously. Major and quite impressive efforts in performance measurement have begun in the private, nonprofit sector—notably by local United Ways, with leadership by United Way of America—and are spreading to many national service and accreditation organizations, such as the Joint Commission on Accreditation of Healthcare Organizations (which is beginning to link accreditation of hospitals and other health care organizations to the outcomes of patient care).

At the same time, a number of countries outside the United States have been active in program evaluation, value-for-money auditing, and performance measurement. The United Kingdom, New Zealand, Australia, and Canada—to name a few English-speaking countries—have begun to focus much more attention on *serving* customers well, including the regular measurement of service quality and outcomes.

This book emerges in part from these programs and in part from the Urban Institute's numerous projects with federal, state, and local (including United Way) agencies between 1971 and 1998. The Institute's efforts to provide practical, detailed material that can help agencies interested in performance measurement to improve their services have encompassed police, fire, solid waste collection, transportation, social services, elementary and secondary education, corrections, environmental protection, and economic development programs.

Chapters 1 through 9 synthesize much of the Urban Institute's work on performance measurement over the past 25 years. These chapters focus on development of measurement procedures for a wide range of public services. The remaining chapters discuss issues, such as results-based budgeting, other major uses of performance information, and the need for ways to monitor the quality and usefulness of performance measurements. Agencies and scholars are only in the early stages of working out satisfactory solutions for these issues.

The Urban Institute's work on results-based performance measurement has been considerably supported, influenced, or both by the following persons:

- William Gorham, president of the Urban Institute, who has supported the effort from the beginning, even while recognizing that it was not a field with a high payoff in terms of grants and contracts;
- Blaine Liner, who has overseen the recent Urban Institute performance measurement work;
- Joseph Wholey, who has been one of the real leaders and pioneers in the program evaluation and performance measurement fields (and who has been kind enough to contribute chapter 13 on assessing the quality of performance measurement systems);
- James Fountain, who, as Assistant Director of Research of the Governmental Accounting Standards Board over the past two decades, has played a major role in encouraging experimentation in performance measurement by state and local governments as a way to achieve better public information and accountability;
- Chris Wye of the National Academy of Public Administration, who has led the academy's effort to provide useful performance measurement information to federal agencies;
- Barbara Moore and Michael Lombardo of the International City/County Management Association (ICMA), who have led ICMA efforts on performance measurement;
- Martha Taylor Greenway and Meg Plantz of United Way of America, who have done a superb job of helping to introduce performance measurement to the private, nonprofit sector;
- My past associates at the Urban Institute—Louis H. Blair, John M. Greiner, John R. Hall, Donald M. Fisk, and Phillip S. Schaenman—who played major roles in developing the early performance measurement concepts and procedures described in these pages, as far back as the early 1970s;
- Malcolm Holmes, of the World Bank and former Budget Division Principal Advisor of the Australian Ministry of Finance, who through numerous discussions on governing-for-results, greatly enhanced my appreciation of the importance of a broad set of performance incentives;
- David Shand, who led the effort at the Public Management Service of the Organization for Economic Cooperation and Development (OECD) and is continuing to press such efforts at the World Bank.

For help on this book in particular, I thank the following persons:

- My current Urban Institute colleagues, Mary Kopczynski, Elaine Morley, and Shelli Rossman, who have been helping to push the frontiers of performance measurement even further;

- Bonnie Harris and Barbara Willis, who provided superb manuscript preparation assistance; and
- Felicity Skidmore and Blair Potter, the editors who spent many days helping to make this work more readable.

For those new to performance measurement, I hope this book is helpful in introducing the many technical and process procedures and issues involved to managers and their staffs at all levels of government and in private, nonprofit organizations. For those with experience in performance measurement, both those inside and outside service agencies, I hope this work will provide at least a few new ideas that improve their performance measurement efforts and spur future advances.

# Foreword

Equity, quality, and accountability in the provision of services to the public are hallmarks of good government. Improving government's performance in these areas is the goal of good managers. Yet if the public and private agencies that deliver services are to succeed in improving their performance, they must have some objective means of measuring it.

It is not difficult to track an agency's outputs, that is, its activities and physical products. In fact, agencies have been tracking their outputs for decades. But outputs are not true measures of performance—outcomes are. Outcomes, rooted in an agency's mission, are the benefits that customers and the larger public realize from services. For example, the number of patients treated at and discharged from a state mental hospital is an output, whereas the percentage of discharged patients who are capable of living independently is an outcome. Thus, to confuse outputs with outcomes is to mistake activity for accomplishment.

Performance measurement enables managers to define and use specific indicators to measure the outcomes and efficiency of their services or programs on a regular basis. Such information can help managers develop and justify budgets and make the best use of the resources available to them. In the process, managers will also be able to gauge and to demonstrate the fairness of programs, thereby building trust in government.

*Performance Measurement: Getting Results* traces the development of performance measurement, describes what managers can reasonably expect from it, provides practical advice on how to set up and use such a system, and ventures into related areas, such as quality control of information, political considerations, and training of personnel. The book distills nearly 30 years of research, experience, and thinking by the Urban Institute's Harry Hatry, a leader in the fields of program evaluation and performance measurement. Former Institute colleague Joseph Wholey, another pioneer in these fields, contributed a chapter on assessing the quality of performance measurement systems.

Hatry's work embodies the Urban Institute's long-standing commitment to helping government improve the quality and outcomes of its services. The Institute has supported and published his extensive research on public services in such areas as prisons, mental health services, and interventions with teenage substance abusers. Seventeen books by Hatry and various colleagues are currently in print on public and private delivery of services; management excellence; program analysis, effectiveness, and innovation; and customer surveys.

Over the years, it has become clear that virtually any public service—police, transportation, education, social services, environmental protection, economic development, and so on—whether delivered by a government agency or a private, nonprofit group, is amenable to performance measurement. Moreover, performance measurement can be used by poor, developing countries as well as wealthy, industrialized ones. Indeed, Hatry notes, the focus on outcomes is gaining ground worldwide.

Performance measurement is not a panacea—it cannot account for why outcomes occurred, it cannot measure all outcomes, and it is an aid to, not a substitute for, good judgment. Yet regularly measuring the outcomes of services provided by government to its citizens—and using those measures to improve outcomes—is as worthy a goal for the next millennium as it has been for this one.

William Gorham
President
The Urban Institute

# Part

# I

## Introduction

# The Scope of Performance Measurement

In New York City, a priest and a taxicab driver died and went to heaven. Saint Peter showed the priest his eternal dwelling place—a shack. Saint Peter then showed the driver his eternal dwelling place—a mansion. The priest was angry and asked Saint Peter, "Why the difference?" Saint Peter said, "When you preach, people sleep. When riders get into his cab, they pray!"

For this book, RESULTS are what count!

## What Is Performance Measurement? Why Do It?

Managers of any sports team need to know the running score so they can assess whether changes are needed for the team to win. Managers of public agencies and private, nonprofit organizations need similar information. For businesses, the running score is data on profits and market share. Costs alone mean little. Measuring that running score and using it for better performance are the subject of this book— a subject popularly called performance measurement.

Performance measurement has many meanings, but it is defined here as *measurement on a regular basis of the results (outcomes) and efficiency of services or programs.* The new element in this definition is the regular measurement of results or outcomes. Regular measurement of progress toward specified outcomes is a vital component of any effort at managing-for-results,[1] a customer-oriented process that focuses on maximizing benefits and minimizing negative consequences for customers of services and programs. The customers may be citizens receiving services directly or citizens or businesses affected indirectly.

If the right things are not measured, or are measured inaccurately, those using the data will be misled and bad decisions will likely follow. As the old saying puts it: garbage in, garbage out.

A major use of performance information is to help develop and then justify budget proposals. But it is at least as important to help managers manage throughout the year. Public and private managers often say that performance information will not help them because their problem is too few resources to do what needs to be done. Yet they need performance information to tell them how to *increase their ability to get the job done with the resources they have*—and to provide evidence to the budget decisionmakers that they are indeed getting the biggest bang for the buck.

Tracking expenditures and the physical outputs programs produce has been done for decades. Tracking these elements is useful to program personnel but says little about what resulted—how customers and the public benefited. Regular tracking of outcomes is intended to fill this gap. Outcome tracking is the new kid on the block for most public and private services and programs, although ample precedents exist. Police and other law enforcement agencies for many years have regularly tracked and reported data such as crime and clearance rates. Transportation agencies have tracked accidents, injuries, and deaths. Health officials have tracked the incidence of serious diseases and mortality. Fire agencies have tracked the number of fires and the resulting injuries and deaths. Environmental protection agencies have tracked the pollutant content of air and water. School districts have tracked test scores. However, *the focus has often been on jurisdictionwide data, not the outcomes related to specific programs, which are essential information.*

Regular tracking is a key characteristic of performance measurement. For budget purposes, annual data are usually sufficient, but agencies need more frequent outcome information to assess how successful the activities of their programs have been, identify where significant problems exist, and motivate personnel to strive for continuous service improvement.[2]

*One final point. A particularly crucial outcome characteristic for public programs—often neglected in discussions of the uses of performance measurement—is equity.* A well-designed measurement system enables agency managers to assess the fairness of a program and make appropriate adjustments. A good performance measurement system will help officials demonstrate to the public and to policymakers that services are delivered fairly—and this will build trust. (Chapter 8's suggestion of categorizing outcomes by the characteristics of the citizens affected is a major way to help assess equity.)

## Limitations of Performance Measurement

All those using performance measurement information, whether inside or outside government or in a private agency, should understand what it can and cannot do and keep their expectations realistic. Performance measurement has three limitations.

**1. *Performance data do not, by themselves, tell why the outcomes occurred.*** In other words, they do not reveal the extent to which the program caused the measured results. This is an important point. The analogy to managers of sports teams helps here. Managers may need to make changes in the game plan, but the score does not tell them why it is what it is or what needs to be changed to improve the score. For that information the managers and their coaches need to watch the game films and have postgame conferences to identify specific aspects that went wrong. It is the same for service delivery. Performance measurement is designed primarily to provide data on outcomes (the score). But to be of most help, performance measurement systems also need to have built into them opportunities to assess the details of program performance and seek explanations for the outcome data such systems produce.

This limitation raises a major issue that is a source of controversy in performance measurement: *accountability.* What should managers be held accountable for? The government of New Zealand has taken the view that responsibility for program outcomes rests solely with officials at the policymaking level, thus removing all accountability for outcomes from the operating departments. Although important outcomes are seldom, if ever, fully under the control of a particular agency (public or private), the agency and its personnel do *share* responsibility for producing those outcomes. As long as a program has any role in delivering a service intended to help produce particular outcomes, the managers of that program—and their personnel—have a responsibility to track the relevant outcomes and use that information to help improve them.

*Agency personnel and other officials are often too ready to believe they lack influence over outcomes. Acknowledging their shared responsibility helps create innovative solutions that can often help agencies improve the outcomes of the services they provide, even in the face of highly limited resources.*

**2. *Some outcomes cannot be measured directly.*** A major example is success in preventing undesirable events, such as prevention of crime or reduction of illicit drug use. In such cases, surrogates can be used, such as indicators that reflect trends over time in the number of incidents that were not prevented.

**3. *The information provided by performance measurement is just part of the information managers and elected officials need to make decisions.*** Performance measurement does not replace the need for basic expenditure data or political judgments, nor does it replace the need for common sense or good management, leadership, and creativity. *A major purpose of performance measurement is to raise questions. It seldom, if ever, provides answers by itself as to what should be done.*

## Outcome-Focused Efficiency Measurement

Efficiency is usually defined in performance measurement as the ratio of the amount of input (dollar expenditure, personnel time, or other physical input) to the amount of product produced by that input. Using unit-cost ratios that relate expenditures to physical outputs has been common in public agencies for years. *The trouble with these ratios is that they can be improved by reducing the quality of the output.* If outcomes are tracked, a more accurate indicator of efficiency becomes possible. For example, "cost per client served" is an output-based efficiency indicator. Efficiency appears to increase when less is spent per client, even if the condition of the typical client deteriorates. "Cost per client whose condition improved after services" is an outcome-focused efficiency indicator. It gives a much more meaningful picture of a program's real accomplishments.

Some people want to use only output-focused efficiency indicators, arguing that such indicators are completely under the control of the program and enable observers to attribute causation confidently. This approach to efficiency measurement presents problems, however.

Take the example of a program that holds regular sessions to help customers stop smoking. "Cost per session" is under the control of the program. "Cost per customer who quits smoking" is not, because whether someone quits something depends on a host of other factors besides the stop-smoking session. But is "cost per session" a true measure of efficiency? Officials and citizens are more likely concerned with efficiency in producing the desired outcome. *Even if the causal link cannot be firmly drawn, the program still has some responsibility for affecting the desired outcome. An outcome-based indicator provides more insight into the extent to which the program is helping accomplish that objective.*

## Which Organizations Are Suitable for Performance Measurement?

Managing-for-results applies to all agencies that provide services to the public, whether the agency has ample or limited resources, is small or large, is public or private, or is in a developing or developed country. As long as the agency is delivering services to the public, its management and elected officials should be intensely concerned with the quality, outcomes, and efficiency of those services and should measure performance.

Even small agencies with very limited resources should be able to track some aspects of service quality and outcomes, probably more than seems possible at first glance, and make operational improvements with their existing resources. Poorer agencies with fewer resources will have to rely on less sophisticated procedures and, perhaps, more volunteers.

*The same principles apply to all. Agency officials and managers need to recognize and support the need for outcome information and be willing to use it to improve the services they are providing, however tight their budgets.*

## Which Services Are Suitable for Performance Measurement?

The procedures and issues of performance measurement are applicable to most public and private services—ranging from public safety programs, to public works programs, to human service programs, to environmental protection programs, to regulatory programs, and to defense programs. Performance measurement is even applicable to internal support services, such as building maintenance, fleet maintenance, information systems, personnel activities, and purchasing. However, outcomes of these services occur primarily within an organization, and it is usually difficult, if not impossible, to estimate the effect these internal services have on the outcomes of external services. Therefore, this book focuses on external services.

*The activities and outcomes to which the regular tracking of performance measurement may not be readily applicable are those whose important outcomes do not occur for years, if not decades.* Long-range planning and basic research are primary examples. The federal government's Government Performance and Results Act of 1993 has been applied broadly to every type of federal program. Nevertheless, basic research programs have had only slight success at fitting tracking systems into the annual outcome-oriented performance measurement process. Regular tracking can be used to assess whether timelines have been met, dollars have been kept within budget, and the quality of any interim product is acceptable (such as by using expert panels to rate the quality and progress of ongoing research. For assessing the major outcomes of research, analytical resources are better spent on later, in-depth evaluations.

### Program Evaluations and Other In-Depth Studies

Performance measurement can be considered a field of program evaluation. However, program evaluation usually refers to in-depth, special studies that not only examine a program's outcomes but also identify the "whys," including the extent to which the program actually caused the outcomes. The procedures involved in such in-depth program evaluations are not the subject of this book.[3]

In actual practice, many of the so-called program evaluations undertaken by government (federal, state, or local) provide information on outcomes but little evidence on the causal linkage between activities and results. Even so, in-depth studies can provide many insights about what happened and why, information ongoing performance measurement cannot provide.

Because of the time and cost involved, in-depth evaluations are usually done much less frequently and only for selected programs. Thus, performance measurement systems and in-depth program evaluations are complementary activities that can nourish and enhance each other. Findings from a program evaluation completed during a given year can add to or even supersede that year's performance measurement data. Data from an agency's performance measurement system can provide program evaluators with data, with useful indications of trends, and raise questions that encourage more in-depth evaluation.[4] Sometimes evaluators can use performance measurement procedures to collect data.

### Relation to Performance Auditing

Performance audits, which are becoming more frequent, are typically conducted by auditors or inspectors general. They are ad hoc studies, often closely resembling in-depth program evaluations, that are applied to a selection of public programs each year. Performance auditors should have considerable interest in performance measurement systems as ways to provide data on outcomes that they can use in their audits.[5]

### Strategic Planning, Budgeting, and Policy Analysis

Performance measurement provides information primarily about the past. Budgeting, strategic planning, and policy analysis are primarily about the future. As discussed in later chapters, performance data provide a baseline for decisions and give clues as to what might happen in the future. These future-oriented processes require estimation and judgment skills that performance measurement systems cannot provide by themselves. This book provides an introduction to these issues (especially in chapters 11 and 12) but does not attempt comprehensive coverage of budgeting, strategic planning, or policy analysis. Rather, these topics are discussed only in the context of the role that outcome-focused performance measurement systems play in these activities.

## Role of Agency Employees

The employees of agencies undertaking performance measurement clearly have a stake in the process. Later chapters address the roles of this important stakeholder group in helping identify appropriate performance indicators and in using performance information. The book does not address the measurement of employee job satisfaction, however, because employees are here considered suppliers of services, not customers.[6]

## A Guide to This Volume

Chapter 2 completes part I by providing the definitions that are the basic background for the material in the rest of the book.

Part II addresses the performance measurement process. Chapter 3 discusses organizational start-up. Chapters 4 through 6 answer the questions of what the program's objectives are and who its customers are (chapter 4); what outcomes should be tracked (chapter 5); and what the specific outcome indicators should be (chapter 6). Chapter 7 addresses the question of how the data can be obtained.

Part III covers the critical issues of how to examine and use the performance measurement data. Chapters 8 and 9 focus on maximizing the usefulness of the data to program personnel and others. Chapter 8 discusses the importance of procedures for providing more detailed breakouts of outcome data. Chapter 9 discusses benchmarking, that is, what comparisons should be made to help interpret outcome levels. Chapter 10 addresses how to decide what analyses can be undertaken, given data availability, and provides suggestions on an all too frequently neglected key element: reporting the findings. Chapters 11 and 12 discuss major uses of performance information, with special attention to results-based budgeting.

Part IV (chapters 13 and 14) addresses a variety of other important performance measurement concerns, including the long-term problem of quality control of the information produced by performance measurement (chapter 13), political considerations, and the need for personnel training (chapter 14).

Part V (chapter 15) provides a summary of the principal points about performance measurement that are important in producing a practical process that is useful in the real world.

## References and Notes

1. "Governing-for-results" and "results-oriented government" refer to the same process. "Managing-for-results" is preferable here because the process is not restricted to government (executive or legislative) but is equally applicable to private service agencies.

2. A distinction is often made between the way in which a service is delivered (such as its timeliness, accessibility, and courteousness to customers) and the results it is intended to achieve (such as actual improvements in the condition of customers). As will be discussed in chapter 4 on the specific content of performance measurement, these service delivery quality aspects are important to customers and should be tracked as intermediate outcomes, but they usually do not indicate how much progress has been made toward service objectives.

3. Considerable literature exists describing in-depth program evaluations and how they might be done.

4. As Marcantonio and Cook note in their discussion of interrupted time-series designs, regularly collected performance data can be an important source of historical data for evaluators. See Richard J. Marcantonio and Thomas D. Cook, "Convincing Quasi-Experiments," chap. 7 in *Handbook of Practical Program Evaluation*, ed. Joseph S. Wholey et al. (San Francisco: Jossey-Bass Publishers, 1994).

5. In addition, these offices are likely to be given the responsibility for periodically assessing agencies' performance measurement systems, the indicators used, and the data being provided. (This quality control responsibility is discussed in chapter 13.)

6. One exception to this is the case of employees of lower-level public agencies through which higher levels of government work. In this context, lower-level agency staff are considered to be intermediate customers of the higher levels of government and their experiences and satisfaction germane to the quality of the higher-level government's program.

# What Types of Performance Information Should Be Tracked?

As Mark Twain said of Wagner's music, "It's not as bad as it sounds."

The central function of any performance measurement process is to provide regular, valid data on indicators of performance outcomes. But performance measurement should not be limited to data on outcome indicators.[1] It should also include information that helps managers measure the incoming workload and gain insight into the causes of the outcomes.

A consistent set of definitions categorizing various types of performance information—to be used across all programs—is the cornerstone of any performance measurement system. All too often, confusion among programs within an agency occurs due to unclear, inconsistent use of terms.

Definitions—or labels—perform the crucial function of enabling users of performance information to distinguish reliably among categories of data that have different implications and different uses. Numerous labels have been used over the years to categorize performance information. Which particular set of labels an agency or program chooses is not the primary issue. The primary issue is to be able to determine which items should be regularly tracked. Appropriate labels help with that.

No two people will categorize every single element in a data set in exactly the same way. Gray areas inevitably exist because it is not always clear where a particular piece of information falls. In addition, for some performance information, the category may depend on the perspective of the agency. For example, to the state agency that develops an educational reform strategic plan, the completion of that plan is an output. However, to the U.S. Department of Education that encourages such plans, their completion by states is an intermediate outcome, as discussed later.

Exhibit 2-1 presents the categories of performance information used throughout this volume. Data on the amount of resources expended for particular programs (inputs) are different from internal information that indicates the amount of activity a program is undertaking (process). These data, in turn, are quite different from the products and services a program has completed (outputs), which should be distinguished from results-based information (outcomes). These distinctions are important in order to avoid misleading those who use the information.

Each of these categories is discussed briefly in turn. Exhibit 2-2 provides summary definitions of key performance measurement terms.

## Categories of Performance Information

### Inputs

Input information is the amount of resources actually used, usually expressed as the amount of funds or the number of employee-years, or both.

This category, when related to figures on the amount of output or outcome (see further below), produces indicators of efficiency or productivity.

---

**EXHIBIT 2-1**

**Categories of Information Used in Performance Measurement Systems**

- Inputs*
- Process (Workload or Activities)
- Outputs*
- Outcomes*
  —Intermediate Outcomes
  —End Outcomes
- Efficiency and Productivity*
- Demographic and Other Workload Characteristics
- Explanatory Information
- Impacts

*These are the categories usually labeled performance indicators in performance measurement systems.

---

EXHIBIT 2-2

**Performance Measurement Definitions**

- **Inputs:** Resources (i.e., expenditures or employee time) used to produce outputs and outcomes.
- **Outputs:** Products and services delivered. Output refers to the completed products of internal activity: the amount of work done within the organization or by its contractors (such as number of miles of road repaired or number of calls answered).
- **Outcomes:** An event, occurrence, or condition that is outside the activity or program itself and that is of direct importance to customers and the public generally. An outcome indicator is a measure of the amount and/or frequency of such occurrences. Service quality is also included under this category.
- **Intermediate Outcomes:** An outcome that is expected to lead to a desired end but is not an end in itself (such as service response time, which is of concern to the customer making a call but does not tell anything directly about the success of the call). A service may have multiple intermediate outcomes.
- **End Outcomes:** The end result that is sought (such as the community having clean streets or reduced incidence of crimes or fires). A service may have more than one end outcome.
- **Efficiency, or Unit-Cost Ratio:** The relationship between the amount of input (usually dollars or employee-years) and the amount of output or outcome of an activity or program. If the indicator uses outputs and not outcomes, a jurisdiction that lowers unit cost may achieve a measured increase in efficiency at the expense of the outcome of the service.
- **Performance Indicator:** A specific numerical measurement for each aspect of performance (e.g., output or outcome) under consideration.

**Source:** Adapted from *Comparative Performance Measurement: FY 1996 Data Report* (Washington, D.C.: International City/County Management Association, 1997), 1–4.

*For performance measurement purposes, the amounts that were actually used, not the amounts budgeted, are the relevant numbers.* An occasional practice has been to call the *workload* that comes into the agency an input. In this volume, workload data are *not included* under this category, because the amount of incoming work is quite different from the amount of cost or staff time expended.

## Process (Workload or Activities)

This category includes the amount of work that comes into a program or is in process but not yet completed. For some agencies, such as human service agencies, the workload is usually expressed in terms of the number of customers that come in for service (individual clients, households, or businesses). For others, the number of customers is not appropriate. Road maintenance programs, for example, might express their workload as number of lane-miles of road needing repair.

Amounts of work are not considered performance indicators because they do not indicate how much product was produced by the program. Workload information is very important to program managers when tracking the flow of work into and through their programs, however. (For example, the amount of work pending from the previous reporting period plus the amount of new work coming in indicates the workload on the program during the current reporting period.)

While amounts of work by themselves are not outputs or outcomes, workload data can be used to produce outcome data. In some programs, the amount of work not completed at the end of a reporting period can be considered a proxy for delays of service to customers (an intermediate outcome). Examples include the size of the backlog of eligibility determinations for loan applications and the size of customer waiting lists. However, more direct, and probably better, indicators of delays and backlogs would be: (a) a direct indicator of the extent of delays, such as the percent of cases in which the time elapsed between the request for a service and when the service was provided exceeded $X$ days, where $X$ is a service standard established by the program; and (b) the percent of customers who reported excessive waiting times to obtain service.

## Outputs

Output information indicates the amount of products and services delivered (completed) during the reporting period. Reporting of output information is standard in agencies throughout the world. Keeping track of the amount of output accomplished is good management. Common examples of outputs include number of miles of roads paved, number of reports issued, number of training programs held, and number of students served by the program. However, outputs do not by themselves tell anything about the *results* achieved, although they are expected to lead to desired outcomes. (Program personnel should ask what results are expected from each output. Those results should be included under the next category, *outcomes*.)

As defined here, *outputs are things that the program's personnel have done,* not changes to outside persons or changes that outside organizations have made.

## Outcomes

In some contexts the word *output* refers to any product of work, whether the product is a program's completed physical product or the outcomes (results) of that work. *The field of performance measurement of public services makes a sharp distinction between outputs and outcomes.*

Outcomes are the events, occurrences, or changes in conditions, behavior, or attitudes that indicate progress toward achievement of the mission and objectives of the program. Thus, outcomes are linked to the program's (and its agency's) overall mission—its reason for existing.[2]

*Outcomes are not what the program itself did but the consequences of what the program did.* An excellent example illustrating the difference between outcome and output comes from the state of Texas:

> The number of patients treated and discharged from a state mental hospital (*output* indicator) is not the same as the percentage of discharged patients who are capable of living independently (*outcome* indicator).[3]

Outcomes may be something the program wants to maximize, such as evidence of increased learning by students, or to minimize, such as crime rates. Some outcomes are financial. For example, for public assistance programs, reducing the amount of incorrect payments (whether overpayments or underpayments) is likely to be an appropriate outcome. Another example, recovering owed child support payments from absent parents, is an appropriate outcome of child support offices. In such cases, outcomes can be expressed in monetary terms.

Outcomes include side effects, whether intended or not and whether beneficial or detrimental. If the program recognizes in advance that such side effects can occur, it should design the performance measurement process to regularly measure them.

As long as they are important and can be tracked, outcomes should be included in the performance measurement system, even if they are not explicitly identified in the program's mission and objective statements. Formal program mission and objective statements seldom include all the outcomes that an agency needs to track. It is not the function of such statements to itemize all the outcomes that the program should seek, just the central, most vital ones. For example, complaints against police officers should be tracked as well as crime clearance rates, even if the mission statement of the police agency does not include statements about providing law enforcement in a fair and honest manner.

It is important to distinguish *intermediate* outcomes from *end* outcomes. This will help programs differentiate between the ends ultimately desired from a program and interim accomplishments, which are expected to lead to those end results (but may or may not). The following discussion highlights the difference with definitions and examples.

*Intermediate outcomes.* These are outcomes expected to lead to the ends desired but are not themselves ends.

Examples of intermediate outcomes:

- People completing employment training programs where program participation is *voluntary*. This reveals how successful the program has been in getting customers not only to participate in, but also to complete, the sponsored training sessions. However, completion is only one step toward the ultimate end of improving the condition of those persons completing the program.
- Citizens doing more exercising or switching to a better diet, as recommended in an agency-sponsored health program (perhaps as measured by surveying clients 12 months after completing the agency's program). Such changed behavior is expected to lead the participants to better health, but since this is uncertain, it is an intermediate outcome.
- A state or local agency completing the development of a comprehensive plan of action encouraged and supported by a federal program (where acceptance of the assistance is voluntary). For the federal government, the fact that states or local governments actually completed a reasonable plan can be considered to be an initial step toward improving services, although it says nothing about the end outcome of service improvement.[4]

For most agencies and products, whether something is an output or an intermediate outcome is clear, but there are exceptions. One example is the number of arrests for a law enforcement program. Many persons believe that arrests are an output because they are actions taken by agency employees. On the other hand, arrests involve citizens outside the agency, the persons arrested, and their families. In that sense, they might be better counted as intermediate outcomes. And they usually indicate that the process of bringing guilty persons to justice has begun.

Other examples include qualities of how well a service is provided to customers, such as response times to requests for service.

*Service quality characteristics: A special type of intermediate outcome.* As used here, quality indicates *how well a service was delivered, based on characteristics important to customers.* It does not tell what results occurred *after* the service was delivered. Since such characteristics are important to program customers, even though the characteristics do not represent final results, they can be considered intermediate outcomes an agency should track. Exhibit 2-3 lists quality characteristics that might be considered by an agency when developing a list of outcomes to track for a program.

Some persons label quality characteristics (such as response times to requests for services) as outputs because they are characteristics of the outputs. However, if a characteristic is expected to be important to customers, it is better to consider it as an intermediate outcome, not an output. Because quality characteristics usually are important to customers, they are better labeled as outcomes to help ensure that they are given proper attention by agencies.

For some customers and under some circumstances, one or more of these quality characteristics might be extremely important—and can even be considered end outcomes. For example, it is vital for low-income families that assistance checks (whether Social Security or any public assistance payment) arrive on time and be accurate. Otherwise, these families will be unable to pay their bills and may be evicted or go hungry.

---

**EXHIBIT 2-3**

**Typical Service Quality Characteristics to Track**

- Timeliness with which the service is provided
- Accessibility and convenience of the service
  — Convenience of location
  — Convenience of hours of operation
  — Staff availability when the customer needs the service (whether by phone or in person)
- Accuracy of the assistance, such as in processing customer requests for service
- Courteousness with which the service is delivered
- Adequacy of information disseminated to potential users about what the service is and how to obtain it
- Condition and safety of agency facilities used by customers
- Customer satisfaction with a particular characteristic of the delivery of the service
- Customer satisfaction with the service overall

*End outcomes.* These are the desired results of the program—conditions of importance to program customers and citizens more generally. End outcomes might, for example, be aspects of health, safety, educational achievement, employment and earnings, or living in decent homes, such as:

- Reduced incidence of specific diseases
- Improved student test scores
- Lower crime rates
- Less violence in schools[5]
- Reduced number of households living in substandard housing
- Increased real household earnings
- Reduced household dependency on welfare

For some programs, customer satisfaction with the *results* of a service can be considered as an end outcome. For example, satisfaction ratings of customers' experiences with parks, recreational activities, libraries, and cultural programs or children's satisfaction ratings of the homes in which they are placed by child welfare agencies are likely to be considered by many citizens as end outcomes—even though those programs have aims that go beyond satisfaction, such as a library's mission to increase public access to information.

Many programs produce *both short-term and long-term end outcomes.* Education is a classic example. Educational programs produce early improvements in student learning, but they also help students obtain employment, and higher salaries, later on. Employment, ability to support a family, and reductions in welfare dependency are long-term outcomes of education programs. Information on long-term end outcomes such as posteducation employment and earnings, however, will not be available early enough to guide program personnel on the success of most of their current activities. Short-term end outcomes need to be tracked to encourage ongoing program improvement. Short-term outcomes related to learning and dropout rates, for example, are outcomes of key concern to education managers, staff, and parents—and can be considered end outcomes for this reason.

Exhibit 2-4 summarizes a number of other issues related to the relationship between intermediate and end outcomes.

## Efficiency and Productivity

The ratio of the amount of input to the amount of output (or outcome) is labeled *efficiency*. Flipping this, the ratio of the amount of output (or outcome) to the amount of input is labeled *productivity*. These are equivalent numbers.

**EXHIBIT 2-4**

## Other Issues Related to the Relationship between Intermediate and End Outcomes

Intermediate outcomes, by definition, occur before—and are expected to help lead to—the end outcomes. *Thus, intermediate outcomes are important to program managers and usually provide more timely information than end outcomes.* For example, customers complete employment counseling programs (intermediate outcome) before they obtain employment (end outcome), which is expected to occur after completion of the program. For long-term end outcomes for which data may not be available for many years (such as reduction in adverse health effects due to smoking and achieving rewarding employment careers), the program can usefully focus on short-term ends (such as reduced smoking and improved learning and skills). Much evidence exists that both reduced smoking and improved learning and skills directly affect the long-term end outcomes and intermediate outcomes.

*Early occurrence of an outcome does not necessarily mean that it is not an end outcome.* For example, family counseling programs hope to produce more stable and happier families in the short run as well as in the long run. Some treatment actions produce quick ends (purification of drinking water), while others require many years before water quality improves significantly (cleanup of rivers).

Another important advantage including intermediate outcomes is that *programs almost always have more influence over intermediate outcomes than they do over end outcomes.* For example, many federal programs (such as education, health and human services, housing and community development, and employment programs) provide assistance to states, local agencies, and/or nongovernmental organizations rather than providing help directly to citizens. Changes sought by the federal programs and made by these other organizations can be considered intermediate outcomes. The federal programs have more direct influence on these outcomes than on the end outcomes, which are also affected by many other factors (such as family circumstances and motivation). The same is true of state programs that work through local governments and of local government programs that work through the business or private, nonprofit community.

*Intermediate outcomes usually are related to the particular way that the service is delivered by the program, whereas end outcomes typically do not vary with the delivery approach.* For example, a government attempting to improve the quality of rivers and lakes can use many ways to achieve this, such as providing funding for wastewater treatment, providing technical assistance to certain classes of businesses, and encouraging lower levels of government to pass stricter laws and ordinances. Each such approach would have its own intermediate outcomes. However, regardless of the approach, end outcomes, such as the quality of rivers and lakes, apply.

Efficiency and productivity have traditionally related costs to outputs (labeled *technical efficiency* by economists). However, to the extent that the performance measurement system provides data on *outcomes* (sometimes called *allocative efficiency* by economists), it provides a much truer picture of efficiency and productivity. This is because focusing on output-to-input ratios carries with it the temptation for managers to increase output at the expense of results and service quality.

Examples of outcome-based productivity indicators:

- Number of persons gaining employment after completing an agency's training program per dollar of program cost (or per program employee-hour).
- Number of customers who reported that the service received had been of significant help to them per dollar cost of that service (or per employee-hour).

Flip these ratios over and they become efficiency indicators.

For example, if 160 customers reported being significantly helped, and the program cost $96,000:

- Efficiency = $96,000/160 = $600 per customer helped.
- Productivity = 160/$96,000 = 1.67 customers helped per $1,000.

Efficiency and productivity ratios can be calculated for any *output* indicator. For *outcome* indicators to be incorporated into these ratios, however, the outcomes need to be expressed as something to be maximized. Let us take crime as an example. "Cost per reported crime," though easy to calculate, makes no sense as an efficiency indicator (although it does make sense in the context of measuring the total costs of crime to a community). The output to be maximized here is *crimes prevented.* "Cost per crime prevented" would be a highly desirable indicator. Unfortunately, valid data on crimes prevented by a program are virtually never available on a regular basis. (Estimation of number of crimes prevented, if it is to yield reliable information, requires ad hoc studies that are usually quite costly and, even then, the estimates are likely to be highly uncertain. This measurement problem applies to most prevention programs.)

Efficiency ratios using outputs are common. Thus far, however, efficiency ratios using outcomes are rare. This is partly because few outcome data have been developed in the past by public or private agencies. With the growth of more outcome-based performance measurement systems at all levels of government and in the private, nonprofit sector, more use of outcome-based efficiency ratios is becoming possible.

### Demographic and Other Workload Characteristics

If agencies are to make full use of their performance data, information on the amount of work coming into a program (sometimes called *demand*) and key characteristics of that work (such as those relating to its difficulty) needs to be collected and linked to outcome information (discussed at length in chapters 8 and 10). Thus, a program that processes applications wants information on the complexity of the incoming workload. A program working with business customers wants information as to each business's industry classification, size, and location. A road maintenance program needs to be concerned with the amount and type of traffic and soil conditions for specific road segments. A hospital needs information on the severity of illness of its patients to help it interpret changes in outcomes of patients.

Similarly, programs that use a variety of service delivery approaches need to have information on the particular approach used to produce particular outputs and outcomes. The number and types of assistance provided to customers with similar problems may vary. Programs may use private contractors for some of their work and their own employees for other, similar work. Programs need to know which work was done using which service approach and then link the outcomes to each approach (see chapter 8).

## Explanatory Information

Programs should be encouraged to provide explanatory information (qualitative or quantitative) to help readers of their performance reports properly interpret the data—especially for outcomes that were poor or much better than expected. In some instances, this will be information about internal factors (e.g., the program unexpectedly lost funds or key personnel during the reporting period). In other cases, the explanations will identify external factors over which the program had little or no control (e.g., a major change in economic conditions or highly unusual weather conditions). (This is discussed further in chapter 10.)

## Impacts

A number of analysts have begun to use the term *impact* to refer to data that estimate the extent to which the program actually *caused* particular outcomes.[6] For example, an indicator of impact would be labeled something like the following: Number of expectant teenage mothers who, *because of the program,* had healthy babies. (Without the program, they would have lost their babies or had babies with substantial health problems.)

However, *the outcome data likely to be obtainable from ongoing performance measurement systems will seldom, if ever, reveal the extent to which the program has caused the outcome.* Other factors—over which the program has only partial control—will inevitably be present. For example, some persons who stopped smoking after completing a stop-smoking program may have stopped because of pressure from family and/or a health care professional, not because of the program. In-depth studies, such as formal program evaluations, may at times be able to estimate the program's impact on some outcomes reasonably well. When available, those data should also be included in the program's performance report.

Because of the time and cost required to obtain impact data, such information is likely to be available only infrequently on any given program (or groups of programs).

## Output or Outcome? Indicators That Are Particularly Difficult to Categorize

Many service attributes are easy to classify, but some are not. Here are some typical attributes that have caused healthy debates.

### Customer Participation

The number of customers participating in a program is an ambiguous indicator because it depends on the particular situation in which it is used.

- If attendance is mandatory, the number participating would, at best, be output information.
- For programs in which participation is voluntary, and which include activities aimed at attracting customers (such as employment training programs and professional development activities), participation can be categorized as an intermediate outcome because it depends on the program's ability to attract participants. Similarly, the program's ability to retain participants until the activities are completed is another intermediate outcome. Completion is more important than participation, because it indicates that the activity has been sufficiently attractive for customers to have stuck with it until the training program's end.
- For public programs such as parks, recreational facilities, libraries, and public transit and for private programs such as those of boys' and girls' clubs (all activities in which participation is voluntary), the number of participants can be considered an intermediate outcome. (Examples of outputs are the number of programs or classes held, number of bus miles, and amount of reading materials purchased.) A good case can also

be made that participation is an end outcome of such programs if enjoyment of the activity is hoped to be a major product of such programs.

## *Customer Satisfaction*

A guiding principle in the search for outcomes, as stressed earlier, is to identify elements of direct concern and value to the public and to direct customers. Since customer satisfaction and similar service attributes, such as courteousness and accessibility, fit this description, they are categorized here as outcomes.[7] Elected officials and donors certainly treat them as outcomes.

What kind of outcomes are these? They are usually *intermediate* outcomes because they cannot take the place of measuring the actual condition of customers after receiving the service. For example, customer satisfaction with the employment and training services they receive is not ultimately as important as whether these customers find employment. (But is not *satisfaction with their jobs* also of major value to these customers?)

For certain services—recreational activities, libraries, and marital counseling, for example—customer satisfaction can be an end outcome. Even here, though, satisfaction is seldom the only outcome sought. In virtually all cases where customer satisfaction is important, other outcomes must also be included to obtain a comprehensive picture of a service's performance.

## *Response Times for Service Requests*

Some people label response time as an output and others label it as an intermediate outcome. Because response time is usually of direct concern to customers, this book includes it in the intermediate outcome category. By the same logic, the level of satisfaction customers have with the response times to their requests is also an intermediate outcome.

## Relationships among Types of Performance Information

Diagramming the continuum of relevant factors for measurement in a performance measurement system in a logic model (outcome-sequence chart) is a highly useful way to summarize the flow across the information categories just discussed. Exhibit 2-5, based on material developed by United Way of America, displays such a system. Chapters 5 (on identifying outcomes) and 6 (on identifying indicators that should be used to measure the outcomes) discuss such flow diagrams further and include a number of additional examples.

EXHIBIT 2-5

**Logic Model (Outcome Sequence Chart) for a Human Services Program**

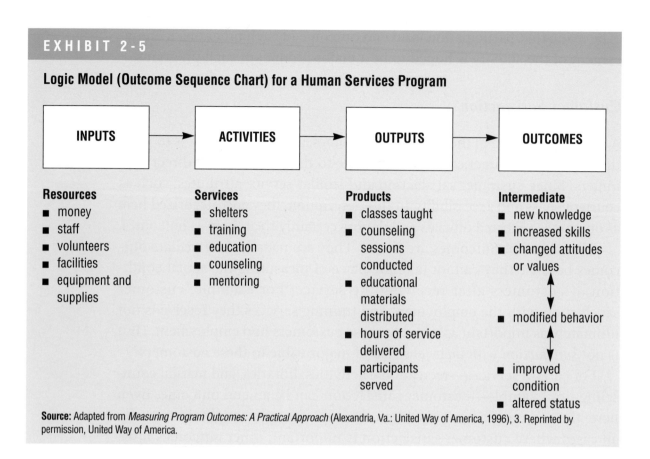

| INPUTS | ACTIVITIES | OUTPUTS | OUTCOMES |
|---|---|---|---|
| **Resources** | **Services** | **Products** | **Intermediate** |
| ■ money | ■ shelters | ■ classes taught | ■ new knowledge |
| ■ staff | ■ training | ■ counseling | ■ increased skills |
| ■ volunteers | ■ education | sessions | ■ changed attitudes |
| ■ facilities | ■ counseling | conducted | or values |
| ■ equipment and | ■ mentoring | ■ educational | |
| supplies | | materials | |
| | | distributed | ■ modified behavior |
| | | ■ hours of service | |
| | | delivered | |
| | | ■ participants | ■ improved |
| | | served | condition |
| | | | ■ altered status |

**Source:** Adapted from *Measuring Program Outcomes: A Practical Approach* (Alexandria, Va.: United Way of America, 1996), 3. Reprinted by permission, United Way of America.

## References and Notes

1. The words *indicator* and *measure* are essentially interchangeable, but *indicator* seems preferable. The word *measure* is ambiguous because it can also mean either an action taken to improve a situation or the act of measuring.
2. The word *effectiveness* has been used by some governments in place of *outcomes*. However, *effectiveness* implies more of a causal linkage than usually warranted by the data, so the word *outcome* seems preferable and is more often used (such as in the federal Government Performance and Result Act of 1993).
3. Texas Governor's Office of Budget and Planning, Legislative Budget Board, *Instructions for Preparing and Submitting Agency Strategic Plans: Fiscal Years 1999-2003* (Austin, January 1998), 39.
4. From the perspective of an individual state or local government, completion of its own plan is an output.
5. Some may prefer to consider this an intermediate outcome needed to achieve improved learning.
6. Some agencies have used the word *impact* to refer to societal outcomes, as distinguished from outcomes to individuals. Such societal outcomes are better considered as broad end outcomes.
7. Some analysts view them as outputs, which demeans their importance. Fortunately, even these analysts often agree that these service characteristics should be measured and tracked.

# The Performance Measurement Process

# Chapter 3

# What Are the First Steps?

Joe expected too much. Excessive expectations about how easy it is to implement performance measurement and what it is capable of doing can also dash the hopes of would-be managers-for-results. This chapter suggests prerequisites and how to start the efforts so as to maximize the chances of success.

## Desirable Prerequisites for Performance Measurement

Results-based performance measurement is a valuable management tool that is widely applicable to public service programs, including those in poor developing countries. Three prerequisites are highly desirable, however, before proceeding.

**1. High-level support for the performance measurement effort.** High-level support is a familiar requirement for almost any significant new agency activity. Performance measurement is no exception. Obviously, explicit, strong support from the top of the organization is the ideal—but it is not a must. Strong support from the head of an individual department, or even the head of a particular division in a department, can be sufficient to support a good performance measurement process within the department or division.

High-level support is needed for two crucial purposes. The first is to secure adequate time and resource commitment to develop, implement, and operate the performance measurement process properly. The second is to help ensure the interest of officials in the performance management work and increase the likelihood that the resulting performance information will be used.

The primary work in developing the performance measurement process will typically be done by program staff, but some outcome measurement elements may require outside support, particularly for ongoing data collection, tabulation, and analysis. The resources for such activities will probably come primarily from the program's own resources, such as contract funds, but such expenditures inevitably depend on upper-level agreement. Certain tasks will require special help from other parts of the agency's operation—such as computer services for data processing or central expertise for customer surveys. The encouragement and support of high-level officials are essential to ensure that such help will be forthcoming.

2. *Reasonable program stability.* Programs that are undergoing major change in mission or personnel are not good candidates for introducing performance measurement. Managers should wait until the situation has settled down.

3. *At least some computerized data-processing capability.* For very small programs, basic performance data collection and processing can be done manually—if necessary, by volunteers. But most programs' data requirements are such that manual data handling would be a highly time-consuming, error-prone nightmare. In the 1970s, when manual data processing was still common, an Urban Institute project had to do manual tabulations with cross-tabulations on detailed outcome indicators for 150 social service clients. No project of that size should be handled manually in these days of the personal computer and standard spreadsheet software.

First steps toward developing or expanding a performance measure process are:

- Determine what program activities to include.
- Establish and implement a working group to oversee development of the performance measurement process.

## Determine What Program Activities to Include

Many programs, even small ones, have more than one major activity. If measurement resources are severely limited, the program manager may need to assess relative priorities for implementing performance measurement and to select the activities that will be covered by the performance measurement activity.

A park or recreation program is likely to sponsor many types of activities (such as many individual support and recreation activities). Should they all be covered or only the major ones?

Programs aimed at helping children's development include a variety of activities, such as information dissemination, parental education, and early childhood programs. Should each activity have its own performance measurement system, or should all of these activities be covered in one integrated performance measurement process?

If the *missions* of a program's various projects are *very similar,* even though the approaches may differ, it is probably feasible (and good practice) to fold them into one combined outcome measurement process. The end outcomes sought will be similar for all projects, even though the intermediate outcomes will differ depending on the service delivery approach used by the individual projects. *To the extent that the missions of the programs are significantly different from one another, separate outcome measurement procedures will be needed and the advantages of combining them into one measurement process shrink.*

## Implement a Working Group to Oversee Development of the Performance Measurement Process

Under this approach, each program manager would form a working group to oversee development and implementation of the outcome measurement process.[1] In addition to the program manager, who normally should act as the group's facilitator, the working group should consist of:

- Members of the program staff
- Representatives of related program areas within the agency
- A representative of the agency's central office (to provide a broader perspective)[2]
- A measurement expert, either from the agency's technical staff (such as from an agency evaluation or analysis office) or an outside consultant or contractor (preferably, someone familiar with the agency's work)
- A representative of the budget office
- A person knowledgeable about information processing

Working groups of 8 to 12 people are typically an effective size. For very small programs, working groups can be smaller. For particularly complex programs, groups may need to be larger.

Initially, the working group should meet frequently and regularly. It should plan on being in existence for at least two years in order to work through the development and initial implementation stages—which should include quality checking of the first products of the performance measurement process. The group needs to undertake a number of steps. Exhibit 3-1 lists these steps and notes which chapter provides further information about them. Exhibit 3-2 organizes the steps into sample agendas for the initial working group meetings.

## EXHIBIT 3-1

### Key Steps for Performance Measurement Working Groups

1. Establish the purpose and scope of the working group (chapter 2).
2. Identify the mission, objectives, and clients of the program (chapter 3).
3. Identify the results (outcomes) that the program seeks (chapter 5).
4. Hold meetings with interest groups such as customer groups (in individual interviews or in focus groups) in order to identify outcomes desired from a variety of viewpoints (chapter 5).
5. Select specific indicators for measuring each outcome and efficiency indicator (chapter 6).
6. Identify appropriate data sources for each indicator and the specific data collection procedures needed to obtain the data. Develop data collection instruments such as survey questionnaires (chapter 7).
7. Identify the specific breakouts needed for each indicator, such as breakouts by customer demographic characteristics, organizational unit, geographical location, type of approach used, etc. Breakout information is extremely useful in determining the conditions under which successful outcomes are occurring (chapter 8).
8. Identify appropriate benchmarks against which to compare program results (chapter 9).
9. Develop an analysis plan—ways that the performance data will be examined to make the findings useful for program officials and others (chapter 10).
10. Select formats for presenting the performance information that are informative and user-friendly (chapter 10).
11. Determine the roles that any program partners (such as project grantees and contractors) with substantial responsibility for service delivery should play in developing and implementing the performance measurement process. For example, many federal and state programs support a number of projects operated by local government agencies (which, in turn, provide services to customers). They are likely to have important roles in both data collection and use (chapter 5).
12. Establish a schedule for undertaking the above steps, for pilot-testing the procedures, and for making subsequent modifications based on the pilot results. (A sample project schedule is shown in exhibit 3-3.)
13. Plan, undertake, and review a pilot test of any new or substantially modified data collection procedures (chapter 7).
14. Prepare a long-term schedule (typically about three years) for implementation, indicating the timing of data collection and analysis relevant to each year's budgeting cycle and the persons responsible for each step in the process.
15. Identify the uses of the performance information by agency personnel (such as in budgeting and helping improve programs, chapters 11 and 12).

Performance Measurement: Getting Results

EXHIBIT 3-2

## Sample Agendas for Working Group Meetings

### Meeting One

1. Identify the purposes and uses of outcome and efficiency data.
2. Discuss working group mission, objectives, and overall schedule.
3. Begin defining program mission, objectives, and customers.
4. Plan for focus groups to obtain input from customers.

### Meeting Two

5. Complete the defining of program mission, objectives, and customers.
6. Begin identifying outcomes and efficiency aspects to be tracked.
7. Role-play as customers.
8. Prepare outcome sequence charts.
9. Work out details of customer focus groups (which should be held before meeting three).

### Meeting Three

10. Review findings from focus groups.
11. Finalize list of outcomes to track.
12. Begin selecting outcome and efficiency indicators.
13. Discuss possible data sources and data collection procedures.

### Meeting Four

14. Work on identifying outcome and efficiency indicators, data sources, and basic data collection procedures.
15. Identify desirable breakouts of indicator data.
16. Plan for development of detailed data collection procedures, such as customer survey questionnaires.

### Meeting Five

17. Finalize outcome and efficiency indicators and data sources.
18. Review initial drafts at detailed data collection procedures, such as customer survey questionnaires, and develop a plan for analyzing the performance data (including specifying comparison benchmarks).
19. Begin planning for pilot-testing of new data collection procedures.

### Meeting Six

20. Complete plan for the pilot test and initiate the test.

### Meetings Seven, Eight, and Nine

21. Review progress of pilot test.
22. Work out test problems.
23. Select performance report formats and identify needed tabulations for the outcome and efficiency data coming from the pilot test.

### Meeting Ten

24. Review pilot test outcome data.
25. Review results of pilot test procedures.
26. Identify and make necessary modifications.

### Meeting Eleven

27. Begin documenting outcome measurement procedures for the ongoing implementation process.
28. Identify specific ways to make the outcome and efficiency data most useful (this includes determining frequency of reporting, improving analysis and presentation of the performance information methods of report dissemination, and developing ways to follow up on findings).

### Meeting Twelve

29. Review all aspects of the performance measurement process.
30. Finalize documentation.
31. Develop a multiyear schedule for full implementation.

EXHIBIT 3-3

## Sample Performance Measurement System Development Schedule (30 Months)*

| Project Steps (see exhibit 3-1) | Month | | | | | | | | | | | | | | | |
|---|---|---|---|---|---|---|---|---|---|---|---|---|---|---|---|---|
| | 0 | 2 | 4 | 6 | 8 | 10 | 12 | 14 | 16 | 18 | 20 | 22 | 24 | 26 | 28 | 30 |

Step 1:
Set overall scope, get top-level support, and establish working group

Step 2:
Identify mission and customers

Steps 3–5:
Identify what is to be measured

Step 6:
Identify data sources and data collection procedures

Steps 7-9:
Determine data breakouts, comparisons, and analysis plan

Steps 10–12:
Prepare for pilot test

Step 13:
Pilot-test, make revisions

Steps 14–15:
Plan for implementation

*At least six more months are likely to be needed to undertake the first round of performance measurement implementation.

Before each meeting, the program manager should prepare and distribute an agenda, making the objectives of the meeting clear. In addition, the program manager should prepare a brief report on the key findings and results of the previous meeting and disseminate it for review by the group *before* the next meeting (detailed minutes are seldom needed).

A sample tight 30-month schedule for developing a program outcome measurement process is presented in exhibit 3-3.[3] The program should also provide regular reviews of the process as it is developing—to make sure that it is providing quality data *and* that the outcome information is being used beneficially.

Most programs require a minimum of three years from the start of the performance measurement development process to production of the first set of comprehensive performance data.[4] The program manager should negotiate with high-level officials for an overall time frame that is reasonable. Pressure on the program to have a *complete* performance measurement system in place can sometimes be reduced if, as is possible for some programs, early data are available on some outcomes and progress can be reported on development of new outcome-oriented indicators.

## Notes

1. Alternative approaches include relying on contractors to design the process or using an in-house team of experts from other parts of the agency. However, the "not invented here" problem and the need for the program to have adequate tailoring for its special features make these latter approaches less attractive. A combination of approaches is, of course, another possible option.

2. Including stakeholders outside the agency, such as representatives of customer groups, is attractive in theory, but it complicates working group scheduling. Nevertheless, as described later, customer input can and should be sought through other means.

3. Seldom, however, are programs given 30 months; invariably, they are rushed to implement a process within a year or so. Unless the program has considerable background in collecting outcome information and already collects most of the needed information, this time span is not enough to do an effective job.
4. This period can be shortened if the program is already producing some outcome information.

# What Are the Program's Mission and Objectives? Who Are Its Customers?

Establishing a performance measurement process begins with identification of a program's, or agency's, mission and its basic objectives. What is the program intended to accomplish? The flow of performance information should flow from, and be based on, the answer to this fundamental question.

Thus, a program's first technical step is to prepare a mission/objectives statement, including identification of its customers. Some mission statements are so general or vague that they provide little help in determining what performance indicators are needed to assess whether or how well the mission is being accomplished. Others can be quite specific but ultimately not very helpful because they indicate only *how* the mission is to be undertaken (the service delivery approach), not what the objectives of pursuing the specified strategies are. Development of a mission/objectives statement provides an opportunity to step back and identify the program's fundamental purposes—the reasons why it exists.

## The Mission/Objectives Statement

The mission/objectives statement expresses the *major results* sought by the program. It is the starting point for identifying the specific outcomes to be measured and the specific performance indicators that are needed. The term *mission/objectives* denotes both the overarching vision of the program (the mission) and the more specific—though still qualitative—program purposes (objectives) that flow from the mission.[1] It is important that these objectives be stated in general, *not quantitative,* terms. They should remain reasonably stable, whereas specific targets are likely to change, often annually, because of new circumstances.

The following are suggestions for developing a mission/objectives statement:

1. Focus on how program activities are expected to affect customers and the public.
2. Identify all the major objectives that the program hopes to achieve. *Most programs have multiple objectives.* It is better to include too many objectives in the statement than to run the risk of excluding objectives that may later be found to be important to one or more customer groups.
3. Call explicitly for *minimizing negative effects of the program.* Transportation is a good example of a program that can have negative effects. Since pollution is an inevitable by-product of transportation, the mission statement of a transportation program might well include ". . . and to minimize air, water, and soil pollution."
4. Include *conflicting objectives,* as appropriate, and *recognize in the statement the need to balance them.* Environmental and economic development programs, for example, have potentially conflicting impacts on each other. Public land management programs, for example, may need to be aimed at a balance between preserving green space, flora, and fauna and promoting economic development.
5. Consider including objectives about *reducing the magnitude of unmet needs,* not just about helping customers who come in for service. For example, "reduce the number of households with incomes below the poverty line."
6. Include objectives related to the *quality of services delivered*—characteristics that are important to customers of the service, such as timeliness and convenience of the help received. While these are intermediate outcomes rather than the end results sought, their importance to customers may warrant their explicit inclusion in a program's objectives, to help ensure that they receive ongoing attention.
7. Include the objective of *providing a service as efficiently as possible.* This is an objective of virtually all programs, even if only implicitly. Its explicit inclusion can serve to remind program personnel of its importance.
8. Include only qualitative, not quantitative, objectives to enhance the likelihood that the statement will remain stable over time. Numerical

targets (such as "improve the outcome by 15 percent") should be avoided because they are unlikely to be valid for more than a particular measurement period.[2]

9. Avoid vague or obscure wording that makes later measurement a guessing game about what was intended. The strategic plan for one state's transportation department included "having all transportation systems and services work smoothly together." Such a statement makes it very difficult to determine how to track progress toward that objective.

The basic form of a mission/objectives statement is as follows:

**To:** [Identify the basic objectives (results) the program seeks and any major negative consequences the program should avoid.]

**By:** [Identify the basic way the service is provided.] WARNING: Do not constrain the options on ways to provide the service. The program is more likely to be stimulated to innovate and try different approaches if it allows managers to choose among specific methods.

An example from a U.S. Department of Education distance learning program (Star Schools) is shown in exhibit 4-1. Note that the **To** statement includes both end outcomes (improved student learning and employability) and intermediate outcomes (improved instruction and student access to a wide range of subjects). The general approach of the program is the use of distance learning technologies. Specific technologies are not included, to avoid limiting the options of those delivering these program services.

Some programs use wording that implicitly places the **By** section first, as in this alternative wording of exhibit 4-1: Use distance learning technologies that improve student learning and employability, including providing access to, and improving instruction in, a wide range of subjects. This is NOT a good practice. Leading with the **To** statement keeps the focus more immediately and therefore more strongly on results.

A **By** statement may not be necessary for programs whose approach is expected to be clear to users of the performance information. Basic municipal services, such as waste collection and recreational programs, for example, are

---

**EXHIBIT 4-1**

**Mission/Objectives Statement for Distance Learning Programs**

**To:** Improve student learning and employability, including providing access to, and improving instruction in, a wide range of subjects.

**By:** The use of distance learning technologies.

EXHIBIT 4-2

**Potential Sources of Information on Program Mission/Objectives**

- Legislation, ordinances, and regulations
- Mission statements contained in budget documents
- Strategic plans
- Program descriptions and annual reports
- Discussions with upper-level officials and their staffs
- Discussions or meetings with customers and service providers

- Discussions with legislators and their staffs
- Input from program personnel
- Complaint information (What have customers complained about?)
- Other levels of government with similar programs
- Program evaluations and performance audits

sufficiently clear that even good statements about service approaches are not likely to be helpful.

Sources of information to help identify the program's mission/objectives are listed in exhibit 4-2.

## Identifying Categories of Customers

Look again at exhibit 4-1. The **To** part identifies the program's primary customers: students. This is good practice. Mission/objectives statements need to identify who the program's customers are, unless it is already obvious to users of the outcome information.[3]

Almost always, programs have multiple categories of customers. Questions such as the following are helpful in identifying customer information from each source listed in exhibit 4-2:

- Who benefits from the program? Who are direct recipients? Who are indirect recipients?
- Who might be hurt by program activities? (This may also help identify potential negative effects of the program that should be identified in the mission/objectives statement.)
- What other persons not directly targeted by the program can be significantly affected by it?
- Which demographic or interest groups are particularly affected by the program? (For example, is its primary focus low-income households?)
- Is the public at large likely to have a major interest in what the program accomplishes (rather than just what it costs)? For programs that

provide assistance to businesses to help them reduce hazardous waste and pollution generated by their activities, for example, the general public clearly is a major customer. But the assisted (and perhaps regulated) businesses are also customers, and the performance measurement process should include outcome indicators that address their concerns as well, such as not being priced out of business.

Examples of key customer (stakeholder) groups for various programs include:

- For school-to-work opportunity programs: students, recent dropouts, parents, and prospective employers.
- For programs aimed at combating teenage pregnancy: teenagers. But should boys as well as girls be targeted by such programs? Are parents also customers?
- For school violence prevention programs: the student body as a whole and school staff.
- For economic development programs assisting U.S. businesses to increase their exports (and profits): businesses and persons seeking employment.
- For local sanitation, crime control, parking and traffic, water services, and code enforcement programs: businesses as well as individual members of the public.

Both *end customers* and *intermediate customers* need to be considered. Intermediate customers can be important groups. State and local government agencies, for example, are the intermediate customers of many federal agency programs. The federal programs work through these lower levels of government to produce favorable outcomes to the end customers. The U.S. Departments of Education, Health and Human Services, Housing and Urban Development, and Labor are particularly dependent on lower levels of government to deliver programs that provide support to citizens.

As with the determination of mission and objectives, determining who are the program's or agency's customers is often more complicated than it appears at first glance. These complications, as well as difficulties in identifying missions and objectives, are not caused by performance measurement. The complications are already there and should not be ignored in a comprehensive performance measurement system. Here are some examples:

*Are the inmates of prisons and jails customers?* The public who are protected from these inmates are the central customers of correctional programs. However, society also is concerned that inmates have some protection in terms of their health and safety. Thus, indicators of correctional activities often include counts of inmate diseases, deaths, suicides, and injuries. Thus, minimizing the frequency of such incidents in correctional facilities is desirable, making such minimization at least an intermediate but probably an end outcome.

*Are the organizations or persons that government regulatory agencies regulate customers?* The effects on those regulated—such as the amount of time, money, and effort required to obtain permits or licenses—should be of concern to regulatory programs. The agencies running regulatory programs should seek to minimize such problems for those regulated, even though the ultimate and more vital outcomes are to protect the health and safety of those whom the regulation is intended to protect. Environmental protection agencies, offices of consumer protection, and boards that regulate doctors, nurses, hospitals, nursing homes, and other health care organizations are among those that can reasonably view the subjects of their regulation as intermediate customers.

Whether or not an agency labels such groups explicitly as customers, its mission statement would do well to articulate the need to reduce undesirable negative effects for them—if only to minimize efficiency-reducing protests from these groups.

## Sort Objectives into a Hierarchy

Many mission/objectives statements include a mix of end objectives, intermediate objectives, and means. Agencies need to determine and make clear which is which.

Working through an example is useful here. The federal government's 1997 drug policy report identified five major objectives: preventing drug use among America's youth; increasing the safety of America's citizens; reducing the health and social costs of drug use; shielding America's air, land, and sea frontiers; and breaking foreign and domestic sources of supply.[4] The first three objectives can be considered ends. Are the last two objectives ends? No. The last two (shielding frontiers and breaking sources of supply) are intermediate (subsidiary) objectives—ways to help achieve the first three.

Chapters 5 and 6 explain ways, such as the use of logic models, to help sort through objectives and develop an appropriate hierarchy.

## A Special Problem for Pass-Through Programs

A special problem arises with federal or state programs that dispense funds (grants) to lower levels of government. Is their sole mission to provide funds accurately and in a timely way? Such tasks should, of course, be tracked as indicators of the quality of the program's service, but would elected officials and the public agree that the purpose of the program is merely to dole out funds accurately and expeditiously? Or should the program's mission statement also include the end purpose for which those funds are to be used: helping improve citizens' health, education, welfare, or whatever the program needs to ultimately achieve? Clearly, the program and its personnel have only partial—perhaps a very small degree of—influence over the ultimate purpose. But program personnel *are* part of the overall service delivery process. *If they are made to feel part of it, they have an incentive to make innovative recommendations that can lead to significant improvements in the service's effectiveness.* Even if those recommendations require legislation, identifying them is a valuable first step in improving program results.

This dilemma frequently confronts agencies in both public and private service delivery. The philosophy in this book is to encourage use of a broad and more proactive outlook for agencies and their programs—to foster innovation. This includes efforts by programs to seek (explicit or implicit) *performance partnerships* with other agencies, other governments, and other private sector organizations that can help in producing the ultimately desired end.

### References and Notes

1. This book avoids the term "goals" because, although it is sometimes used to refer to what are here called objectives, it is also often used to refer to specific numerical targets, which generally should not be included in a mission/objectives statement.
2. Numerical targets should be developed separately, as discussed in later chapters, for each performance indicator that flows from the mission/objectives statement.
3. This book uses the word "customers" to refer to any category of persons that a program serves or affects (other than those involved in delivering the service). Some people object to considering direct service customers as the primary customers, believing that the public, the taxpayers, are the real customers and pointing out

that the latter two groups are sometimes ignored when staff are developing objectives. While agreeing that taxpayers and citizens at large should not be left out, it does not seem necessary to explicitly include them in all mission/objectives statements.

4. Office of National Drug Control Policy, *Performance Measures of Effectiveness: A System for Assessing the Performance of the National Drug Control Strategy*, Report no. NCJ 168953 (Washington, D.C.: Office of National Drug Control Policy, 1998).

# What Outcomes Should Be Tracked?

"If you don't know where you have been, how can you know where you are going?"

A performance measurement system is only as good as the outcomes it tracks. Each program needs to develop a specific list of outcomes important to it. (The next chapter discusses transforming each outcome into specific, measurable outcome indicators.) A checklist of broad, basic categories of outcomes to be considered in the outcome identification process appears in exhibit 5-1.

Selecting the outcomes that should be tracked is essentially a judgment call (as is the identification of a program's mission and objectives, described in chapter 4). Public service agencies almost always have multiple objectives and multiple categories of customers. Thus, those making the selection should attempt to include all these perspectives, at least to the extent practical.

The sources listed in chapter 4 for identifying a program's mission/objectives can also be useful in the search for outcomes. They are listed again in exhibit 5-2 for the reader's convenience. This chapter discusses four promising approaches to identifying outcomes and then briefly discusses how the candidate outcomes obtained from all sources might be combined.

The four approaches described in this chapter are:

- Focus groups
  — customers

EXHIBIT 5-1

## Checklist of Types of Outcomes to Consider

Consider for inclusion outcomes that:

- *Produce the results sought by the specific program* (either that prevent unwanted incidents or remedy existing problems).
- *Minimize undesirable or negative effects* that are likely to occur (such as complaints about the service, excessive harassment by public officers to increase traffic tickets or arrest counts, environmental problems from transportation or economic development programs, and adverse economic effects from environmental protection programs).
- *Improve the quality of service delivery.* *
- *Reduce the amount of unmet need.* Many programs focus on customers who come in for assistance. Customers may represent only a portion of the citizens eligible for the assistance.
- *Produce benefits that accrue to the general population from providing effective services to specific customer groups* (such as reduction in crime from programs aimed at keeping youths in school).
- *Provide equitable outcomes to customer groups.* As noted in chapter 4, this outcome is not often explicitly stated in program mission/objectives statements other than those of programs that directly address equity issues, such as equal opportunity programs.

*See exhibit 2-3 for a list of potentially applicable service quality attributes.

EXHIBIT 5-2

## Other Information Sources for Outcomes

- Legislation and regulations
- Mission statements from budget documents
- Strategic plans
- Program descriptions and annual reports
- Discussions with:
  — upper-level officials (and staff)
  — legislators (and staff)
  — customers and service providers
- Input from program personnel
- Complaints in the file from customers
- Other jurisdictions with similar programs
- Program evaluations and performance audits

— program staff (especially field personnel and any contractors or grantees that help deliver services)

- Input from meetings with other partners (such as federal, state, and local personnel)
- Role-playing by program staff acting as customers
- Outcome-sequence charts (logic models)

## Focus Groups

Focus groups of customers are an excellent way to obtain input on a program's outcomes and service delivery quality. But be prepared to hear them air their gripes about the program before they identify the things they like about it. Gripes—which include such matters as delays in providing services—are often extremely useful in identifying program characteristics that represent important outcomes to be tracked.[1] Focus groups of program or project personnel, especially those who frequently work in the field with customers, are also a useful way to obtain a perspective on outcomes of concern to customers.

Exhibit 5-3 identifies typical steps for focus group planning and implementation.

The direct costs of focus groups are not high. Participants do not usually need to be paid, and the meetings, which should be held in a number of locations within the area served by the program, do not need to be held in luxurious surroundings. BUT considerable staff preparation and administrative effort are needed to ensure that the process goes smoothly and is effective in gaining the information sought. Refreshments generally should be provided to participants.

## Meetings and Related Input from Other "Partners"

Many federal, state, and local programs involve participation by other agencies or organizations. These are usually public or private nonprofit agencies but can also be the business community (such as with school-to-work and economic development programs). Seeking the input of these other agencies and organizations into identification of outcomes that should be tracked is usually advisable.

The program can obtain such input through meetings, telephone and conference calls, mail, fax, internet, and any other form of communication, as well as focus groups.

EXHIBIT 5-3

### Focus Group Steps

- Plan the sessions. Determine the information needed, the categories of participants, and the timing, location, and other administrative details of the sessions.
- Select a facilitator who is experienced in conducting focus groups to manage the meeting and a person to take notes on the information provided by the participants.
- Invite 8 to 12 customers to participate in each focus group meeting.

    Members can be chosen from lists of customers without regard to the statistical representativeness of the selection. The information obtained from focus group participants does not provide statistical data, so statistical sampling, though an optional selection method, is not necessary. The main selection criteria are that the participants have experience with the program and be at least somewhat varied in their characteristics.*
- Set a maximum of two hours. Hold the meeting in a pleasant and comfortable location. Soft drinks and snacks help provide a relaxed atmosphere.
- Begin with introductions and an overview of the purpose of the meeting.
- The facilitator can then ask the participants two questions. For customer focus groups, the questions should be:
  — What do you like about the service?
  — What don't you like about the service?**
- The facilitator can ask these questions in many different ways. The fundamental requirement is to establish an open, nonthreatening environment and to obtain input from each participant. *Facilitators should not debate or argue with the participants.*
- The recorder and the facilitator should work together to provide a meeting report. The report should identify outcome-related characteristics raised explicitly or implicitly by one or more participants. The program should consider tracking these characteristics.

*Program personnel groups should include a broad representation of staff familiar with customer concerns—in particular, personnel who work in the field and first-line staff.

**For a program personnel focus group the questions would be:
  — What do you believe customers like about the service?
  — What do you believe customers don't like about the service?

Caution: If a program seeks input from these other organizations, as is desirable, the program should expect to use it or face the possibility that spurned advice will offend those organizations.

*Preferably, programs would work with other organizations as partners in designing and implementing the whole performance measurement process.* For example, service agencies at various levels of government, private nonprofit organizations, business organizations, and churches might all be delivering services aimed at the same objective. Partnerships are warranted when the program believes that desired outcomes would be best achieved by obtaining voluntary agreement among organizations as to (a) the outcomes and outcome indicators to be tracked; (b) how the data should be collected; (c) the short- and long-term targets for each outcome indicator; and (d) the roles and responsibilities of each organization in providing the particular service. The involvement of these organizations from the outset can facilitate future data collection efforts and possibly reduce the costs of data collection to any one organization. Such a process is not easy, however, and takes considerably more effort than the traditional go-it-alone approach.

Such agreements are called performance partnerships. They are a new concept and require significant time and effort to work out with other organizations.

## Role-Playing by Program Staff

An easy procedure for helping identify program outcomes, which can also be fun, is to have program staff role-play as customers—with each staff member taking the role of a particular category of customer. For example, a state child welfare agency might ask its program staff to play the roles of local county and city office personnel, parents and other child care givers, and the children themselves. Staff who work directly with customers (including staff from field offices) are likely to be particularly valuable participants.

This procedure is especially useful for programs that are not able to hold customer focus groups.[2]

The sessions should last perhaps two hours. Each participant, in his or her customer role, should be asked the same questions posed to customer focus groups: "What do you like about the program? What don't you like about it?" Participants then draw on their own knowledge of the program and what their experiences have indicated are the likely reactions of customers.

As with focus groups, someone should act as the recorder, to take down the findings of the role-playing session, especially the potential outcome characteristics identified during the session. The recorder should then draft a report listing all outcomes explicitly or implicitly identified by the role players as either intermediate (including service quality) or end outcomes.

## Outcome-Sequence Charts (Logic Models)

Programs are likely to find preparation of outcome-sequence charts (often called logic models) helpful in identifying outcomes.[3] This is because such charts provide a visual depiction of what a program is expected to produce, and they allow staff to construct the anticipated time path of program activities from initial inputs through end outcomes.[4]

Every program implicitly has a set of hypotheses about what actions will produce what results. The charts attempt to identify these hypotheses by showing the outputs, intermediate outcomes, and end outcomes expected to flow from program activities.

Exhibit 5-4 illustrates a sequence of expected events for a dropout prevention program focused on parental involvement. The program's activity (workload) here is providing classes to help parents be more supportive of their children's learning efforts. Holding classes (block 1) is the program activity or output. The number of classes completed is an output of the program. Parents attending these classes (block 2) and parents completing the program (block 3) are intermediate outcomes. These outcomes indicate, respectively, the program's success in attracting parents into the program and retaining them through the end of the program. Parents then encouraging their children to learn (block 4) indicates that the program actually affected those parents—a more advanced intermediate outcome. This is *expected* to lead to improved student learning, but it does not reveal what end outcomes actually *resulted*. Increased attendance (block 5a), fewer behavioral problems in school (block 5b), and improved grades (block 5c) of students whose parents completed the program activities are desired short-term end outcomes for the education system. Fewer students dropping out of high school (block 6) is also hoped for, but this outcome cannot be completely determined until all current students are through their final year of high school. It is, therefore, a longer-term end outcome. The logic goes even further to include work and earning histories of the students as very long-term end outcomes (block 7).

Each outcome (and output) on the chart is important to the program and should be included in the program's performance measurement process.[5] This example considers improved attendance (5a), fewer behavioral problems (5b), and improved grades (5c) to be end outcomes. Other analysts might show them as intermediate outcomes. People can legitimately disagree over outcome categories. Whether something is classified as an intermediate or end outcome rarely affects the measurement process itself. It can affect the importance the program attaches to the outcome, however, and thus the relative amount of resources applied to achieving it as opposed to other outcomes.

**EXHIBIT 5 - 4**

**Outcome-Sequence Chart: Parental Involvement in Dropout Prevention Program**

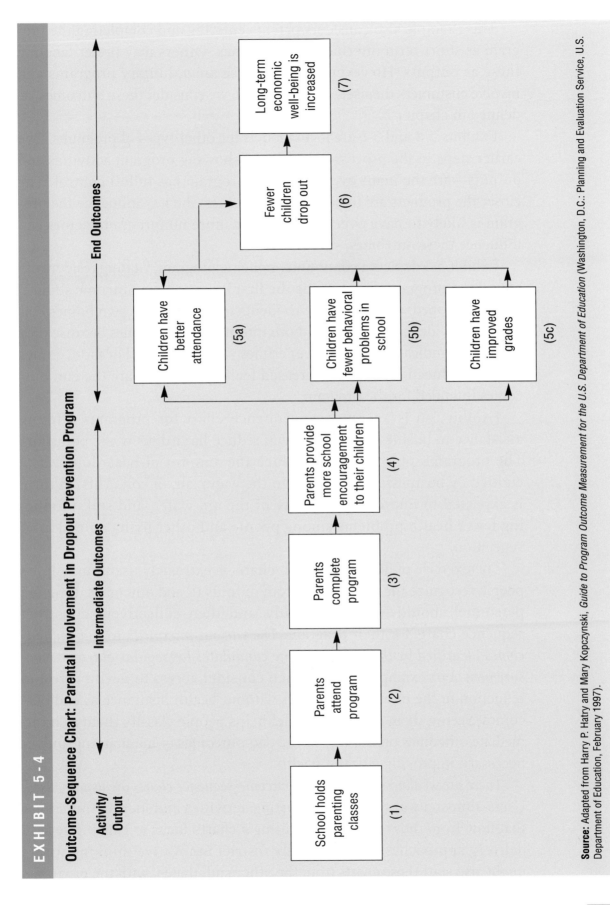

**Source:** Adapted from Harry P. Hatry and Mary Kopczynski, *Guide to Program Outcome Measurement for the U.S. Department of Education* (Washington, D.C.: Planning and Evaluation Service, U.S. Department of Education, February 1997).

This example also considers parents entering and completing the program as short-term intermediate outcomes. Others may prefer labeling these as outputs. However, because these are voluntary programs and involve customers themselves taking steps, we consider these outcomes, as defined in chapter 2.

Exhibits 5-5 and 5-6 are logic models for other types of programs. The earlier steps in the process—the blocks showing program activities and outputs—are the items over which the program has fullest control. The closer the products are to being end outcomes, the less influence the program is likely to have over them because more nonprogram factors can influence these outcomes.

Exhibit 5-5 depicts a community policing program. Getting residents to attend the program's meetings is the first intermediate outcome sought. This, it is hoped, will encourage residents to protect their own homes better and provide leads to police—both intermediate outcomes because they still do not indicate whether fewer crimes were committed or more crimes solved. Reduced crime and increased feelings of safety are the end outcomes intended for the program.[6]

Exhibit 5-6 is an outcome-sequence chart for programs offering assistance to businesses to help them reduce hazardous waste pollution. The program's objective is to reduce the amount of hazardous waste emitted by businesses, whether into the water, air, or soil. This, in turn, is expected to improve the quality of the air, water, and soil, producing fewer health problems among people and other living animals and vegetation.

The exercise of developing such charts is extremely useful in helping people recognize the progression from outputs to end outcomes. Program personnel should first individually, and then collectively, construct sequence charts for their program. *The various intermediate and end outcomes identified by them then become candidates for regular outcome measurement.* For example, people often consider access to health care and reduction in the number of families without health insurance as end outcomes. Seeing them in a logic model helps people classify them as intermediate outcomes on the way to the end outcomes of maintaining and, as necessary, improving citizens' health.

*There are weaknesses in the way outcome-sequence charts are usually used.* Users almost always start from *existing* activities and identify outcomes that flow from those activities. Limiting a chart's focus to existing service delivery approaches can potentially restrict innovative thinking. Users might also start these charts from the other end, that is, with the program's

EXHIBIT 5-5

## Outcome-Sequence Chart: Community Policing Program

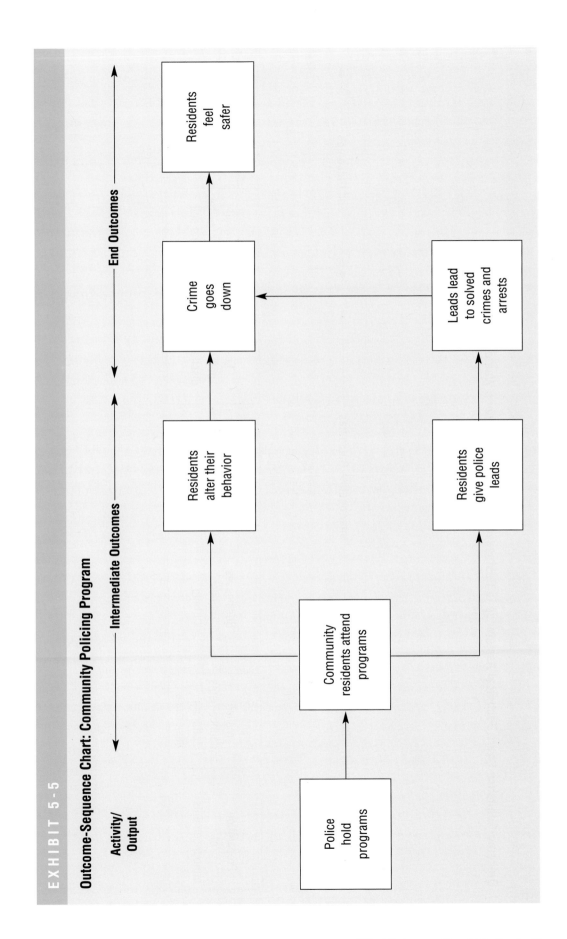

Activity/
Output

Intermediate Outcomes

End Outcomes

Police
hold
programs

Community
residents attend
programs

Residents
alter their
behavior

Residents
give police
leads

Crime
goes
down

Leads lead
to solved
crimes and
arrests

Residents
feel
safer

EXHIBIT 5-6

**Outcome-Sequence Chart: Technical Assistance to Businesses to Reduce Hazardous Waste Pollution**

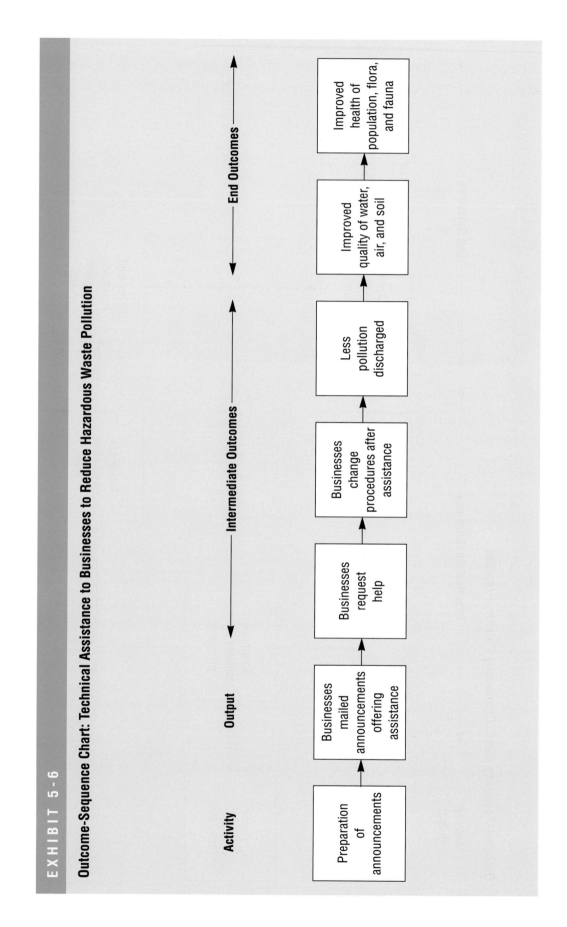

mission and objectives, and work back. This is more difficult but is likely to be well worth the extra effort. *In any case, outcome-sequence charts should be used only in combination with other outcome-identifying procedures, such as those described in this chapter.*

## Combining Candidate Outcomes from All Sources

Before completing the list of candidate outcomes, program staff should ask the following questions:

1. Do the outcomes assembled cover all the objectives identified in the mission/objectives statement?
2. What bad things would happen to customers if the program's budget and resources were substantially cut or deleted? What would the consequences be? What benefits would customers receive if the program's budget and resources were increased? Thinking through the answers to these questions may help identify outcomes that have not yet been included and should be added to the list.
3. Are there any potentially bad consequences or effects associated with the program that should also be monitored? If these can be tracked on a regular basis, they should be included as outcomes. (Some of these may have been identified in the mission/objectives statement as something to be minimized, or at least contained, by the program.)

When these additional questions have been answered satisfactorily, the outcomes obtained from all sources described in this chapter should be assembled together into one list. At this stage, outcomes should be categorized as intermediate or end, and overlaps and duplications should be identified.

The resulting list of outcomes is likely to be very long. Even so, it is best not to screen any out at this stage, except for those that appear truly trivial or those identified as being duplications. *Outcomes should not be deleted simply because no feasible way to measure them is currently known.* The list of outcomes should be trimmed only after specific performance indicators (chapter 6) and associated data collection procedures (chapter 7) have been identified and the cost of additional data collection estimated.

### References and Notes

1. These gripes might be summarized by the focus group facilitator (retaining the anonymity of the complainers) and presented to the program manager and staff for possible action—a side benefit of focus groups.

2. Role-playing has the additional advantage of sensitizing program staff to customer concerns more generally.

3. The first publication of which I am aware that used the term "logic model" and provided examples of them was published two decades ago in Joseph S. Wholey, *Evaluation: Promise and Performance* (Washington, D.C.: Urban Institute, 1979).

4. This process can also be an excellent component in training on performance measurement—for any and all levels of personnel. And the process itself can stimulate program personnel to consider alternative ways to achieve outcomes.

5. Regular measurement of the longest-term outcomes, such as future earnings of students who are now in elementary and secondary school, may not be feasible for the program.

6. Some persons believe that the solving of crimes and arrests are intermediate outcomes.

# What Outcome Indicators Should Be Tracked?

Selecting the specific indicators to be measured is a key part of developing a performance measurement system. Too often, agencies base their selection of indicators on how readily available the data are, not how important the outcome indicator is in measuring the extent to which the outcomes sought are being achieved.

**What Gets Measured and Reported Gets Attention!**

This chapter focuses primarily on outcome indicators—a major focus of results-based performance measurement systems. It touches briefly on efficiency indicators as well.

## What Outcome Indicators Are

Outcome indicators are not the same as outcomes. Each outcome to be tracked needs to be translated into one or more outcome indicators. An outcome indicator identifies a specific *numerical measurement* that indicates progress toward achieving an outcome. Thus, performance indicators usually begin with *number of . . . , percent of . . . , ratio of . . . , incidence of . . . , proportion of . . .* or similar words.

Some people argue that, since change between reporting periods is the fundamental objective, indicators should directly measure this change. In such a case, indicators would start with such words as *the change in. . . .* If the change version is used, the indicator needs to be calculated as the *difference* between the values for different reporting periods. The outcome indicator would be, for example, "number of cases correctly resolved during the time period" or "the percentage by which the number increased this reporting period as compared to the previous period." Indicators that show the value for particular reporting periods, not the change between periods, are probably preferable. They provide added information by showing the level of performance rather than merely the change. Changes over time can be readily calculated for any two (or more) periods for which values are available.

Translating outcomes into outcome indicators sounds like a relatively straightforward activity, but numerous measurement issues can arise to complicate the task.

A fundamental guide to the development of successful indicators is to ask about each: Is its wording sufficiently specific? Addressing this question often reveals words in the indicator that need to be defined in more depth, perhaps with the help of experts. Often it reveals problems that need to be hammered out with experienced program personnel. For example, a program that seeks to track "the percent of clients completing the program in this reporting period who were helped to a significant extent" needs to define specifically four concepts in this wording:

- What exactly is meant by significant extent?
- What exactly is the time period covered (see box)?
- How much service is required before a person is counted as a client (in order to determine the correct number for the denominator of the percents)?
- What constitutes completion?

Data sources and data collection procedures (discussed in more detail in the next chapter) often dictate the specific wording of an indicator. For example, if service timeliness is being assessed by customer surveys, the indicator will be something like "percent of customers giving satisfactory ratings to service timeliness." But if program records are the data source, the indicator will be something like "percent of service requests for which the program exceeded its standard for responding."

If a transportation system outcome is "roads will be in good rideable condition," the outcome indicator might be "percent of roads in good condition." However, this needs to be defined more precisely. Should roads be expressed as lane-miles? Should unpaved roads be included? And what determines whether a lane-mile is in "good" condition? Numerous road-rating procedures exist; technical personnel need to use them to work out the detailed definition. An option is to measure "good rideable condition" from the viewpoint of customers, transforming the outcome indicator into "percent of sampled respondents who rated the rideability of roads as either good or excellent." In this situation, the program will need to decide which of these two basic indicators (or both) it wants to track. Data collection procedures and their costs often affect the decision as to the specific indicator to be used (as described in chapter 7).

Exhibit 6-1 lists criteria for selecting outcome indicators. It is useful to rate each candidate indicator on each of these. Exhibit 6-2 shows a specific example: a set of indicators recommended for solid waste collection services.

*A major potential criticism of performance measurement systems* is that they focus attention on the indicators being measured. If important outcome characteristics are neglected, this can lead to misallocation of a program's resources and effort. The system needs to include a comprehensive set of indicators (see exhibit 6-1). This includes indicators that track undesirable outcomes. For example, a law enforcement agency that focuses solely on number of police arrests or a tax collection agency that focuses solely on the amount of dollars collected (by auditing federal, state, or local tax returns) will tempt staff to harass individual citizens (and businesses) to increase these values. Including other indicators, such as the number of validated complaints, considerably reduces such problems by altering the incentives facing staff.

Often, more than one indicator will be appropriate for measuring an outcome. For example, "improvement in the quality of life of senior citizens" might be measured by such indicators as (a) "the percent of served senior citizens reporting that their life situation has improved since service receipt" and (b) "the percent of key family members who reported finding the senior citizens more pleased with life since service receipt." An agency could decide to use only one of these but would probably obtain a more comprehensive perspective on the outcome by using both.

---

### The Need to Be Clear about Time Covered by an Indicator

Each outcome indicator needs to be clear as to the time covered. For example:

- Some indicators report on the number of incidents that occurred during a specified reporting period, such as *number of traffic accident deaths occurring in the past 12 months.*
- Some indicators apply to a particular point in time, such as *number of cases of tuberculosis on record as of December 31, 19xx.*
- Some indicators track clients over a period of time. The period needs to be carefully specified, such as *percent of clients whose condition had improved substantially as of 12 months after the client began service* AND *whose condition was assessed during the current 12-month reporting period.*

This last indicator is particularly complex (but can be particularly important for health and human service programs). To calculate the required indicator, the program needs to (a) have assessed the clients' condition at the time they started service (i.e., sometime during the previous 12 months) AND (b) assess each client 12 months after that date (i.e., during the following 12-month period).

### Criteria for Selecting Outcome Indicators

- *Relevance* to the mission/objectives of the program and to the outcome the indicator is intended to help measure.
- *Importance* to the outcome it is intended to help measure. Does the indicator measure an important aspect of the outcome?
- *Understandability* to users of what is measured and reported.
- *Program influence or control over the outcome.* Do not use this criterion as a way to avoid measuring important outcomes. Almost always a program will have less than full influence over most outcomes, especially end outcomes. As long as the program is expected to have some tangible, measurable effect on a specific outcome, an indicator of that outcome should be a candidate for inclusion—whether the effects are direct or only indirect.
- *Feasibility* of collecting reasonably valid data on the indicator.
- *Cost of collecting the indicator data.* This is another criterion to be used with caution. Sometimes the most costly indicators are the most important.
- *Uniqueness.* To the extent that an indicator is duplicated by, or overlaps with, other indicators, it becomes less important.
- *Manipulability.* Do not select indicators that program personnel can easily manipulate to their advantage.*
- *Comprehensiveness.* The set of indicators should include outcomes that identify possible negative or detrimental effects. Classic examples are harassing citizens to achieve large numbers of arrests, indictments, or tax collections. Where negative effects are a danger, indicators such as the number of valid complaints should be tracked as a counterbalance. Other questions about comprehensiveness include: Does the list of indicators cover all the quality characteristics of concern to customers, such as service timeliness? Does the list of indicators include relevant feedback from customers of the program relating to the outcomes?

*This depends to a considerable extent on the particular data collection procedure used, as discussed in chapter 7.

Seeking comprehensiveness will be constrained both by available measurement resources and by inherent data problems. For some outcomes that cannot be measured directly, reasonable surrogates can be found (see discussion later in this chapter). For some outcomes, it may not even be possible to find a reasonable surrogate. *In such a case, the performance measurement system should explicitly identify the omissions.*

*The aim is to provide valid, useful data on which managers and other officials can rely—and to recognize explicitly the limitations of those indicators.*

## Using Outcome-Sequence Charts to Help Identify Outcomes and Indicators

The previous chapter discussed the usefulness of logic models to identify outcomes. Exhibits 6-3 and 6-4 repeat the outcome-sequence charts for parental involvement and community policing presented in chapter 5,

EXHIBIT 6-2

## Objectives, Outcomes, and Outcome Indicators for Solid Waste Collection

Overall objective: To promote the aesthetics of the community and the health and safety of the citizens by providing an environment free from the hazards and unpleasantness of uncollected refuse with the least possible citizen inconvenience.

| Objective | Outcome | Specific Indicator |
|---|---|---|
| **Pleasing aesthetics** | Street, alley, and neighborhood cleanliness | 1. Percentage of (a) streets, (b) alleys the appearance of which is rated satisfactory (or unsatisfactory) |
| | | 2. Percentage of (a) households, (b) businesses rating their neighborhood cleanliness as satisfactory (or unsatisfactory) |
| | Offensive odors | 3. Percentage of (a) households, (b) businesses reporting offensive odors from solid wastes |
| | Objectionable noises | 4. Percentage of (a) households, (b) businesses reporting objectionable noise from solid waste collection operations |
| **Health and safety** | Health | 5. Number and percentage of blocks with one or more health hazards |
| | Fire hazards | 6. Number and percentage of blocks with one or more fire hazards |
| | Fires involving uncollected waste | 7. Number of fires involving uncollected solid waste |
| | Health hazards and unsightly appearance | 8. Number of abandoned automobiles |
| | Rodent hazard | 9. Percentage of (a) households, (b) businesses reporting having seen rats on their blocks in the past three months |
| | | 10. Number of rodent bites reported per 1,000 persons |
| **Minimum citizen inconvenience** | Missed or late collections | 11. Number and percentage of collection routes not completed on schedule |
| | | 12. Percentage of (a) households, (b) businesses reporting missed collections |
| | Spillage of trash and garbage during collections | 13. Percentage of (a) households, (b) businesses reporting spillage by collection crews |
| | Damage to private property by collection crews | 14. Percentage of (a) households, (b) businesses reporting property damage caused by collection crews |
| | Citizen complaints | 15. Number of verified citizen complaints, by type, per 1,000 households served |
| **General citizen satisfaction** | Perceived satisfaction | 16. Percent of (a) households, (b) businesses reporting overall satisfaction with the solid waste collection service they receive |

**Source:** Adapted from Harry P. Hatry et al., *How Effective Are Your Community Services? Procedures for Measuring Their Quality*, 2nd ed. (Washington, D.C.: The Urban Institute and the International City/County Management Association, 1992).

adding illustrative outcome indicators. Exhibit 6-5 displays an outcome-sequence chart for a stop-smoking program.

These charts can also be used to help identify efficiency indicators, especially outcome-based indicators. As noted in chapter 2, dividing outcome indicator values by inputs (dollars expended or employee hours) yields outcome-based efficiency ratios. For example, in exhibit 6-5, the number of persons reporting that they had stopped smoking 12 months after program completion, when divided by the cost of the program, yields program cost per person who stopped smoking, the end outcome–based efficiency indicator. Number of persons who completed the program, when divided by the cost of the program, yields cost per person completing the program, the intermediate outcome–based efficiency indicator.

The latter is a less meaningful indicator of program efficiency, because program completion has a less direct relationship to the ultimate goal of the program. But it is based on data that are available more quickly and is still a more meaningful indicator of program efficiency than the output-based efficiency indicators commonly used by government, such as cost per program held.

As with all indicators based on outcome data, outcome-based efficiency data do not guarantee that the outcomes were due to the program. (The problem of attribution is discussed further in the last section of this chapter.)

*Reminder from chapter 2:* Outcome values expressed as something to be minimized or as a percent make no sense when used in efficiency indicators. For example, number of children dropping out of school (exhibit 6-3) and number of reported crimes (exhibit 6-4) cannot be used to provide indicators of efficiency (but the number *prevented* can be used, if measurable).

## Numerical Forms for the Indicators

Outcome indicators are often expressed as the number or percent (proportion or rate) of something. Programs should consider including *both* forms. The number of successes (or failures) in itself does not indicate the rate of success (or failure)—what was not achieved. The percent by itself does not indicate the size of the success. Assessing the significance of an outcome typically requires data on both number and percent.

Numbers can be expressed in a variety of ways, including:

- *Number,* such as the total number of customers that had a particular condition, that improved, or that reported satisfaction with a service.

EXHIBIT 6-3

## Outcome-Sequence Chart with Indicators: Parental Involvement in Dropout Prevention Program

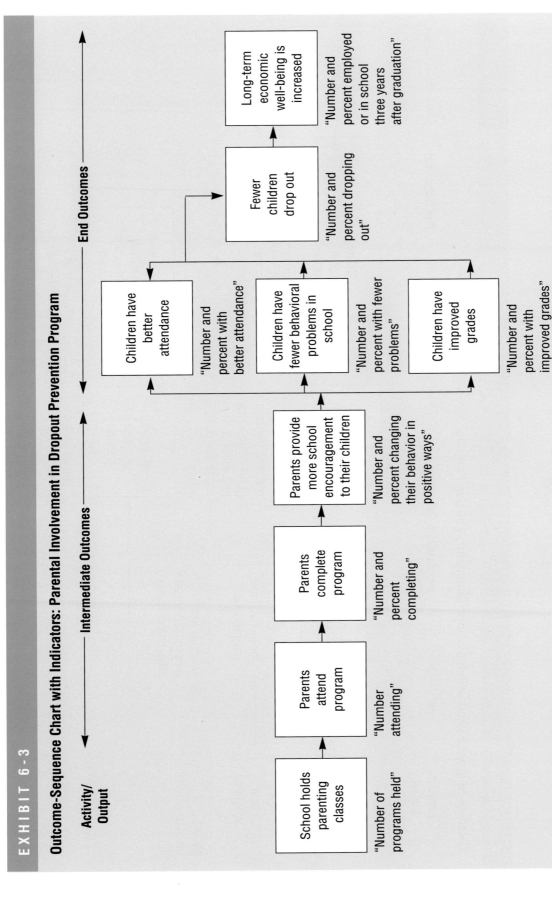

Activity/
Output ————— Intermediate Outcomes ————— End Outcomes

School holds parenting classes
"Number of programs held"

Parents attend program
"Number attending"

Parents complete program
"Number and percent completing"

Parents provide more school encouragement to their children
"Number and percent changing their behavior in positive ways"

Children have better attendance
"Number and percent with better attendance"

Children have fewer behavioral problems in school
"Number and percent with fewer problems"

Children have improved grades
"Number and percent with improved grades"

Fewer children drop out
"Number and percent dropping out"

Long-term economic well-being is increased
"Number and percent employed or in school three years after graduation"

**Source:** Harry P. Hatry and Mary Kopczynski, *Guide to Program Outcome Measurement for the U.S. Department of Education* (Washington, D.C.: Planning and Evaluation Service, U.S. Department of Education, February 1997).

What Outcome Indicators Should Be Tracked?

EXHIBIT 6-4

## Outcome-Sequence Chart with Indicators: Community Policing Program

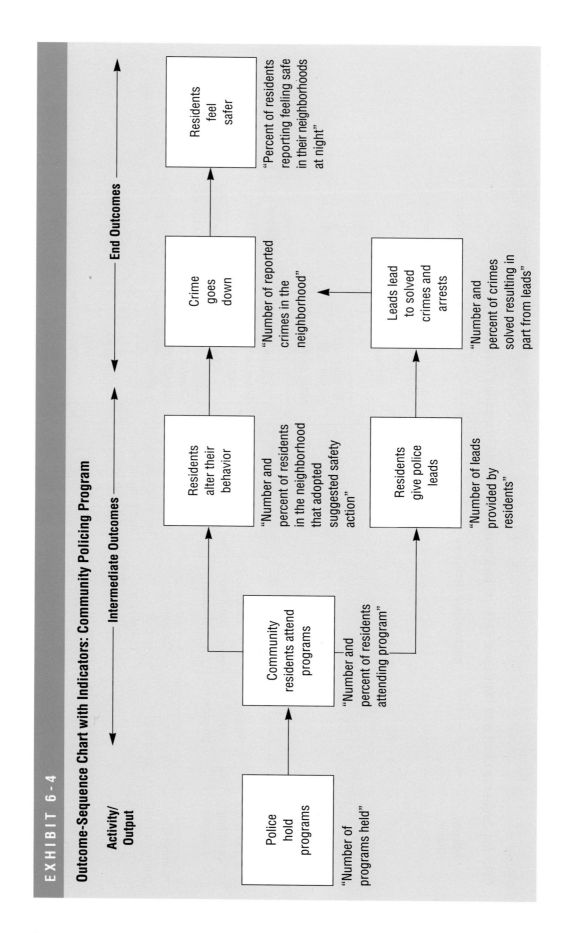

EXHIBIT 6-5

**Outcome-Sequence Chart with Indicators: A Stop-Smoking Program**

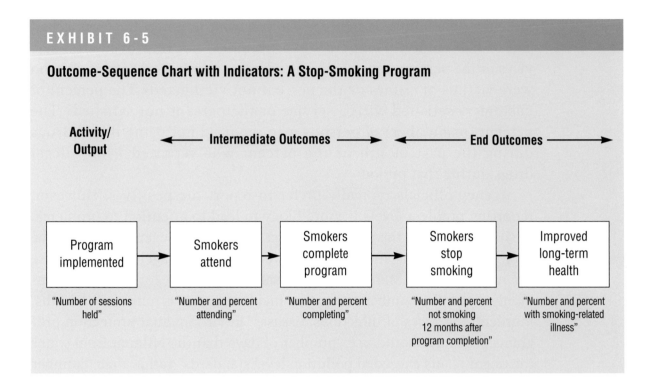

- *Mean*, the arithmetic average of a set of numerical values. A typical example is the average time between a call or request for a service and the response. Arithmetic averages have the advantage of being widely understood. Their disadvantage is that they can be greatly affected by extreme values.
- *Median*, the middle value of a set of numerical values. (If the set includes an even number of values, the median is usually determined by taking the arithmetic average of the two middle values.) Medians have the advantage of not being influenced by extreme values, as arithmetic averages are.

Percents can also be expressed in a variety of ways, including:

- Percent that fell into a particular outcome category, such as the percent that rated some service characteristic as good.
- Percent that fell above (or below) some targeted value, such as the percent of persons with blood pressure above an identified danger level.
- Percent that fell into particular outcome intervals, such as the percent between two specified values representing too high and too low blood pressure, respectively.

Some indicators are expressed as something the program wants to *maximize*. Others are expressed as something the program wants to *minimize.* Often there is a choice: Do you want to report the glass as half full or half empty? The percent (or number) not improved after services or the percent improved? The percent (or number) of citizens who were victims of crimes or the percent not victimized? The percent of customers satisfied with a service or the percent not satisfied? The percent (or number) of persons who reported not using illegal drugs during the past month or the percent who reported using illegal drugs during that period.

Agency officials typically prefer to report the positives. However, reporting problem levels is more likely to lead to attention to problems. In situations where the number or percent of negative events is likely to be very low, but the negative events are very important, agencies should use the negative form. Many health and safety programs, for example, commonly report the number of negative incidents, such as numbers of deaths, murders, and cases of infectious diseases. Environmental protection programs probably should use "number of days that the effluent from water treatment plants exceeded pollution level standards" rather than "number of days in full compliance."

## Key Factors Affecting Selection of Outcome Indicators

For any given outcome, a program is likely to be faced with many indicator choices. These choices will depend on factors such as the following:

- *The data collection procedure needed to provide the indicator.* The specific indicator will be affected by the data collection procedure. Procedures are discussed at length in chapter 7. They can vary considerably in data collection cost and validity.
- *The particular data source.* For example, in an educational program, customer surveys might be used to track perceptions of school safety. Three groups—children, teachers, and parents—might be surveyed. If so, each group would provide its own perspective and require its own outcome indicator.
- *Presence of different aspects of the outcome.* For example, the outcome *improved water quality* might be measured by a variety of pollutant-count indicators, by fish-kill counts, or by some combination of these. Multiple indicators are likely to be needed.
- *Different points in time at which the measurement is taken relative to when the service was provided.* For many outcome indicators, programs have a choice as to when the measurements will be made and at what frequencies.

For example, changes in a customer's condition for many human services programs (such as health, social service, and employment programs) might be measured (a) at the time the service was last provided, (b) at different lengths of time after the service ended, or (c) at specified periods from the time the customer entered the service.

## Cautions

Programs will be tempted to confine their measurements to the customers' condition while still receiving services or at their last official visit because of the relative ease of measurement and lower measurement cost. For programs that are meant to have lasting effects after customers finish receiving services, however, this restriction will prevent the program from tracking considerably more important outcomes.

Some organizations have urged or required that their programs limit the indicators sent to upper levels to some fixed number. Although officials who receive performance data from many different programs often prefer to see only those indicators the program believes to be most important, other indicators may be crucial for *internal* program tracking. *Program management should retain as many indicators as it believes will be useful and for which it has sufficient resources for regular data collection.* Data on some of these other indicators may occasionally be valuable to upper-level officials as supplementary information.

Exhibit 6-6 illustrates a set of outcome indicators identified for external reporting by the "Star Schools" distance learning program. These 7 intermediate outcome indicators and 5 end outcome indicators were selected by the program from a full set of 34 indicators. The rest were for internal use.

*Do not exclude an outcome indicator merely because the program has been doing very well on it for a period of time.* Include *any* outcome indicator that is important for the program. Continue to take credit for good accomplishments and continue to monitor for possible change. Suppose, for example, that the number of new cases of a particular disease drops to virtually zero for two years. This does not mean there will never be new cases in the future. Excluding the indicator prevents the program from monitoring possible reappearance.

## Difficult-to-Measure Outcomes

"Not everything that counts can be counted." Performance measurement, by definition, is undertaken on a regular basis. Some activities and some

EXHIBIT 6-6

**Selected Outcome Indicators for External Reporting: Star Schools Program**

*For Intermediate Outcomes*

1. Number and percent of (a) K-12 students (ethnicity, age and grade level, gender); (b) teachers (ethnicity, level of experience); and (c) others participating in the program.
2. Number and percent of K-12 students who are disadvantaged, have limited proficiency in English, or are disabled who are participating in the program.
3. Number of students enrolled in Star Schools high school credit courses, college preparatory courses, or advanced placement courses that had not been available previously.
4. Number of school administrators reporting changes or improvements in classroom teaching and learning practices related to distance learning.
5. Number and percent of teachers reporting that the learning materials for students were an effective means of covering the subject topics.
6. Number and percent of schools reporting that the distance learning materials they had received were (a) understandable, (b) adequate and complete, and (c) being used.
7. Number of schools that continue to use distance learning services (courses, staff development) when no longer receiving Star Schools funding, by characteristic of activities that continue.

*For End Outcomes*

1. Percent of students who report that the distance learning activities added significantly to the quality of the course or subject, by various student characteristics such as age, gender, and ethnicity.
2. Percent of students reporting increased interest in school because of distance learning activities in their classes.
3. Percent of teachers reporting (a) increased learning by their students; (b) improved student attendance; (c) increased interest in subject area; and (d) improved critical thinking and problem solving attributable at least in part to the use of distance learning activities in their classes.
4. Percent of students whose test scores improved significantly in courses in which distance learning technologies had been introduced and had become a significant part of the instruction.
5. Number of non–college-bound students who are employed within (a) six months or (b) one year of completing high school and who report that participation in the program was a contributing factor in being selected for employment.

**Source:** Prepared for the U.S. Department of Education Star Schools working group, reported in Harry P. Hatry and Mary Kopczynski, *Guide to Program Outcome Measurement for the U.S. Department of Education* (Washington, D.C.: Planning and Evaluation Service, U.S. Department of Education, February 1997).

outcomes are extremely difficult or expensive to track, in which case in-depth evaluations are likely to be preferable. The following are particularly difficult to measure activities:

- *Prevention programs.* These include programs such as crime and fire prevention, child abuse prevention, and disease prevention. Regulatory programs such as environmental protection and state licensing boards face the same dilemma: They also are ultimately intended to prevent a variety of public health and safety problems. But how can one measure the number of incidents that were prevented? Such a determination typically requires highly sophisticated and expensive program evaluation designs that attempt to provide some way to measure what would have happened in the absence of the program.

For regular performance measurement, less sophisticated and less expensive alternatives are needed. The traditional approach is to use the number of incidents that were *not prevented* as a surrogate for cases prevented. In addition, sometimes surrogates can be found that track reduction in major factors known to lead to undesirable incidents, such as *risk factors*—factors that, if reduced, are expected to help prevent the unwanted incidents. However, risk factors are intermediate outcomes. For example, the U.S. Department of Health and Human Services has undertaken regular surveys of behaviors presumed to lead to health and safety problems among young people. These risk factors include poor diet, inadequate physical activity, alcohol and other drug abuse, tobacco use, and unsafe sexual behavior.[1] Surrogates used for prevention of communicable diseases include age-appropriate vaccination rates (or nonvaccination rates).[2] The survey data provide indicators of the presence of each risk factor among youth in the United States.

For regulatory programs, useful indicators of intermediate outcomes track the detection and correction of violations and complaints.

- *Basic research and long-range planning activities that take many years before outcomes can be expected.*

As the period of time until major outcomes can be expected lengthens, the usefulness of regular measurement declines and more and more factors are likely to have intervened—making the task of relating outcomes to these activities extremely difficult. What can be done in such cases? Agencies can track some early intermediate outcomes—such as the percent of time that reports and plans were provided on schedule; the results of peer reviews; or, for research programs, the number of citations in the technical literature. This information, however, tells little about results. End outcomes are better assessed, if they can be assessed at all, by in-depth special studies.

- *Programs in which the customers are anonymous, such as hotlines.* How can the program tell if the customers have been helped?

Some hotlines have asked callers if they would permit a call-back in a few days and ask for a telephone number for a later survey to find out what happened.[3]

- *Programs in which major outcomes apply to a very small number of events.* For some programs, the results of a small number of particularly important events may have significance far beyond their statistical incidence. For example, the results of a very small number of major federal or state litigation programs may be extremely important, even though the program has also litigated a large number of other cases that individually and collectively are much less important. Tabulations of overall litigation success rates, though useful, do not adequately consider the impact of the few very important cases. Another example is that of emergency response programs if only a few major emergencies occur during a reporting period.

In these instances, quantitative data are not sufficient. A pragmatic option is to provide qualitative information separately for these few but very important cases. This procedure will not be very satisfactory to persons who only like numbers, but it is reasonable and can provide important performance information to users of the data. Separate quantitative measurements for these small numbers of cases would also be provided.

For emergency response programs, these might include the response times and the number of persons provided food and shelter. For periods in which no emergencies actually occurred, surrogates that measure the degree of preparedness would need to be used—such as response times to simulated or test events—as is typically done by the Department of Defense (using war games and simulations).

- *The jurisdictionwide impact of programs whose scope is limited to a small part of a problem.* Sometimes communities or larger units of government want to know the effects of a program on the whole jurisdiction, but the program can only assist such small portions of the total population needing assistance that it is unlikely to affect the relevant value of the outcome indicators.

  What can be done in such cases? Not much. The program's measurement effort should track the outcomes for the population to whom it did provide service. For example, a program that attempts to reduce a jurisdiction's teenage pregnancy rate but only has resources to work with in-school youth at a small number of schools would track the intermediate and end outcomes for youth *attending those schools.*

- *Internal support services.* Should performance measurement systems be used for internal support services, such as facility maintenance, fleet maintenance, purchasing, information technology, personnel, and accounting? The relationships of these activities to the end outcomes of operating programs are typically extremely difficult to assess, but most agencies, particularly those applying substantial resources to these activities, would find performance measurement a useful planning and management tool.

  Even though support activities do not produce external outcomes, they should be tracked. They have their own customers—the personnel in the agency's operating programs that they service. Tracking "outcomes" such as the timeliness and accuracy of their work and internal customer satisfaction is feasible and an important aspect of good management.

## Constructing Outcome Indicators to Help Identify Causes

Outcomes do not necessarily reveal anything about what caused them. In almost all cases, a program will have only partial influence over the values of its outcome indicators. External factors beyond the control of the program will also affect indicator values. This applies to most intermediate outcomes and even more strongly to end outcomes. But sometimes it is possible to construct an outcome indicator that sheds light on the extent to which the service affected outcomes. Two major approaches are the following:

1. *Ask customers to rate the extent to which the program contributed to the outcomes they reported.* For example, for a health program, customer surveys (discussed in the next chapter) can ask customers whether their condition has improved since the service began to provide the indicator "number, and percent, of customers whose condition improved since the service began." But surveys can go further than that. They can also ask for customer ratings of the extent to which the service contributed to the improvement. In this case, the outcome indicator would be "percent of customers who reported both having improved and that the service had contributed significantly to the improvement."
2. *If data can be obtained on the reasons for a problem, whether that information comes from agency records or surveyed customers, tabulate the data.* Surveys of households can provide measurements of the percent of households using a park or a library. To get some idea of causes, follow-up questions can ask those who have not used the program for the reasons why, with options such as "locations not convenient," "hours not convenient," "cost too high," "used service and didn't like it," or "not interested." Tabulations can be made of the number and percent of citizens giving each reason. The program can then use the information to help identify effective action.

   Another example: When measuring the frequency of traffic accidents, an agency can also group the accidents by cause, producing such indicators as the number of traffic accidents in which faulty traffic signs or signals played a role.

### Providing for Qualitative Outcomes

For some—perhaps many—programs, managers may believe that one or more important outcomes are not covered by the performance data. Many, if not most, program managers will believe that quantitative measurement cannot capture all the benefits of their programs—and, indeed, a good case can be made that this is so. To help allay this concern, *a performance measurement system should include explicit provision for programs to report such outcomes even though they have only qualitative evidence. Not everything that is important is measurable!*

For example, a program aimed at encouraging students with disabilities to consider science or math careers might believe that improving students' confidence in their ability to do well in academic courses is an important intermediate outcome. The program may not have reliable quantitative data on improved confidence (although data from professionally done customer surveys, in which respondents provide their ratings of outcomes, can be considered quantitative rather than qualitative information).

Programs should provide as much evidence as possible to back up qualitative statements. In the above example, the program should provide any evidence that student confidence has improved, even though only qualitative information is available. Qualitative evidence is, in general, considerably weaker and less convincing than quantitative evidence of progress.

## An Option: Identify the Extent of a Program's Influence on Individual Outcomes

As long as a program can have some effect on the value of an outcome indicator it should be a candidate for inclusion. *But agencies can alert users to a more accurate and fairer picture of performance by also identifying and reporting the approximate degree of influence they have over each outcome indicator.*

This author knows of no agency, public or private, that rates its influence over individual outcome indicator values, but this is a task that agencies should consider in their efforts to provide a fair picture of their performance.

The program might, for example, assign categories to each indicator, such as whether the program had little, some, or considerable influence. Such categories should be defined as specifically as possible to help users understand them. Agencies will also want to ensure that similar category definitions are used by all their programs—so that users of agency performance reports will be provided comparable judgments as to degree of influence.

Ratings would likely be made by the program manager, but with review by higher-level managers to ensure comparable ratings across programs.

## References and Notes

1. Centers for Disease Control and Prevention, "Youth Risk Behavior Surveillance—United States, 1997," *Morbidity and Mortality Weekly* Report (August 14, 1998).

2. For more discussion, see National Research Council, *Assessment of Performance Measures for Public Health, Substance Abuse, and Mental Health*, eds. Edward B. Perrin and Jeffrey Koshel (Washington, D.C.: National Academy Press, 1997).

3. If the hotline has caller ID, the call-back is potentially available, though its use is probably unethical. Caller ID has been used in cases of obvious danger—primarily to provide help if the caller sounds dangerously suicidal. Even caller ID will not reach people who have used a pay phone.

# What Methods of Data Gathering Should Be Used?

A schoolteacher, telling his students that their final test had gone to the printer, asked whether they had any questions. The first student asked how many questions there were on the test. The second asked how many essay questions there were. The third asked, "Who's the printer?"

Data collection procedures and sources are indeed vital considerations. It is impossible to finalize a set of performance indicators before choosing data collection methods. Each method has different strengths and weaknesses and different costs.

This chapter discusses four major alternatives for collecting quantitative performance indicator data:[1]

- Administrative data from program and/or agency records
- Customer surveys
- Trained observer ratings
- Special technical equipment

## Program and Agency Records

Most agencies and programs routinely record data on customers and/or transactions for administrative purposes.[2] This data collection procedure has been by far the most widely used for producing performance data. Agency records can be used to calculate performance indicators. Records may come from the program itself, from other programs within the agency, or from other agencies (including other levels of government). The relevant information needs to be extracted from those records and tabulated (if not already tabulated) in order to yield the desired outcome indicators.

In addition to being a source of outcome information, agency records are also the main data source on the amounts of input (both dollars and employee time) and output produced by the program. This information is needed for efficiency indicators. Records can also be a source of demographic characteristics of customers and other characteristics of the workload for use in providing breakouts of outcome indicators (see chapter 8).

Examples of outcome indicators for which agency records will be the source:

- Data on timeliness and response times for police, fire, and emergency service calls or for any other requests by customers for services or information.
- Number of complaints received, preferably broken out by the subject of the complaint and the severity of the problem. If the data are not already in the database, staff will have to develop a reliable procedure for producing the information. Number of legitimate complaints is the preferred indicator. Staff will also have to develop a way to assess which complaints are legitimate.
- Number of persons who participated in services, such as for particular recreation, library, or social service programs. This information is needed in calculating customer success rates.
- Number of traffic accidents, injuries, and deaths.
- Number of reported crimes and fires.
- Clearance rates for each crime category.
- Incidence of various illnesses and deaths and their rates among program customers.
- Number of persons receiving public assistance payments.
- Number and rates of low-weight births.
- Recidivism rates.

Agency record data may be based in part on other procedures, such as trained observer ratings. For example, child welfare agency data on the number of children removed from unsafe homes may be based on staff members' observations of home conditions routinely recorded in agency records.

## Advantages of agency records:

- The data are readily available at low cost.
- The procedures for transforming the data into indicators are familiar to most program personnel.

## Disadvantages of agency records:

- Agency records seldom contain enough service quality and outcome data to create an adequate set of performance indicators.
- Modifications to existing record collection processes are often needed to generate useful performance indicators. For example, though collecting data on program response times to requests is common for some types of services, others will need to modify their procedures to make sure that the following are provided:
  — Time of receipt of the service
  — Definition of what constitutes a completed response
  — Time of completion of response
  — Data-processing procedures to calculate and record the time between receipt of request and completion of response
  — Data-processing procedures for combining the data on individual requests into aggregate response-time indicators
- Obtaining data from the records of other programs or agencies, which is sometimes needed to calculate an indicator, can be administratively difficult and can raise issues of confidentiality. For example:
  — Indicators of the success rates of health and social service treatment programs may take the form of recidivism rates. Such data might need to be obtained from hospitals, police, courts, and other health and social service agencies where "failed" clients end up.
  — Indicators on bringing criminals to justice need information from prosecutors and/or court systems on the dispositions of arrests (often difficult for other agencies to access).

---

## Customer Surveys

Customers—whether citizens, clients, or businesses—are an important source of information about service quality and outcomes. A major way to obtain reliable feedback from customers is through professionally prepared surveys.[3] Exhibit 7-1 lists the variety of information obtainable from such surveys.

Statistically valid surveys of customers, properly designed and implemented, are an excellent way to obtain information on such outcomes as customer condition, behavior, experiences, and satisfaction—especially after customers have completed services. Complaint data, while useful, do not cover the full range of information on service performance, because complainers are not likely to be representative of the full population of

EXHIBIT 7-1

**Information Obtainable from Customer Surveys**

1. Customer condition and attitudes after receiving services, as well as the results of those services
2. Customer action or behavior after receiving program services
3. Overall satisfaction with a service
4. Ratings of specific service quality characteristics
5. Extent of service use
6. Extent of awareness of services
7. Reasons for dissatisfaction with, or for not using, services
8. Suggestions for improving services
9. Demographic information on customers

those served. Focus groups—though a very good means of helping to identify what outcomes should be measured and how to interpret data findings—are not designed to collect statistically representative data.

### Advantages of customer surveys:

- Surveys are often the most feasible, if not the only, way to obtain data for some outcomes. Much of the information listed in exhibit 7-1, for example, is unavailable from other sources.
- Surveys provide direct input from the program's customers, adding not only valuable information but also credibility.

### Disadvantages of customer surveys:

- Surveys require special expertise, especially for development of the questionnaire and sampling plan and for training of interviewers.
- They can require more time and are more costly than other forms of data collection, especially if the work is contracted out.
- Evidence based on respondents' perceptions and memory may be less convincing than data obtained from agency records.
- Some customers may not respond or will not be honest in their response. This potential problem can be alleviated by well-worded questions and good interviewing. It is also alleviated with regularly repeated performance measurement, assuming the proportion of disaffected persons is likely to be about the same in each instance, with no significant net effect on measured changes over time.

## Content of Customer Surveys

The types of information listed in exhibit 7-1 fall into five major categories:

*Questions related to the outcomes of services (items 1–4).* Responses to these questions can be used to develop indicators of outcomes. Questions should be asked about both *specific* service characteristics (to help program personnel identify specific service problems) and *overall* service ratings.

*Questions seeking information about the type and amount of the service used (items 5 and 6).* In some instances, amount of services can be used as an outcome indicator (such as to calculate the number and percent of families who used a park, library, or public transit during the past month). These data can also be used to relate service outcomes to the types and amounts of services respondents received. If the agency links the service information from its records to individual survey respondents, data from agency records can be used for this purpose. This option allows the survey questionnaire to be shorter and is presumably more accurate, since it does not rely on respondents' memories of services received.

*Diagnostic questions (item 7).* These questions ask why respondents gave particular answers or ratings, especially unfavorable ones.[4] In addition to being used in the performance measurement process, an edited list of such responses should be provided to program personnel, anonymously of course, to help them identify needed improvements.

*Requests for suggestions on improving the service (item 8).* Usually, suggestions for improvement should be requested at the end of the questionnaire. These suggestions should also be provided, again anonymously, to program personnel.

*Questions seeking demographic information (item 9).* Demographic information allows the program to break responses out by specific customer characteristics. For a school program, for example, relevant characteristics could include grade level, age, gender, school lunch participation status, disability status, race or ethnicity, state, urban vs. rural vs. suburban school system, and so on. (Major uses for demographic breakouts are discussed in chapter 8.)

## Survey All Potential Customers or Only Service Users

Managers must decide what kind of survey to use. *Household surveys* include representative samples of all potential customers in a jurisdiction, regardless of whether or not they have used the services about which they are being asked. *User surveys* include samples of customers who have actually used a particular service. (User surveys can seek responses from all customers or a representative sample.)

### Advantages of household surveys over user surveys:

- Household surveys can obtain information about several services simultaneously.
- If they cover several services, their costs can be shared among agencies, reducing the costs to each.
- They can obtain information from and about nonusers, enabling programs to estimate *rates of participation* by different types of households.[5] Furthermore, they can obtain feedback from nonusers on reasons why a service is not used.
- Since they are usually administered centrally, they are likely to have better quality control.
- They are less of a burden on individual agencies. In addition to being usually administered centrally, they do not require information on the addresses or telephone numbers of specific agency customers.

### Advantages of user surveys over household surveys:

- User surveys usually provide more in-depth information on a particular service because users are familiar with it and do not need to be asked about nonuse or other services.
- They involve less work at the sample selection stage because addresses and/or telephone numbers of users are usually available to the agency. For household surveys, the sample needs to be drawn from some census of households or businesses.
- They can sometimes be conducted at the facilities customers use (such as parks, libraries, public assistance offices, and schools).
- Higher response rates are likely because users have a personal interest in and knowledge of the service.
- They are likely to be less expensive because of the advantages cited above.
- The information is likely to be considerably more useful to program personnel because it is more extensive and detailed.

### Examples of Customer Survey Questionnaires

- Exhibit 7-2 is a very simple user questionnaire. An on-site, written user survey that has been used by the Long Beach, California, Community Development Agency, this questionnaire is about as short as one can

EXHIBIT 7-2

**Example of Simple User Questionnaire**

*How Are We Doing?*

Date _____

The quality of service I received today was:

**HELPFULNESS**                                                                    Please circle one
       1                    2                    3                    4                    5
  Unsatisfactory                          Satisfactory                          Excellent

**WAIT TIME**                                                                      Please circle one
       1                    2                    3                    4                    5
  Unsatisfactory                          Satisfactory                          Excellent

The primary reason for my visit was:

_____

Comments _____

_____

_____

_____

(Use reverse side for additional comments)

Optional _____
                              Name                                        Date

FOR STAFF USE ONLY

Action taken _____

_____

_____

_____
                              Name                                        Date

be. It asks service users to provide comments and suggestions for improvement, but it does not ask about any end outcomes. Note that the questionnaire also calls for entry by the agency of any action taken.

- Exhibit 7-3 is an extract from a questionnaire for users of specific public facilities. Originally designed to obtain feedback on park and recreation facilities in Saint Petersburg, Florida, it asks about specific quality aspects of services, as well as an overall satisfaction rating. Such questions can be readily adapted to most types of services and facilities.
- For internal support activities, other government staff and departments are customers. Exhibit 7-4 is a written survey for internal customers used by Seattle, Washington's Fleet Services Division for its motor pool.

EXHIBIT 7-3

**Survey of Facility Users**

| How Would You Rate the Following? | Excellent | Good | Fair | Poor |
|---|---|---|---|---|
| 1. Hours of Operation | ☐ | ☐ | ☐ | ☐ |
| 2. Cleanliness | ☐ | ☐ | ☐ | ☐ |
| 3. Condition of Equipment | ☐ | ☐ | ☐ | ☐ |
| 4. Crowdedness | ☐ | ☐ | ☐ | ☐ |
| 5. Safety Conditions | ☐ | ☐ | ☐ | ☐ |
| 6. Physical Attractiveness | ☐ | ☐ | ☐ | ☐ |
| 7. Variety of Programs | ☐ | ☐ | ☐ | ☐ |
| 8. Helpfulness of Personnel | ☐ | ☐ | ☐ | ☐ |
| 9. Overall | ☐ | ☐ | ☐ | ☐ |

All customers are given a copy when they obtain a vehicle and are asked to complete it and send it back. This survey was printed on heavy paper with the return address printed on the outside. To return it, the user had only to fold the form and put it in the interoffice mail. Similar foldover forms can be used for brief mail surveys to citizens. Seattle has also undertaken surveys for other internal services, such as its copy center, janitorial services, and personnel.

- Exhibit 7-5 shows three questions from a mail survey of customers of family counseling services, used by what was then called the Family Services Association of America.

This series of questions illustrates the multiple uses of surveys:

- The first question focuses only on satisfaction with the client's counselor. It does not ask about the results of the service, so it provides only information on an *intermediate outcome*.
- The second question asks for information about customer improvement, an *end outcome* indicator.
- The third question asks respondents to identify the extent to which the agency's service *contributed* to the improvement (as the respondents saw it). This is also an end outcome indicator, but it has the additional value of addressing the issue of attribution. The responses from questions 2 and 3 can be combined into the following end outcome indicator: "percent of clients reporting [a particular level] of improvement AND reporting that agency services contributed to the changes reported."[6]

EXHIBIT 7-4

**Department of Administrative Services Fleet Division**
**Motorpool Customer Service Checklist**

1. How often do you use the pool?
   ☐ Daily      ☐ Weekly      ☐ Monthly      ☐ Other

2. For this trip, did you call to make a reservation?      ☐ Yes      ☐ No

3. Was a car available when you needed it?      ☐ Yes      ☐ No

4. If not, how long did you have to wait? _____

5. Have you ever been turned down when you wanted to use a car?      ☐ Yes      ☐ No
   If yes, what did you do?

   ☐ Waited until a car was available      ☐ Used a private car

   ☐ Other: _____

   _____

6. Was the car clean?      ☐ Yes      ☐ No

7. Was the car in good mechanical condition?      ☐ Yes      ☐ No

8. Were you treated courteously by motorpool staff?      ☐ Yes      ☐ No

9. Please rate our quality of service:
   ☐ Excellent      ☐ Good      ☐ Fair      ☐ Poor

Comments or suggestions: _____

_____

_____

_____

_____

_____

Name: _____ Department: _____ Phone: _____

Please fold in half and send back to DAS in interoffice mail. This form is preaddressed. If you
have any questions or need additional information, please call 684-0137. Thank you.

**Source:** City of Seattle.

## Survey Administration Methods and Their Trade-Offs

*Mail surveys.* This is the cheapest method, but second and third mailings
and/or telephone follow-ups are necessary to secure high enough response
rates to yield reliable information. Mail questionnaires are not, of course,
useful for respondents who cannot read them. To obtain satisfactory completion rates, mail questionnaires generally need to be short and simple.
Cluttered, complex questionnaires and questionnaires that are longer than
four to five pages are likely to yield excessively low response rates.
Response rates are also likely to be much higher among users than among

EXHIBIT 7-5

**Mail Survey Questions on Family Counseling**

1. How satisfied were you with the way you and your counselor got along with each other?
   - Very satisfied
   - Satisfied
   - No particular feelings one way or the other
   - Somewhat dissatisfied
   - Very dissatisfied
2. Since you started at the agency, has there been any change for better or worse in the way the members of your family get along with each other? Would you say you now get along:
   - Much better
   - Somewhat better
   - Same
   - Somewhat worse
   - Much worse
3. How do you feel the service provided by the agency influenced the changes you have reported?
   - Helped a great deal
   - Helped some
   - Made no difference
   - Made things somewhat worse
   - Made things much worse

a general sample of households in the area. (See exhibit 7-6 for suggested ways of increasing response rates to mail surveys.)

*Telephone surveys.* Telephone surveys can achieve good response rates from households at lower cost than the in-person alternative. They are more expensive than mail surveys, however, because they require considerable interviewer time and training. They also cannot cover populations without ready telephone access.

*In-person surveys administered at the respondent's home or business.* These tend to yield high response rates and can provide detailed information since they can be longer and more complicated than mail questionnaires. They are the most costly to administer, however, and are usually too expensive for data collection on the repeated basis needed for performance measurement.

*In-person surveys administered at a service facility.* In-person survey administration at a facility—such as a park, library, school, or social service agency—has the advantages of obtaining high response rates and detailed information without the high cost of finding respondents at their homes or businesses.[7] This option cannot, by definition, be used for outcomes that occur after the customer leaves the facility, but it can be a very efficient method if the whole population of interest uses the facility and can respond on past circumstances.

EXHIBIT 7-6

**Suggestions for Increasing Response Rates to Mail Surveys**

- Include a transmittal letter signed by a respected, high-level official. Guarantee complete confidentiality of responses. Address the letter to a specific individual whenever feasible.
- Emphasize the need for information *from customers* to *improve future services*.
- Mail an advance postcard notifying recipients that they will soon receive a questionnaire and asking explicitly for their help.
- Since a mail questionnaire must be short and simple, make sure each question has a clear purpose and stick primarily to response categories that only require a check mark. Open-ended questions (requiring an answer in the respondent's own words), though rich in information, should be limited to a very small number and to the most crucial issues of concern.
- Keep skip pattern (instructions to respondents to skip certain questions depending on their response to a previous question) to *an absolute minimum*, and when unavoidable *be sure skip patterns are crystal clear.*
- Go for a professional, polished look. Even if the questionnaire is prepared in-house, it should look typeset and be printed on high-quality, preferably colored paper. *Cutting corners by using low-quality copiers and so forth risks unacceptable response rates.*
- Enclose a stamped, self-addressed envelope in each questionnaire mailing.
- Use two or three mailings. One mailing is seldom enough. Postcard and telephone reminders can also be used, especially for small samples.

The survey might ask only about the service provided by the facility or about other services. For example, the Centers for Disease Control and Prevention of the U.S. Department of Health and Human Services has used the method effectively in surveying school-age children in school facilities on a number of health risk factors (such as tobacco and drug use, physical inactivity, and unhealthful dietary behaviors). These surveys yield intermediate outcome indicators on important health and safety programs.

*Combination of survey methods.* The best alternative is often the use of mailings supplemented with telephone calls to persons who failed to respond to follow-up mailings.

For some programs, it may be feasible to survey *all their customers*, such as by routinely mailing questionnaires to each customer. This will apply, for example, when a federal agency is surveying a small number of state agencies.

When very large numbers of citizens, businesses, or clients are the population to be surveyed, a sampling of the population is needed. The program will then have to decide on the sample size. Larger samples are needed if the program wants higher rates of precision, but high rates of precision are seldom needed in the customer survey area. Larger samples will be needed if the program wants separate outcome information on a number of population subgroups. If, for example, the program wants outcome data for each of the

50 states, it will need to have large enough samples of respondents from each state to provide information at the desired level of precision.

In choosing which method is best, an agency needs to weigh the tradeoffs between getting higher response rates (providing greater confidence that the findings represent the views of the population surveyed), larger sample sizes (providing greater precision), and cost of administration. *Whichever method is used, agencies should seek at least a 50 percent response rate.* (Techniques such as enclosing questionnaires with all utility bills will seldom yield high enough returns to make the data credible.)

### Tips on Customer Survey Design and Administration

- *Establish a working group to help develop content.* This should include key service agency representatives, perhaps a representative of the chief administrative officer, a survey expert, and a spokesperson for program customers.
- *Beware of biased or muddled wording.* Always have a professional survey expert review final question wording and sequencing.
- *Always test a questionnaire on a small number of customers* before full implementation to catch (a) awkward, ambiguous, or redundant questions; (b) confusing or incorrect instructions; and (c) wording that sounds offensive or just plain foolish.
- *Translate questionnaires* if substantial numbers of the desired respondents are unlikely to speak English.
- *Use outside contractors for the administration of regular surveys if resources are available.* Contracting is usually easier than in-house administration, even for a mail questionnaire. Suggestions about what to include in a survey contract are provided in exhibit 7-7.

### Ways to Reduce Survey Costs

Survey costs depend on the number of persons surveyed, the frequency of the survey, the mode of administration, and efforts to increase response (and completion rates). Here are suggested ways to cut survey costs.

- *Sample the population rather than surveying everyone.* When a program has only a small number of customers (perhaps no more than one or two hundred each year), it may be feasible to survey all of them. But when very large numbers of citizens, businesses, or clients are the customers, selecting a representative sample is an efficient way to go.

EXHIBIT 7-7

**Elements to Include in Contracts for Customer Surveys**

- Number of *completed* questionnaires, including minimum sizes for each major category of customer for whom data are sought, and minimum acceptable response rates.
- Survey administration details, such as (a) whether mail, telephone, or both are to be used; (b) the number of mailings or number of follow-up telephone calls; and (c) the time between mailings and telephone follow-ups.
- Contractor's role in questionnaire development.
- The amount of testing of the questionnaire that the contractor will do.
- Provisions for maintaining respondent confidentiality.
- Any special coding to be done by the contractor (e.g., transforming location data provided by respondents into a more compact grouping of geographical areas).
- Specification of how tabulations are to be handled, such as whether "nos" and "don't knows" should be included in the denominators for the percents calculated.
- Products, and their formats, that will be provided to the agency. Products should include, at a minimum, (a) a detailed description of survey procedures used and response rates achieved; (b) frequency counts for each question; (c) a fully legible printout of the responses for each returned questionnaire (with confidentiality preserved) in case the agency wants to do any of its own tabulations.
- Time frame for the work.
- Any restriction on release of the data to the media.
- Overall cost.

- *Reduce required sample size by avoiding excessive precision.* For most programs, 99 percent confidence limits are overkill. Even 95 percent limits, though well accepted, are excessive for most performance measurement work. Ninety percent limits are likely to be sufficient. To gain any particular level of precision, the required sample will increase as the number of population groups for which the program wants separate outcome information increases. If a program needs outcome data for each of the 50 states, it will need to set large enough sample sizes for each state to yield acceptable levels of precision.
- *Do not seek higher response rates than you really need.* Statisticians often recommend achieving response rates in the neighborhood of 75 percent. As noted, a 50 percent response rate is adequate for most outcome measurement work. Survey administration costs rise steeply as response rate requirements increase.
- *Use agency personnel when appropriate and possible.* However, do *not* use as interviewers persons who are delivering the service. This undermines survey credibility.
- *If your questionnaire can be mailed and the sample size is small, administer it in house.*

- *Use or adapt questionnaires that are already available.* They might, for example, be available from other agencies or from universities. After a questionnaire has been developed, keep it reasonably stable from year to year. It should be used to obtain the same data on the same performance indicators in future reporting periods. Some changes in questions and question wording from year to year are probably inevitable, but these should be minor and kept to a small number to avoid compromising the year-to-year comparability of data. This practice also avoids the need to invest in major new questionnaire development efforts.
- *Look for expert help within the agency* or other low-cost sources.
- *Use commercially available software for tabulations.*
- *Use volunteers to administer surveys whenever possible.* This is particularly practical for private, nonprofit agencies. Be warned, however, that volunteers need extensive training and may not be dependable. They need to be carefully monitored.
- *Do not attempt to cover every category of customer in the sample.* Consider dropping groups that (a) are extremely costly to survey; (b) are only a very small proportion of the population of interest; and (c) are not vital to the survey objectives. Be sure that all such omissions are clearly identified in survey reports.
- *Add questions to already scheduled surveys, such as those of other agencies or universities.* For example, city and county governments might collect questions from a number of their agencies into one community household survey. Programs with related functions (such as various public or private child development programs) might develop a joint questionnaire and questionnaire administration process.

## Trained Observer Procedures

Trained observers[8] are used to rate outcome conditions that can be perceived by the eyes or other physical senses of an observer.[9] The key element for performance measurement is that the rating scales and procedures provide values that are reliable enough to withstand challenge. The goal is to ensure that different observers at different times give the same or very similar ratings to similar conditions.

The following procedures will ensure a high degree of reliability:

- Systematic rating scales that provide well-defined yardsticks against which the observers can assess observed conditions

- Adequate training and supervision of the observers and the process
- Periodic checking of the quality of the ratings

For trained observer ratings to be a suitable performance measurement procedure, the outcome needs to be measurable by physical observation and reliable on a scale that identifies several variations of the condition to be measured.

In the past, inspections have been used to assess health, fire, and food safety at a variety of facilities. For the most part, however, these findings were not aggregated for use in providing regular condition assessment ratings. In recent years, however, trained observer procedures have begun to be used to track systematically these and other conditions. Trained observer ratings are also used for assessing the cleanliness of streets, condition of roads, condition of parks and playgrounds, condition of facilities (such as schools, hospitals, and prisons), condition of traffic signals and signs, and quality of food served to customers.

Trained observer procedures are used for human services as well. For many years, agencies have rated the ability of clients with physical and mental problems to undertake basic activities of daily living. Another example is the kindergarten teacher checklist used by North Carolina to make periodic assessments of its Smart Start program. Samples of kindergarten teachers rate children on 40 characteristics based on their observations of each child in their classes. The data collection instrument uses a 1 to 5 scale (never, seldom, sometimes, often, or always) to rate physically observable items on each child's preacademic and social skills—such as whether the child recognizes his or her own name in print, hurts other children or animals for no apparent reason, and speaks in sentences of more than three words.[10] Averages and other statistics are calculated from the ratings, which are also used to measure time trends.

### Advantages of trained observer ratings:

- Trained observer ratings can provide reliable, reasonably accurate ratings of conditions that otherwise are difficult to measure.
- Periodic ratings can be used to help allocate program resources throughout the year. For example, the New York City Sanitation Department has for many years regularly used trained observer ratings of street cleanliness to help allocate and reallocate its street-cleaning crews over time.
- The data can be presented in an easy-to-understand format, which is important in reaching officials and the public.

## Disadvantages of trained observer ratings:

- They are labor-intensive procedures that require significant personnel time, including time for training observers. Some social service and mental health agencies have used caseworkers to rate their own clients' progress. This does not require significant added expense and is appropriate for internal tracking of client progress. For performance measurement purposes, using an agency's own caseworkers should be avoided, however, because their potential self-interest in the ratings reduces the perceived, if not the actual, credibility of the results.
- The need for periodic checks of observers to ensure that they are adhering to the procedures adds costs.
- Program personnel may be uncomfortable with observer ratings, as evidenced by their relatively infrequent use.

## Types of Rating Systems

Three major types of rating systems are in use by trained observers:

- Written descriptions
- Photographs
- Other visual scales such as drawings or videos

*Written descriptions.* This, the simplest and most familiar type of rating system, depends entirely on specific written descriptions of each grade used in the rating scale.

An abbreviated written scale for building or street cleanliness is the following:

- Rating 1: **Clean.** Building or street is completely or almost completely clean; a maximum of three pieces of litter per floor or block is present.
- Rating 2: **Moderately Clean.** Building or street is largely clean; a few pieces of isolated litter or dirt are observable.
- Rating 3: **Moderately Dirty.** Some scattered litter or dirt is present.
- Rating 4: **Dirty.** Heavy litter or dirt is present in several locations throughout the building or along the block.

A citizens' group, the Straphangers Campaign, used 77 volunteers and a written scale to rate the quality of subway car announcements in each of 17 subway lines of the Metropolitan Transit Authority's New York City Transit, making over 5,300 observations over a three-month period.[11] In addition,

Straphangers provided ratings for each of 20 New York City subway lines, assessing the cleanliness of floors and seats of 2,257 subway cars over a three-month period.[12]

Assessing the need for repairs is an additional, very important use for outcome information from observer ratings. The city of Toronto used the information obtained from the scale in exhibit 7-8 not only to help track road conditions but also to determine what repairs were needed in each location, as noted in the right-hand column comments. That is, the ratings were used both for performance measurement and for determining needed actions.

## EXHIBIT 7-8

### Condition Rating

| Rating | Condition | Description | Comments |
|--------|-----------|-------------|----------|
| 9 | Excellent | No fault whatsoever | Recently constructed work |
| 8 | Good | No damage, normal wear, and small cracks | |
| 7 | Fair | Slight damage, crackfill or minor leveling required | Average rating for City of Toronto pavements and sidewalks |
| 6 | Repair | 10% of complete replacement cost | Pavement requires preventive overlay. Level of Tolerance for City of Toronto pavements |
| 5 | Repair | 25% of complete replacement cost | Eligible for reconstruction programme. Condition Rating 4—Level of Tolerance for City of Toronto curbs and sidewalks |
| 4 | Repair | 50% of complete replacement cost | |
| 3 | Repair | 75% of complete replacement cost | Total reconstruction probably indicated |
| 2 | Repair | More than 75% of complete replacement cost | Requires complete reconstruction |
| 1 | Impossible to repair | | |

*Photographic rating scales.* Photographic scales can be more precise than written scales in providing clear definitions of each rating grade. Generic photos are used to represent grades on the rating scale. Observers are given (and trained in the use of) a set of photos, with several representing *each grade* on the rating scale.

Exhibit 7-9 is an extract from a 16-photograph scale (four photographs for each grade on the scale) that was used by the District of Columbia. A similar photographic scale has been used for many years by New York City's Sanitation Department to track street cleanliness.

*Other visual scales.* Visual rating scales can also use drawings or sketches that represent each grade on a rating scale. Exhibit 7-10 provides an example of sketches representing conditions of school buildings—in this case, the condition of schoolroom walls. This rating scale was used by the New York City school system to track the physical condition of its schools and to help make decisions about building repairs.

### Implementing a Trained Observer Process

Implementing a trained observer process requires the following steps:

- Decide what conditions should be rated.
- Develop a rating scale for each condition. If possible, adapt an existing scale. Use photographs and written guidelines as appropriate.
- Determine which facilities or areas should be rated, when, and how frequently. Ratings can be applied to all or selected facilities or areas. If resources are only available to rate a subset of locations, choose them by using random sampling so that the locations chosen will be representative.
- Select and train observers, who might be program personnel, college or graduate school students, or volunteers. Technical ratings, such as safety hazards, will require persons with the requisite professional training.
- Test the scale and observers on a small number of sites in the facility or area to make sure that reasonably trained observers give consistent ratings.
- Establish procedures for supervising the observers and for recording, transcribing, and processing the data they collect.
- Conduct the ratings regularly.
- Develop and disseminate reports on the findings from each set of ratings for the current period and changes from previous periods. The reports should show the number and percent of locations that fell into particular rating categories. *Do not report only the average scores, which can hide very important distributional information.*

EXHIBIT 7-9

**Example of Street Litter Conditions**

Condition 1=Clean; 2=Moderately clean; 3=Moderately littered; 4=Heavily littered

**Source:** Harry P. Hatry et al., *How Effective Are Your Community Services? Procedures for Measuring Their Quality*, 2nd ed. (Washington, D.C.: ICMA and the Urban Institute).

EXHIBIT 7-10

**Trained Observer Rating Scale: Condition of School Classroom Walls**

School Scorecard
Rating Scale

Scale Value: 0

Scale Value: 1

Scale Value: 2

Scale Value: 3

Scale Value: 4

Scale Value: 5

Scale Value: 6

**Source:** New York City Department of Education.

- Establish procedures for systematically checking the ratings of trained observers to provide quality control. One way to do this is for the supervisor to check periodically a small sample of the ratings done by each observer.

The following additional steps are needed for a photographic rating system:

- Take a large number of photographs in settings representative of the range of conditions to be rated. These photos should reflect the actual types of conditions the program wants to assess.
- Select a panel of judges comprising persons with varied backgrounds who are not associated with the measurement activities. Select a set of familiar labels, each representing a condition that the program expects to find, such as clean, moderately clean, moderately dirty, and dirty. Ask the judges to sort the photographs into groups that represent each condition.
- For each condition, select the photographs (perhaps four or five) that the largest number of judges identified as representative. These sets of photographs then become the rating scale.
- Develop written guidelines to accompany the photographs, if needed.
- Train observers in the use of the photographic scale and field-test it with those observers to determine the extent of agreement among them. Revise the ratings and procedures as needed.
- Develop the final scale. Package copies of the photographs selected for the final scale in a kit for each trained observer.

## Automating Trained Observer Ratings

Hand-held computers, now available at surprisingly low prices, can be programmed to record observational data. This can considerably ease the amount of clerical work needed and reduce errors introduced by manual recording. New York City has been using such hand-held computers to report on the condition of city buildings (including schools), as required to meet a legislative mandate. The Fund for the City of New York (a public interest organization) has also used them to collect data on a number of physically observable conditions in samples of locations within the city. The conditions observed include, among others, defective street signs, abandoned cars, the presence of rodents or other pests, and defective street lights.[13] This information is used to identify both summary and specific conditions. Data entry, tabulations, and reports can be done quickly.

# Use of Special Technical Equipment

Special equipment is needed to collect data for outcome indicators that require scientific measurement, such as:

- Noise levels
- Air pollution levels
- Water pollution levels
- Road condition (using road meters)

Many state transportation agencies have been using road meters for a number of years. The Fund for the City of New York used a special car outfitted with a "profilometer" to measure street roughness on a sample of 12 percent of the city's blocks. Exhibit 7-11 is a product of this initiative. Two outcome indicators were generated from these readings for each of the city's 59 community districts: a smoothness score (percent of blocks rated acceptable) and number of "significant jolts" encountered per mile.[14] (Acceptability was determined by correlating citizen ratings of sample blocks with the profilometer's readings.)

### Advantages of technical equipment:

- Appropriate technical equipment usually provides accurate, reliable data.
- It may be the only reasonable way to achieve completely credible information on important environmental outcomes such as those listed above. Programs can obtain subjective outcome data using trained observers or user surveys to assess the quality of roads, water, air, and so on, but such information is likely to lack the credibility provided by technical measurement.

### Disadvantages of technical equipment:

- The equipment can be expensive to procure, operate, and maintain.
- The information obtained must be interpreted to be useful to program personnel and outsiders. For example, vertical displacement measurements need to be converted into an excellent, good, fair, or poor ride scale or similarly self-explanatory grouping, and air pollution measurements need to be converted into overall air quality levels understandable to the public, such as good, moderate, approaching unhealthful, and unhealthful.

EXHIBIT 7-11

## Use of Special Equipment to Measure Rideability

# How Smooth Are New York City's Streets?
(Community District Distribution)

Results of a Study Conducted by the
**Fund for the City of New York**
Center on Municipal Government Performance

**Significant Jolts
Encountered per Mile**

▲ fewer than 5    (3 Community Districts)

▲▲ 5 – 9    (34 Community Districts)

▲▲▲ 10 – 14    (17 Community Districts)

▲▲▲▲ 15 or more    (5 Community Districts)

**Smoothness Score**
(Percent of Blocks Rated "Acceptable"* in Each District)

80% or more    (1 Community District)

70 – 79%    (4 Community Districts)

60 – 69%    (20 Community Districts)

50 – 59%    (25 Community Districts)

fewer than 50% (9 Community Districts)

Parks, airports, cemeteries and other
large areas not measured

*"Acceptable" blocks have a City Roughness Index (CRI) of 7.12
or less. Roughness index computed from profilometry readings
conducted by Galaxy Scientific Corporation. Findings derived by
driving once through the City on randomly selected streets in all
community districts. For description of methodology and the range
of ratings see report *How Smooth Are New York City's Streets?*
Data collected Fall 1997.

Note: Numbers and boundaries within the 5 boroughs are
community district designations. There are 59 community districts
in New York City.

0   1   2   3   4   5 mi.

The Bronx
Manhattan
Queens
Brooklyn
Staten Island

### Citywide and Borough Findings

| | Smoothness Score (Percent of Blocks Rated "Acceptable") | Significant Jolts Encountered per Mile |
|---|---|---|
| New York City | 60% | 9.5 |
| The Bronx | 58% | 8.7 |
| Brooklyn | 63% | 8.4 |
| Manhattan | 45% | 14.2 |
| Queens | 64% | 9.3 |
| Staten Island | 56% | 7.5 |

This study was made possible by a grant from the Alfred P. Sloan Foundation.
© Fund for the City of New York, 1998

**Source:** Fund for the City of New York, Center on Municipal Government Performance, *How Smooth Are New York City's Streets?*
(New York: Fund for the City of New York, September 1993), 37.

## Selecting Appropriate Data Sources and Data Collection Procedures

Following are criteria for selecting data collection procedures:

- *Cost.* This is always a primary concern. Sometimes bargain-basement procedures can be used effectively (such as the use of mail rather than telephone surveys), depending on the response rates and types of data required. Also, some outcome indicators can ride the coattails of other procedures. For example, *data for a number of outcome indicators might be obtainable from a single customer survey; or trained observers might be able to collect data simultaneously for a number of different outcome indicators*, such as street cleanliness, road bumpiness, and condition of traffic signs, with little added cost.
- *Feasibility.* This criterion covers identification of nonfinancial obstacles that are likely to make data collection very difficult or impossible. For example, if data are needed from other agencies, will they permit access to it?
- *Accuracy and reliability achievable with the procedure.*
- *Understandability.* The data must be understandable to program managers and persons outside the program, including the public.
- *Credibility.* This includes the potential for data manipulation, especially by persons with an interest in making the data look good (such as the example of caseworkers doing follow-up of their own clients). Because of the potential for data manipulation, surveys by outside contractors are likely to be more credible than surveys administered by the agency itself. Such problems will be reduced to the extent that an agency has a data quality control process that is recognized as good. (See chapter 13 for further discussion of quality control issues.)

## Using a Pilot Test

All new or substantially modified data collection procedures should be pilot-tested before full implementation to identify and eliminate bugs. The pilot test should approximate the conditions that will exist during full implementation, but it will usually be enough to test the procedures only on some segments of the program. For example, a pilot test might cover:

- Only those outcome indicators that are new or require substantial modifications to existing data collection procedures
- Only some of the activities

- Only some of the locations or customers
- Only for part of a year

The working group developing the performance measurement process should oversee this test if possible, working with program and project personnel to identify problems. Modifications should then be made to alleviate problems found in the pilot test—such as problems with the sampling plan, questionnaires and other data collection instruments, and individual outcome indicator definitions.

The working group should also keep track of the staff time and out-of-pocket costs required for the new procedures during the test and use this information to estimate the annual cost to the program. If this estimated cost seems high, the group should make recommendations regarding possible elimination of particularly difficult outcome indicators, reduced sample sizes, shorter data collection instruments, and so on. The group should also be on the lookout for additional outcome indicators that should be tracked.

## Other Potential Problems in Data Collection

These problems include the following:

- Definitions that are likely to be unclear to those responsible for collecting the information.
- Missing data. For example, an economic development program might not have a complete list of businesses served. If missing data are a major problem, the program may need to modify its record-keeping process.
- Confidentiality requirements, such as permission from parents to survey their children. Such requirements can add considerably to the effort required to obtain the data.

Resolutions may involve correcting the problem, deciding to delete an outcome indicator, or accepting less accuracy.

## Frequency of Data Collection and Reporting

Programs need to think hard about how frequently their performance measurement data should be collected. Higher frequency typically leads to higher cost, and some data need to be collected less frequently than others. Indicators such as number of traffic accidents or crimes reported are tabulated and reported at least monthly. At the other end of the frequency scale, some data might be collected every other year.

The drive for accountability and performance information for budget planning has led agencies to focus on annual reporting. But *for the basic performance measurement purposes of monitoring and continual program improvement, data collection at least quarterly should be the goal.*[15]

With careful planning, quarterly data collection does not need to add substantially to costs. With respect to agency records, for example, once the data have been computerized, frequent tabulations are feasible at minimal additional cost. Routine follow-up questionnaires sent to customers a certain period after service receipt (say, nine months) also may yield year-round data at little added cost.

For customer surveys, if sampling is needed, consider splitting the annual sample size—defined by a budget constraint—into smaller subsamples. A questionnaire would be administered to each person surveyed once a year but at a different time during the year. For example, splitting the total annual sample into four subsamples (25 percent of the total sample for each) would provide quarterly data collection—*providing managers with timely feedback and seasonal information*—at an annual cost of only about 10 percent more than if one large survey were conducted. The findings for each calendar quarter would be statistically less precise because the samples are smaller,[16] but accumulating the data would yield annual data as precise as if the whole sample had been surveyed at a single point in time.

Some outcomes need to be measured at a specific time after service started or was completed, as is the case for many social service programs. In these cases, the program will probably need to collect outcome data throughout the year. The data can be tabulated at any useful intervals, such as monthly, every other month, or quarterly.

Note that *questions whose responses are not expected to change appreciably from quarter to quarter, or even year to year, need not be asked every time.* Agencies and their programs may also want to reserve space on the questionnaire for a small number of especially timely questions that are asked on a one-time basis. These need not be performance measurement questions: They might seek opinions from citizens on policy or program changes that the agency or program is considering.

## Final Comment

When making choices among data collection procedures in terms of cost and accuracy, programs need to trade off a high degree of accuracy against less statistical precision. *It is better to be roughly right than precisely ignorant.*

---

## References and Notes

1. Obtaining quantitative data is not always possible for all indicators. The program needs to be explicit about important outcomes for which there is no quantitative performance information and provide qualitative judgments about performance on those outcomes.

2. The term "archival data" is sometimes used to refer to the use of records.

3. For full detail on the material summarized here and information on important technical issues regarding sample size and selection, administrative procedures, data accuracy, required response rates, and analysis of survey results, see Harry Hatry et al., *Customer Surveys for Agency Managers: What Managers Need to Know* (Washington, D.C.: Urban Institute Press, 1998) and other materials in the Selected Readings listed at the end of this book (appendix A).

4. In my experience, questions asking for explanations of good ratings have yielded little useful information. Since every question is an added burden on respondents, as well as requiring added coding time by those processing the responses, I recommend not asking respondents why they gave favorable responses.

5. Attendance counts are useful but do not indicate how many *different* persons or households used the service during a particular reporting period unless the names of particular users are available.

6. Two other questionnaire examples appear in appendixes B and C. For further examples of questionnaires for household, business, and user surveys for local government services, see Harry Hatry et al., *How Effective Are Your Community Services? Procedures for Measuring Their Quality*, 2nd ed. (Washington, D.C.: ICMA and the Urban Institute, 1992).

7. For administration at a facility that is not under the agency's immediate control, permission from the facility is required. For surveys of minors, parental permission may be required.

8. For further details on trained observer procedures, see John Greiner, "Use of Ratings by Trained Observers," chapter 10 in *Handbook of Practical Program Evaluation*, ed. Joseph S. Wholey et al. (San Francisco: Jossey-Bass Publishers, 1994); and Hatry et al., *How Effective Are Your Community Services?* chapter 12 and appendixes 3 and 6 (chapters 2, 3, 4, and 8 provide examples).

9. The physical observation can be through any of the five senses (sight, hearing, smell, taste, touch). Since most public sector applications use sight, the text discussion focuses primarily on visual scales.

10. Kelly Maxwell, Donna Bryant, Lynette Keyes, and Kathleen Bernier, *Kindergartners' Skills in Smart Start Counties in 1995: A Baseline from Which to Measure Change* (Chapel Hill: The University of North Carolina, 1997). The checklist was adapted from the Maryland Systematic Teacher Observation Inventory, an instrument developed by the Maryland Department of Education.

11. Straphangers Campaign, *How Does Your Subway Line Rate?* (New York: New York Public Interest Research Group Fund, Inc., June 1998).

12. Straphangers Campaign, *Subway Shmutz: Cleanliness in New York City Subway Cars* (New York: New York Public Interest Research Group Fund, Inc., April 1998).

13. Fund for the City of New York, *Computerized Neighborhood Environment Tracking* (New York: Fund for the City of New York, 1999).

14. Fund for the City of New York, Center on Municipal Government Performance, *How Smooth Are New York City's Streets?* (New York: Fund for the City of New York, September 1998).

15. Quarterly program reporting has been common in government agencies for many years, but little of it has included systematically collected data on outcomes.

16. Take an annual sample of 1,000 customers split into quarterly samples of 250 each. At a 90 percent confidence level, the sample size of 250 would yield a confidence interval of approximately +5.4 percentage points, versus +2.7 percentage points for the full sample of 1,000. If 50 percent of those sampled gave a certain rating to a particular service characteristic, the confidence intervals would be, respectively, 44.6 percent to 55.4 percent and 47.3 percent to 52.7 percent. If the first two quarters are added together, giving a total sample of 500, the confidence interval would be +3.8 percentage points. Further data and information on the trade-offs among sample sizes, confidence intervals, and confidence levels are given in Hatry et al., *Customer Surveys for Agency Managers.*

# Analysis and Use of Performance Information

# Making Outcome Information Useful: Providing Indicator Breakouts

Producing data does not mean that they will be useful. The average depth information was accurate, but the following elements should be included in a performance measurement system to help transform outcome data into really useful information:

- *Breakouts* (disaggregations) of the outcome data for each indicator
- *Comparisons* of the program's data to benchmark data
- *Explanations* as to why the data are the way they are—particularly when they do not meet expectations
- *Clear presentation of the information* in understandable, user-friendly formats

This chapter discusses the first of these elements—how to choose outcome indicator breakouts for a program.[1]

## Why Are Breakouts Important?

> **Caution:**
> Watch Out for Overly Aggregated Data!

Breakouts can reveal highly useful findings on performance that are hidden by aggregation. Two functions of breakouts are particularly important.

First, breakouts can distinguish *differences in performance among relevant groups*. Identifying such differences is the first step toward asking:

- Why is *high* performance occurring in some places and not others? Answers to this question can lead to transferring successful practices to less successful work.
- Why is *low* performance occurring in some places? Answers to this question can ensure that appropriate improvement options are identified and addressed.

Second, breakouts can help identify inequities among customer groups—situations in which some groups had significantly better outcomes than others. An agency or program can also use performance indicators that reflect the size of the gap between groups. For example, Minnesota's Department of Health has as a specific objective reducing the disparity in infant death rates between racial groups. The department could have displayed the gap by breaking out the overall infant death rate for each group. Because of the importance of the objective, however, the department included in its 1996 agency performance report three indicators that directly reported the gaps: the disparity ratios (infant mortality rates relative to that of white infants) for African Americans, Native Americans, and Asian Americans. It uses these data to help guide its allocation of resources.

Here are two examples of the types of questions programs need to address as they determine their breakouts:

- *For a state or local school system.* For which specific grades should outcome data be provided: groups of grades, such as K–6, 7–9, 10–12; every grade; or just those grades for which academic testing is commonly done? Should the data be divided by age groups rather than by grade, and if so, which ones?
- *For a water quality protection program.* If the Environmental Protection Agency wants intermediate outcome data on state progress, should the

---

**EXHIBIT 8-1**

**Basic Types of Breakouts for Outcome Data**

- Organizational unit or project
- Workload or customer characteristics
- Geographical location
- Difficulty of workload
- Type and amount of services provided
- Reason for outcome or rating

data be broken out by state, or is region sufficient? If region, how should the states be grouped? Should the data be grouped by pollutants? If so, which ones?

## Breakout Categories

Exhibit 8-1 lists basic breakout categories.

### By Organizational Unit or Project

Each manager or supervisor should have outcome information for his or her area of responsibility. Outcome data that only lump the service responsibilities of several managers or supervisors together limits considerably the value of performance information.

Similarly, if a program sponsors different projects—perhaps using different grantees or contractors—outcome data for each project, available both to the program and to the grantees or contractors for that program, will greatly increase the usefulness of the data.

Examples of organizational units for which breakouts are likely to be relevant include:

- Individual facilities (such as individual hospitals, libraries, recreation centers, parks, prisons, or jails)
- Particular offices that are each the responsibility of a specific supervisor or manager (such as federal, state, or local public assistance or health offices)
- Groupings of offices or facilities that are an upper-level manager's responsibility (groups of parks or fire stations)

The organizational breakout of a computer facility is shown in exhibit 8-2. It displays data from six different supervisory divisions. Each unit was provided data on the response time of its own activities. The outcomes from the other units were also available so that each unit could compare its performance to that of the others.

Exhibit 8-3 compares three units of a family services program.

Providing outcome data on every organizational unit can become expensive. Customer surveys, in particular, can become expensive if large samples are needed for each unit. In such cases, the program needs to make a choice: Be satisfied with less than complete coverage of all individual units, or use smaller sample sizes (and obtain less precise data).

## EXHIBIT 8-2

### Computer Facility Callback Timeliness

| Division | Percent of Customers Called Back the Same Day* | |
| | March 1998 | April 1998 |
|---|---|---|
| 1 | 98 | 88 |
| 2 | 52 | 59 |
| 3 | 88 | 97 |
| 4 | 67 | 100 |
| 5 | 30 | 38 |
| 6 | 60 | 52 |
| **Overall** | **61** | **59** |

**Source:** Adapted from a report of a U.S. Department of the Navy computer facility.

*Information on the number of calls received from customers by each division should also be provided. If the number is very small for a division, the percentage may not be meaningful. In this example, division 4's percentage for April (100%) was based on very few calls.

One hybrid option is to combine organizational units that have small workloads (e.g., units with small numbers of customers).

### By Workload or Customer Characteristics

Breakouts by categories of customers or other forms of program workload are likely to be very useful in providing information to program personnel about the extent to which particular categories are achieving the desired outcomes (and which categories are not). Such breakouts also provide important information about *the distribution (and therefore equity) of benefits.*

Programs for which **individual persons** are customers should consider such breakout categories as the following:

- Age
- Gender
- Race or ethnicity
- Household income
- Household composition (such as size and number of children)
- Disability status
- English-speaking capability
- Other special status (such as migrant worker family)

Performance Measurement: Getting Results

EXHIBIT 8-3

**Outcomes by Organizational Unit and Difficulty of Preservice Problems (Family Services Program)**

| | Percent of Clients Whose Adjustment Level Has Improved 12 Months after Intake[a] | | | |
|---|---|---|---|---|
| **Difficulty of Problems at Intake** | **Family Services Unit 1** | **Family Services Unit 2[b]** | **Family Services Unit 3[c]** | **All Units** |
| Minor | 52 | (35) | 56 | 47 |
| Moderate | 35 | 30 | (54) | 39 |
| Major | 58 | 69 | 61 | 63 |
| **Total** | **48** | **44** | **57** | **50** |

a. Tables such as these should also identify the number of clients in each cell. If a number is overly small, the percentages may not be meaningful.
b. Unit 2 clients with minor problems at intake have not shown as much improvement as hoped. Unit 2 should look into this (such as identifying what the other units are doing to achieve their considerably higher success rates), report on their difficulties, and provide recommendations for corrective actions.
c. A substantial proportion of Unit 3 clients with moderate problems at intake showed improvement. The program should attempt to find out what is leading to this higher rate of improvement so Units 1 and 2 can use the information. Unit 3 should be congratulated for these results.

Programs for which ***businesses*** are customers might use breakout categories such as the following:

- Business size (*e.g.*, number of employees and annual sales volume, each grouped into a manageable number of size ranges)
- Product type (using standard industrial code classifications, for example)
- Ownership characteristics (*e.g.*, whether minority- or female-owned and whether classified as a small business)

For some programs, outcomes may focus on *types of workload rather than customers*. For example, for road maintenance programs, road condition might be grouped according to one or more of the following characteristics:

- Amount of traffic and the proportion that is truck traffic
- Type of pavement
- Soil conditions
- Historical weather conditions

For water and sewer programs, the condition of various parts of the distribution network might be grouped by:

- Pipe size
- Pipe materials
- Soil conditions

For federal and state education programs, breakouts for groups of school districts or schools might be based on:

- Size (student enrollment or number of teachers)
- Urban, rural, or suburban location
- Percent of student body enrolled in subsidized meal programs (as a surrogate for family income)
- Status of educational reform

In all these cases, programs will need to define clearly each category to be used for each characteristic, bearing in mind the importance of having a manageable number of categories that together form a complete set. For example, a program interested in breaking out its outcomes by customer income will need to decide how many income categories should be used and what income range should define each category. If services are targeted to low-income households, for example, suitable income categories might be less than $5,000 a year; $5,000–$15,000; and over $15,000. For a clientele that is typically middle-income, better categories might be less than $15,000 a year; $15,000–$30,000; $30,001–$45,000; and over $45,000.

## By Geographical Location

This will be a key breakout for many programs. Knowing the outcome of services in each geographical area will provide information about where performance is good and where it is not. (Recent developments in Geographical Information Systems, GIS, have greatly increased the practicality of breakouts by geographical area, including neighborhood, by facilitating the coding of geographical coordinates.[2])

For example, a state might track indicators of health, employment, and education test scores—not only for the state as a whole but also for each of its counties and cities or for various regions within the state. The state can use such data to identify assistance needs for those areas where performance has been subpar. Each county or city, in turn, may want such data broken out by key districts or neighborhoods.

Useful geographical breakouts include:

- Neighborhood
- Areas within organizational boundaries (such as districts or precincts)
- Political boundaries (such as electoral districts)
- Counties or cities
- Zip codes
- Regions
- States

Exhibit 8-4 is an example from New York City's street cleanliness rating. Such a map has been published for many years by the city in its annual *Mayor's Management Report* to the public. The darker the shading on the map, the dirtier the streets. The data simultaneously show the outcomes of cleaning efforts and where cleanup activities are most needed. The city uses such cleanliness ratings to help allocate crews to areas most in need. Reviewing the differences in data over time indicates the extent to which long-term progress is being made in each geographical area. (Since 1990, the date of this map, the number of dirty and marginal districts has shrunk dramatically.)

Exhibit 8-5 presents data from a Portland, Oregon, annual household survey, administered as part of its annual performance measurement process. The data identify differences by geographical area in residents' feelings of security in their neighborhoods during the day.

## By Difficulty of Workload

All programs receive work that covers a range of difficulty. The proportion and degree of difficulty are likely to vary from one reporting period to another and from one organizational unit to another. The more difficult the workload, the more time-consuming, and probably the more expensive, it is to achieve desired outcomes. For example:

- Some customers are more difficult to help than others, perhaps because of type of complaint or language problems.
- Some roads are more difficult to keep in good condition than others, perhaps because of the amount of total traffic, the amount of truck traffic, soil conditions, and/or weather conditions.
- Some applications are much easier to process than others. Applications for eligibility to participate in a program or for permits, licenses, or loans are likely to be easy for staff to process, whereas other applications could

EXHIBIT 8-4

## Department of Sanitation Street Cleanliness

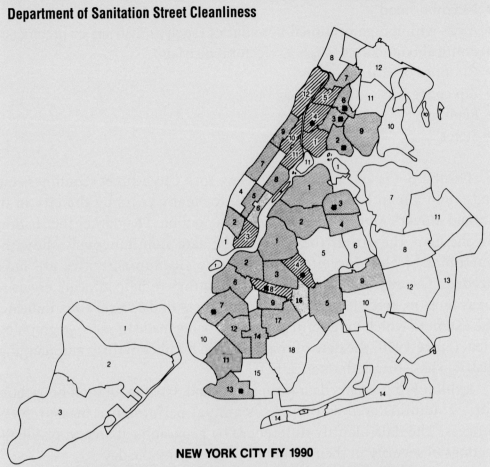

**NEW YORK CITY FY 1990**

**CHANGE IN LEVELS OF CLEANLINESS FOR THE 59 SANITATION DISTRICTS**

| Number of Districts | | Cleanliness Level |
|---|---|---|
| **FY 90** | **FY 89** | |
| 0 | 0 | Very Dirty |
| 9 | 8 | Dirty |
| 29 | 25 | Marginal |
| 21 | 26 | Clean |

| Number of Districts | Degree of Change - FY '89 - '90 |
|---|---|
| 0 | ▲ Significant Improvement in Cleanliness of +5.0% or More. |
| 9 | ■ Significant Decline in Cleanliness of –5.0% or More. |

**Source:** City of New York, *The Mayor's Management Report* for fiscal year 1990 (New York: City of New York), 170.

**Residents Rating Their Neighborhood
"Safe" or "Very Safe" during the Day**

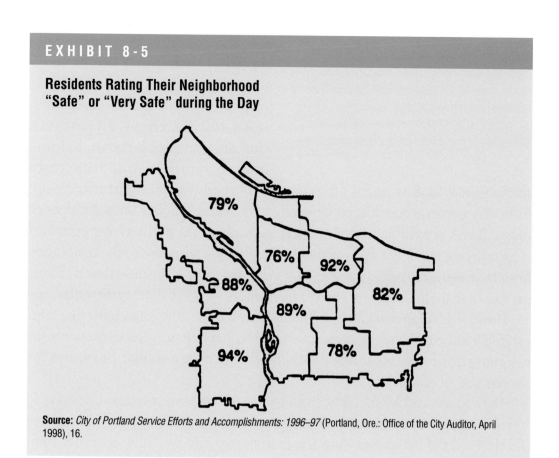

**Source:** *City of Portland Service Efforts and Accomplishments: 1996–97* (Portland, Ore.: Office of the City Auditor, April 1998), 16.

require staff to obtain confirmations and do other checks before accepting or denying them.

Although difficulty is a workload characteristic (discussed above), it is especially important to performance measurement.

For some programs, risk factors may be a good way to capture workload difficulty. For example, to the extent that smoking, lack of exercise, and existing health problems (such as diabetes) are risky conditions that lead to more severe health problems, persons with more risk factors will be more difficult to help.[3] In this case, outcome indicator breakouts reflecting the condition of patients after they have participated in health care programs should be reported by degree of risk—with higher percentages of success expected for patients at less risk.

***The importance of workload difficulty breakouts.*** Aggregate outcomes can be misleading and unfair if the difficulty of the incoming workload is not considered. Exhibit 8-6 shows how easy it is to jump to the wrong conclusion if only aggregate data are reported. Unit 1 helped a higher proportion of its total cases (60 percent vs. 47 percent) than unit 2, but the breakout data show that unit 2's percentages are better than unit 1's. What happened? Unit 2 had a much higher proportion of difficult cases than unit 1 (60 percent vs. 20 percent). The greater problems in helping difficult rather than routine cases make unit 2 look worse if all cases are lumped together, but when each difficulty group is considered by itself, unit 2 scores higher on both types of cases. (Look at exhibit 8-3 for another example of the perils of aggregation.)

*Reporting breakouts by workload difficulty will also reduce the temptation for service delivery (public agencies or private agencies) to cream—that is, focus on easier-to-help (and less costly) customers—to get their ratings up.*

***How to develop workload difficulty categories.*** The key challenge is to establish difficulty categories that are reliable. All staff persons responsible for assigning difficulty categories should be able to assign similar categories for similar sets of conditions.

The easiest and least costly strategy for developing such categories is to have a group of key personnel familiar with program agency operations develop a set of categories—no fewer than two and probably no more than five—and detailed definitions of each category. The category names might be simple ones, such as high, medium, and low difficulty, but each category should be defined thoroughly. The definitions need to be based on the specific workload characteristics for which information is expected to be available.

The categories and their definitions should then be pilot-tested on a small number of workload units (such as customers, loan applications, or road sections).

A variety of program personnel, including some of those who will be responsible for assigning the difficulty categories to the workload units, should be asked to select which category is most appropriate for each sampled case. The categories chosen by each person for each test workload unit should then be compared to determine whether they are sufficiently similar to represent reliable categorizations. If the level-of-difficulty categories selected for each case are not similar,

**EXHIBIT 8-6**

**Workload Difficulty Breakout (Clients)**

|  | Unit 1 | Unit 2 |
|---|---|---|
| Aggregate Data |  |  |
| **Total Clients** | **500** | **500** |
| Number Helped | 300 | 235 |
| Percent Helped | 60% | 47% |
| Breakout Data |  |  |
| **Difficult Cases** | **100** | **300** |
| Number Helped | 0 | 75 |
| Percent Helped | 0% | 25% |
| **Routine Cases** | **400** | **200** |
| Number Helped | 300 | 160 |
| Percent Helped | 75% | 80% |

the definitions will need to be reworked (and/or the persons assigning the categories given more training).

This procedure will be sufficient for many agencies and programs. A more sophisticated approach is to use statistical analysis to relate available data on outcomes to the characteristics. For example, statistical regression analysis might be used to determine the relationship between past data on outcomes for individual clients and the characteristics believed to be related to difficulty in achieving successful outcomes. For human service programs these characteristics might include educational level and household income. Such statistical procedures have been used by the federal Job Training Partnership Act program, for example, to enable states to take into account local economic conditions when comparing the success of programs in getting their customers employed. Statistical analysis has also been used by the U.S. Health Care Financing Agency to take the entering condition of patients (an indicator of difficulty) into account in comparing mortality rates among hospitals.

## By Type and Amount of Service

Outcomes can be grouped by the amount and type of service provided and/or the procedure used to deliver the service. This provides managers and their staffs with key information to help them assess which service delivery approaches are working well and which are not. This breakout applies when the program varies the service given to individual items in its workload so that comparisons can subsequently be made. In a social service program, for example, the agency might apply more caseworker time for some clients, use a greater proportion of telephone rather than in-person assistance for some clients, use more paraprofessionals for some clients, and so on, depending on resources available on a given day or during a given week. Another example is a program that contracts some of its work and uses its own personnel to perform similar work. As long as the type of assistance is not tailored to particular categories of clients, breakouts by type of assistance can be helpful.

If the agency classifies each item of workload by the particular type or amount of service applied to the item and then links that information to the outcome data on the workload, the program personnel can then obtain and compare outcome information for each type or amount of service.

Exhibit 8-7 presents an example adapted from data in a pilot of performance measurement for social service programs in North Carolina local governments. In these data, the number of interviews (and the severity of problems at intake) did *not* increase the percentage of clients whose condition improved. (The program analysts would need to investigate further in

EXHIBIT 8-7

**Outcomes by Level of Service Received**

| Problems at Intake | Percent of Clients Whose Problems Improved after Nine Months | | | |
| | Service Level (Number of Interviews) | | | |
| | 1 | 2–10 | Over 10 | Total |
| --- | --- | --- | --- | --- |
| Minor | 50 | 36 | 0 | 28 |
| Moderate | 57 | 53 | 56 | 55 |
| Major | 67 | 77 | 47 | 63 |
| **Total** | **60** | **58** | **45** | **53** |

order to understand the relationship between category of client and number of interviews.)

A good example of what breakouts by type of procedure can reveal is Hawaii's audit of procedures for licensing nurses. The audit examined complaints involving nurses' use of drugs. It broke out the complaint data by procedure used to check on the nurses' license applications. It found that 81 percent of all such complaints involved nurses who had been licensed by an endorsement procedure rather than by a check of the applicant's nursing history. The audit recommended that the endorsement procedure be altered.[4]

*Type and amount of service can be used to encourage innovation.* Managers who want to test new service delivery procedures can try the procedures while continuing to use existing procedures on *the remainder*. This will help them determine which are better. To ensure against compiling biased evidence, the workload should, to the extent feasible, be randomly assigned to each candidate procedure.

Outcome data obtained during the test period can then be tabulated for each procedure. Here is the basic sequence of steps to be followed in such a test:

1. Identify the procedures to be compared.
2. Choose a procedure for selecting which incoming workload will be served using each of the candidate procedures. The purpose here is to select a *representative* sample of the workload for each procedure (and thus maximize the likelihood that the same proportion of difficult workloads will be included in each of the groups). For this purpose, a coin toss (or random number table) can be used to ensure representativeness.

**Cautionary Tale**

*Avoid assignment procedures that lead to different types of workloads being assigned systematically to different procedures.* Many years ago, one city government wanted to compare its existing process for maintaining city vehicles in-house to a second process that involved more preventive maintenance and to a third process that used private contractors to provide the vehicle maintenance. The agency assigned one-third of its vehicles to each of these three methods—a fine idea. Unfortunately, the city chose to assign all Fords to the first process, all General Motors cars to the second, and all Chryslers to the third. By choosing this assignment process, the city eliminated the possibility of telling whether different outcomes were due to the particular procedure or to the make of car.

If the arrival of workload is essentially random, assigning every unit of incoming workload on a rotating basis to each of the procedures would serve the same purpose.

3. Assign each unit of incoming workload to a procedure, based on the randomizing scheme.
4. Record the procedure used for each workload item.
5. Track the outcome indicators for each item.
6. Tabulate the value of each outcome indicator for each procedure.

### By Reason for Outcome or Rating

If information is available on reasons for outcomes, *particularly reasons for poor outcomes*, breakouts by reason can be used to suggest actions needed to correct problems.

A number of programs, such as social, health, and crime and justice programs, maintain case records. At some point, these cases are closed. Some results will represent successes and some will not. For unsuccessful cases, there are typically several alternative reasons for failure. For example, unsuccessful litigation may have occurred because witnesses died, evidence became contaminated, adequate staff time was not available to handle the case, or the litigation work was poor. Health treatment may be unsuccessful because patients did not follow the regimens prescribed, physicians or nurses made errors, or the health problems were essentially incurable. Tabulating outcomes for each such reason should help the program identify corrective actions.

In customer surveys, respondents can be asked why they expressed dissatisfaction with a particular service or why they did not use it. For example, respondents might not have used a service because:

- Location not convenient
- Location not safe
- Hours of operation not convenient
- Had a previous bad experience with the service
- Did not know the service was available
- Had no time available to use the service
- Had no need for the service

For traffic accidents, agencies usually identify a reason, such as weather, car defects, traffic signal or sign problems, or driver or pedestrian error. Tabulations of these for each location and time provide performance measurement data by cause and suggest what, if any, corrections are needed.

For all these situations, recording and tabulating reasons for each case allows agency and program managers to identify prominent reasons and decide what corrective actions are appropriate. *To be most useful, reasons should be grouped into those the program can do something about and those it cannot.* In the example above, no time available for use and no need for a service are reasons over which the program typically has no influence.

Exhibit 8-8 shows reasons why students who needed help for substance abuse found it difficult to get (based on survey data). The performance indicator is *percent of students who needed help but found it difficult to get.* All the reasons are relevant for improving program performance but in different ways. The first two reasons indicate the need to get information to students on sources of help. The other reasons indicate the need for specific changes in program approaches. (The exhibit also indicates the use of breakouts by grade, usually important for educational outcomes.)

## Other Types of Breakouts

Programs should examine each of their outcome indicators to determine what additional breakouts would help them identify where the desired outcomes are occurring and where they are not. Examples of special breakout characteristics include:

- Vehicle ownership—for transportation programs in which accessibility to transportation is important
- Home ownership and type of dwelling—for housing-related programs that base benefits (or regulations) on criteria such as owner or renter, single family or multifamily dwelling
- The extent to which business customers have past experience in exporting—for interpreting the outcomes of export promotion programs

EXHIBIT 8-8

**Reasons Why Students Who Needed Help for Their Alcohol and Other Drug Use Found It Difficult to Get, Hawaii, 1989–1996, by Grade**

| Reason | Students (%) in Grade | | | |
|---|---|---|---|---|
| | 6 (N=164) | 8 (N=229) | 10 (N=183) | 12 (N=109) |
| 1. Had no idea who to ask or where to go for help | 54 | 57 | 50 | 60 |
| 2. Didn't think that people your age could get counseling/treatment | 47 | 39 | 28 | 24 |
| 3. Were afraid to talk to a counselor or anyone else because your parents or teachers would find out | 43 | 58 | 57 | 52 |
| 4. Were afraid of getting in trouble with the law | 46 | 38 | 28 | 27 |
| 5. Were afraid of what your friends would think | 43 | 38 | 28 | 27 |
| 6. Thought you could handle the problem yourself | 41 | 55 | 58 | 61 |
| 7. Could not get the kind of help that you needed or wanted | 27 | 31 | 25 | 24 |

**Source:** Adapted by the Center for Substance Abuse Research (CESAR), University of Maryland, from data from Renee Klingle and Michael Miller, *Hawaii Adolescent Treatment Needs Assessment Results from the Hawaii Student Drug Use Study, 1989–1996* (Honolulu: The University of Hawaii Speech Department for the Hawaii Department of Health, Alcohol, and Drug Abuse Division, 1996).

## Procedures for Choosing Breakouts for a Program

Final decisions on which breakouts are needed should be made before final decisions on data content and procedures. This is to ensure that the data collection needed for the preferred breakouts is built into the final data collection plan. Going back after the fact and trying to reconstruct data from records, for example, is usually very inefficient and can be very expensive.

The program should consider the breakout categories discussed earlier in this chapter and determine which are applicable. A sensible approach is to have program staff do the selection with input from other parts of the agency. (The sources discussed in chapter 6 for identifying outcome indicators can also help identify breakout candidates.)

The number of categories for a given breakout and how each category is defined will be determined to an important degree by the inevitable trade-offs among: (a) data collection procedure used, (b) data collection resources available, and (c) degree of data accuracy needed. Programs are likely to need help from statistical experts to help them understand these trade-offs in the context of their program needs.

## References and Notes

1. Comparisons are discussed in chapter 9, explanations and presentation formats in chapter 10.
2. For a good discussion of using geographical information, especially at the community level, see U.S. Department of Housing and Urban Development, *Mapping Your Community: Using Geographic Information to Strengthen Community Objectives*, HUD-1092-CPD (Washington, D.C., October 1997).
3. For more discussion of risk factors, see National Research Council, *Assessment of Performance Measures for Public Health, Substance Abuse, and Mental Health*, eds. Edward B. Perrin and Jeffrey J. Koschel (National Academy Press: Washington, D.C., 1997).
4. Auditor, State of Hawaii, *Sunset Evaluation Update: Nurses: A Report to the Governor and the Legislature of the State of Hawaii* (Honolulu, October 13, 1994).

# Making Outcome Information Useful: Comparing Findings to Benchmarks

Once a program has outcome data, how can it find out whether the level of performance they reflect is good or bad? By comparing the outcomes for the period of interest with benchmarks—that is, measures of what can be expected. This chapter identifies the types of benchmarks likely to be useful as comparison measures.

Major types of benchmarks used to assess performance for a particular reporting period are:

1. Performance in the previous period
2. Performance of similar organizational units or geographical areas
3. Outcomes for different workload or customer groups
4. A recognized general standard
5. Performance of other jurisdictions or the private sector
6. Different service delivery practices
7. Targets established at the beginning of the performance period

The breakout data discussed in chapter 8 provide the information for comparisons using benchmarks 2, 3, and 6. Other data sources are needed for comparisons using benchmarks 1, 4, 5, and 7. Each of these benchmarks is discussed in detail below.

## Performance in the Previous Period

This comparison is almost always relevant and important. Comparisons of current to previous performance are the most common type of comparison and are applicable to all programs. They help agency officials assess whether performance in a given service environment has improved or deteriorated over time. They can also be used to help assess the impact of a new procedure on performance.

Data on past performance should be readily available, except for first-time performance indicators. Reporting periods compared should be of the same length, whether monthly, quarterly, annually, or whatever.

Two important questions need to be answered by an agency in establishing its performance measurement system: How frequently should the data for each indicator be reported? To which particular past period should the current period be compared?

### Frequency

*The more timely the feedback, the more useful it is to program managers and staff.* Many agencies prepare internal program reports on process and output indicators on a quarterly, if not a monthly, basis. This same frequency is likely to be desirable for data on outcomes. For data already in administrative records, greater frequency can be obtained at minimal cost. As noted in chapter 7, the timeliness problem can often be solved at only a small additional cost. If survey data are desired quarterly, for example, a quarter of the annual budget can be devoted to collecting a quarter of the anticipated annual data. The quarterly data will be less precise than suveying all respondents at once, but the desired precision will still be achieved when the quarterly observations are combined into an annual estimate. The total additional cost will be about 10 percent. (Two types of exceptions should be mentioned. The first covers performance indicators for which even annual data are inherently too expensive to collect. The second covers indicators whose values are not expected to change significantly over a 12-month period, such as some water quality measurements.)

### Comparison Period

Comparing a particular 12-month period with the previous 12-month period is almost always appropriate, but should quarterly data be compared with data from the previous quarter or with data from the same quarter of a previous year? Programs whose outcomes are believed to be significantly affected by seasonal factors should compare data for a particular quarter with data for the same quarter in previous years. To track changes in outcomes after the introduction of new program practices, data for several periods after the introduction of the new practices should be compared to data for several periods before their introduction.

## Performance of Similar Organizational Units or Geographical Areas

An important use of breakouts by organizational units and geographical areas is to compare outcomes when providing essentially the same service to essentially the same type of customers. Such comparisons indicate which units or areas are performing well and which are performing badly relative to one another. In addition to the monitoring value of such comparisons, they can have motivational value for program personnel in each unit.

Plausible units to be compared include:

- Offices
- Service districts
- Facilities (such as libraries, parks, community centers, hospitals, correctional facilities, day care centers, landfills)
- Regions

For such comparisons to be valid, the missions and types of customers must be reasonably similar across units. Exhibit 8-2 in chapter 8 shows a breakout by operating divisions of a computer facility; exhibit 8-3 shows a breakout by service unit of a family services program.

Some programs will want to compare performance across geographical areas of the program's jurisdiction. For example, many local programs, such as street cleaning, road maintenance, parks and recreation, and libraries, find it useful to compare outcomes across neighborhoods. Exhibits 8-4 and 8-5 illustrate breakouts that allow managers to make comparisons by geographical area.

## Outcomes for Different Workload or Customer Groups

Once workload and customer breakouts are available, comparisons can be made among the categories to enable managers to focus on the ones that seem to need special actions. In other words, comparisons indicate whether the program is more or less successful on particular outcome indicators with certain categories of customers or workload than with others—men compared to women, the young compared to the elderly, Hispanics compared to whites, blind customers versus wheelchair customers, rural roads versus urban roads, and so on.

Exhibit 8-3 in chapter 8 shows comparisons across both organizational units and customer difficulty levels for a social service agency. Family services unit 3 had a substantially higher overall success rate than units 1 and 2, but, as usual, the outcome data do not tell why unit 3 did better. Program staff can use breakout by difficulty to help explore the whys. For example:

- Unit 2, compared to the other units, did very well with clients who had major problems but not so well with clients who had minor or moderate problems. Unit 2's procedures for clients with minor and moderate problems should be looked into in order to ascertain whether its procedures differ significantly from those of the other two units and whether unit 2 might be able to obtain improvement ideas from those other units.
- Unit 3 had substantially better outcomes on clients with moderate problems and did relatively well on other clients. Should this unit's practices be transferred to the other units?

## A Recognized General Standard

When another level of government or a professional association has developed a standard for an outcome indicator, this standard can be used to assess performance.[1]

For example:

- The federal government periodically sets standards on drinking water quality and on emissions from wastewater treatment plants. Some of these are mandated, some are not. Individual jurisdictions can use these standards as a benchmark against which to compare their own levels.
- The U.S. Department of Labor's performance measurement process for the Job Training Partnership Act (JTPA) calculated and disseminated annual national performance standards based on the most recent data on outcomes achieved by local programs. Individual programs at both state and local levels have used these national standards to assess their own performance.[2]

Exhibit 9-1 lists the six indicators JTPA used as the primary outcome measurements. (The first five are end outcomes. The last is best considered an intermediate outcome.) JTPA recommended adjusting these standards (statistically) to reflect local difficulty conditions, including economic factors and participant characteristics.

## Performance of Other Jurisdictions or the Private Sector

For some outcome indicators, comparable outcome data might be available from other jurisdictions or the private sector. This type of comparison can be useful as long as (a) the activity of the other jurisdictions or private firms is sufficiently similar to that of the program being evaluated and (b) compatible data on the indicators are available in a timely way.

For all such comparisons, the outcome values need to be "normalized" to produce meaningful (and fair) assessments. That is, the outcome values need to be related to some factor that adjusts for differences in scale, often a population count. Normalization procedures produce indicators such as *number of crimes per capita* or *percent of road-miles in good condition* (the number of miles in good condition divided by the total number of road-miles in a jurisdiction).

Making these comparisons has the added benefits of (a) indicating what performance level is realistic to target and (b) identifying exemplary practices of high-performing organizations that can be adapted by managers to enhance their own agency's performance.

Comparative outcome indicator data that have been available to local or state jurisdictions for many years include:

---

### EXHIBIT 9–1

**Job Training Partnership Act Performance Indicators and National Standards**

|  | Performance Indicators | National Standards |
|---|---|---|
| **Adult** | Employment Rate at Follow-Up* | 62% |
|  | Weekly Earnings at Follow-Up* | $204 |
| **Welfare** | Employment Rate at Follow-Up* | 51% |
|  | Weekly Earnings at Follow-Up* | $182 |
| **Youth** | Entered Employment Rate | 45% |
|  | Employability Enhancement Rate | 33% |

* The follow-up period was defined as 13 weeks after employees had finished the training or employment program.

- Traffic accidents, injuries, and fatalities
- Crime rates (aggregate clearance rates for various categories of crime are also reported annually for local governments in various population-size categories)
- Fire incident rates and losses
- Levels of air and water pollution (for larger cities and counties)
- Health statistics
- Standardized test scores for school districts within a state, collected and reported by districts and state education agencies

Private businesses that provide services similar to publicly provided services—and therefore have outcomes that can provide useful benchmarks—include private bus companies, solid waste collection firms, vehicle maintenance shops, and food service companies. Data on frequency of in-service breakdowns, response times, and/or unit cost might be available to provide relevant benchmarks for comparisons.

In recent years, a number of formal efforts to compare public agency performance measurements have begun, especially comparisons of local government agencies. The latter include efforts in the United Kingdom, Germany, and the United States. The Australian government has begun comparing a variety of performance data from its states. Exhibit 9-2 illustrates such comparisons using U.S. public library data.

A problem here is obtaining the outcome data in a timely way. Regular reports providing intergovernmental data may not be available for many months, if not years, after the reporting period and thus may not be very useful to program managers. Programs and agencies may be able to shorten this lag considerably by arranging to share data prior to public release.

## Different Service Delivery Practices

Programs periodically consider new or different practices. As discussed in chapter 8, the outcome measurement process can be used to help programs assess the results and outcomes of different ways of doing things, such as:

- Different operating procedures
- Different technologies
- Different staffing arrangements
- Different amounts or levels of service provided to individual customers
- Different providers (such as private contractors)

EXHIBIT 9-2

## Annual Circulation per Capita for Libraries, FY 1996 (End Outcome Indicator)*

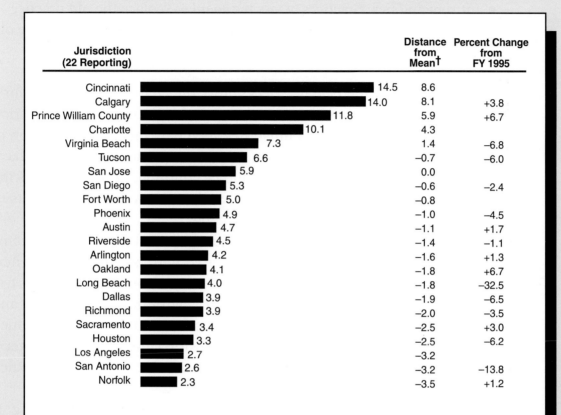

| Jurisdiction (22 Reporting) | | Distance from Mean† | Percent Change from FY 1995 |
|---|---|---|---|
| Cincinnati | 14.5 | 8.6 | |
| Calgary | 14.0 | 8.1 | +3.8 |
| Prince William County | 11.8 | 5.9 | +6.7 |
| Charlotte | 10.1 | 4.3 | |
| Virginia Beach | 7.3 | 1.4 | −6.8 |
| Tucson | 6.6 | −0.7 | −6.0 |
| San Jose | 5.9 | 0.0 | |
| San Diego | 5.3 | −0.6 | −2.4 |
| Fort Worth | 5.0 | −0.8 | |
| Phoenix | 4.9 | −1.0 | −4.5 |
| Austin | 4.7 | −1.1 | +1.7 |
| Riverside | 4.5 | −1.4 | −1.1 |
| Arlington | 4.2 | −1.6 | +1.3 |
| Oakland | 4.1 | −1.8 | +6.7 |
| Long Beach | 4.0 | −1.8 | −32.5 |
| Dallas | 3.9 | −1.9 | −6.5 |
| Richmond | 3.9 | −2.0 | −3.5 |
| Sacramento | 3.4 | −2.5 | +3.0 |
| Houston | 3.3 | −2.5 | −6.2 |
| Los Angeles | 2.7 | −3.2 | |
| San Antonio | 2.6 | −3.2 | −13.8 |
| Norfolk | 2.3 | −3.5 | +1.2 |

**Source:** *Comparative Performance Measurement: FY 1996 Data Report* (Washington, D.C.: International City/County Management Association, 1998).

*Circulation includes all items of any format (e.g., written and audiovisual materials), including renewals that are checked out for use outside the library. Circulation per capita includes combined circulation reported by jurisdictions from central libraries, branches, and bookmobiles. Some of the variation in circulation rates among jurisdictions may be due to differences in factors such as the availability of branch libraries, the overall number of facilities, number of hours open, size and scope of library holdings, and economic or demographic characteristics of the population served.

†The mean is 5.9 items; the median is 4.6; and the standard deviation is 3.5.

The two principal approaches to using an outcome measurement process to compare alternative policies, processes, or procedures to those currently being used are:

- Introducing new practices *across the board* to replace the old practice
- Introducing new practices into *part of an operation* and running the old and new practices side by side for a period of time

When introducing new practices across the board, outcome data for a period before the change should be compared with outcomes for a period after the change. Exhibit 9-3 illustrates such data for the introduction of automated dispatching equipment. The new equipment appears to have improved response times. Its use should be continued (other factors being equal), according to this comparison, and even added to other parts of the system, assuming its costs are reasonable.

When introducing new practices in just part of the program, outcome data for the old process should be compared with outcomes for the new process over the same period. This type of comparison helps managers test alternative procedures and innovative ideas without making a full (and irreversible) commitment. Exhibit 9-4 illustrates outcome data obtained for a computer versus manual loan-processing comparison. (Chapter 8 describes how to set up an experiment to generate the data needed for such a comparison.)

The data in exhibit 9-4 indicate that computer processing is considerably faster but that error rates are slightly higher. This outcome information may well lead the agency to review the errors made under

---

**EXHIBIT 9–3**

**Comparison of Outcomes before and after Procedure Change**

| | 1998 Quarters | | | | 1999 Quarters | | | | 2000 Quarters | | | | 5-Qtr. Average Before | 6-Qtr. Average After |
|---|---|---|---|---|---|---|---|---|---|---|---|---|---|---|
| | 1st | 2nd | 3rd | 4th | 1st | 2nd | 3rd | 4th | 1st | 2nd | 3rd | 4th | | |
| Average Response Time (Minutes) | 5.2 | 5.7 | 5.8 | 5.3 | 5.5 | 5.6 | 4.8 | 4.5 | 4.5 | 4.4 | 4.8 | N/A | 5.5 | 4.8 |

↑

**Introduction of Automated Dispatching Equipment**

Performance Measurement: Getting Results

the new procedure in order to identify and correct problems and then run the experiment again to check error rates after the corrections have been made. If the error rates fall, the program may choose to move completely to computer processing. If error rates do not fall, the program must decide whether to tolerate higher error rates in return for greater speed or look for an automated system that is less error-prone.

**Computer versus Manual Procedures for Processing Eligibility Determinations***

| Processing Procedure | Error Rate (%) | Applications Taking More Than One Day to Process (%) |
|---|---|---|
| Computer | 9 | 18 |
| Manual | 8 | 35 |

*About 250 applications processed by each procedure.

Exhibit 8-7 compares various levels of service provided to customers of a social service program. This is an example of a "natural" experiment. The program did not purposely set up an experiment to test whether more sessions made a difference. Rather, in the normal order of doing business, incoming clients varied in the scale of their problems and staff had more sessions with some clients than others, regardless of the difficulty of the client's problem. Natural experiments can provide useful comparisons if the requisite outcome data are recorded.

The exhibit presents data on clients' number of sessions and problem difficulty. The data suggest that more sessions are not associated with improved outcomes. However, these data are not sufficient to draw a firm conclusion. In-depth analysis is needed before a program takes action based only on this type of pattern. Other factors that should be investigated are customer age, ability to speak English, and so on.

Virginia, in a deliberate experiment, compared the collection performance of its existing publicly operated child support enforcement offices with that of privately run offices contracted for the purpose. When the state's performance measurement process compared total dollars collected for the two groups of offices in FY 1997, the privately operated offices were revealed to have done better. But when the state broke out the collections data by source, it found that the publicly operated offices had larger collections for families on welfare than did the privately run offices.[3] On yet another indicator, number of support orders established, the publicly run offices also did better, although their operations cost somewhat more. After two years, the agency concluded that the overall difference between the two approaches was small. As a result, the General Assembly approved outside contracting as an option *but did not mandate its use.*

## Targets Established at the Beginning of the Performance Period

Establishing targets (or at least projected values) for each outcome indicator for the coming performance period is a highly useful management tool. The Government Performance and Results Act now requires federal programs to set targets at the beginning of each year for that year—and to report to the President and Congress after the end of the year the actual values and how they compared to the targets.

Experience with an indicator is important in setting firm targets. If an outcome indicator is new, it is wise to defer setting firm targets until the program has collected enough data to be confident of setting plausible values. Alternatively, a program might set targets for the initial data collection periods and be explicit in labeling them experimental.

Annual targets (or projections) are likely to be required for an agency's budget preparation process. These should be compatible with any goals or targets in the program's strategic plan, if one exists. Programs will typically find it useful to set not only annual targets but also targets for shorter reporting periods, such as quarters.

Out-year targets, perhaps for five years into the future, can encourage long-range thinking by program personnel and reduce the temptation to overemphasize current results at the expense of future progress.

In deciding on out-year targets, managers need to consider the timing of outcomes in relation to program activities. Some outcomes, especially end outcomes, should not be expected until one or more years after the year in which the activity takes place. This is particularly true for state and federal programs that work through local service delivery agencies. (In such instances, a program's current year outcomes may be based primarily on expenditures and activities undertaken in previous years.)

Preferably, different targets should be established for each outcome indicator in each breakout category (see chapter 8). This is especially important for each level-of-difficulty category. Different targets will make the comparisons much more useful, more meaningful, and fairer. They will also reduce the temptation for program personnel to concentrate on easier cases in order to show high performance.

### Things to Keep in Mind When Selecting Targets

Targets can be set in many different ways. Chapter 12 discusses the process in detail. In the meantime, here are some pointers:

- *A target does not have to be a single value.* A range is a perfectly reasonable alternative. For example, if the outcome indicator is expressed as a percent, the target might be expressed as the most likely achievable percent, plus or minus 5 percentage points.
- *Consider previous performance.* This is almost always a major factor in determining targets.
- *Consider benchmarking against the best.* If the program has more than one unit that provides the same service for the same types of customers, consider using the performance level achieved by the most successful managerial unit as the target for all units. In exhibit 8-6 of chapter 8, for example, benchmarking against the best would select unit 2's outcome rate for both difficult and routine cases (25 percent and 80 percent, respectively) as the next year's target—at least for internal agency reporting. Reports going outside the agency might use only the aggregate success rate as the target. Since aggregate targets are based, at least implicitly, on some assumption about the distribution of workload by difficulty category, the program should explicitly estimate the percentage of customers expected to fall into each difficulty category in the next reporting period.
- *If benchmarking against the best is considered too great a challenge, use the average performance of all units.* If the program wants to be even more conservative, it could use the worst value as the target, to emphasize the need to achieve at least that minimum level of success. Avoid the temptation to underestimate targets in order to look good each year; program reviewers will eventually catch on.
- *Consider the outcomes achieved in the past for different customer or workload categories.* For example, use the highest or average outcome achieved for any one demographic category as the target for all categories. If a program indicated successful outcomes for, say, 53 percent of men and 48 percent of women, setting a future overall target of 53 percent—for each gender and in the aggregate—would encourage high performance with all customers.
- *Consider the performance levels achieved by other jurisdictions or by private firms with similar activities and workload or customer compositions.* Benchmarking against the best in this case means setting targets at or near the best outcomes achieved by other organizations.
- *Make sure the targets chosen are feasible, given the program's budget and staffing plan for the year.* Keeping the same target despite reduced budgets can probably be achieved up to a point, but eventually cutbacks in resources should be reflected in reduced targets.
- *Identify any new developments—internal and external—that may affect the program's ability to achieve desired outcomes.* For example, legislative

changes (whether affecting policy or budget) that have just occurred or are expected to occur during the next reporting period may make it more or less difficult to achieve desired outcomes.

- *Target setting for periods shorter than a year needs to be done in the context of seasonal factors*—job availability, changes in service demand, and so on.

---

### Reference and Notes

1. These standards, however, for the purpose of outcome measurement comparisons need to be *outcome* standards. Most professional standards pertain to process and staffing characteristics, which do not help calibrate outcomes.
2. The Workforce Investment Act of 1998 (Public Law 105-220, August 7, 1998) replaces JTPA, but it appears to call for quite similar outcome-tracking procedures.
3. Reported in Diane Kittower, "Counting on Competition," *Governing Magazine* 11, no. 8 (May 1998).

# Analysis and Reporting of Performance Information

Using performance measurement only for accountability to higher levels would be a great waste. *Performance measurement data should be used to help improve programs.* After an agency has collected all these data, it needs to examine and analyze the data to identify appropriate actions that may be needed. This chapter suggests a variety of ways in which agencies can analyze performance data to help make such improvements. The last sections also discuss how to report results to maximize the chance that they will be used to good effect.

## How Performance Data Can Help

Analysis of data from a well-conceived performance measurement system can help an agency:

- Identify the conditions under which a program is doing well or poorly and thus stimulate remedial actions
- Raise key questions regarding a service that can help staff develop and carry out improvement strategies
- Provide clues to problems and sometimes to what can be done to improve future outcomes
- Help assess the extent to which remedial actions have succeeded

Chapters 8 and 9, respectively, identify breakouts a program should consider for each outcome indicator and potentially useful comparisons the program might make to interpret its outcome data. Such breakout and comparison information should be a major focus of a program's analysis effort.

Always keep in mind that almost all performance data have substantial limitations. The major limitation is that data on outcomes seldom, if ever, tell what caused the outcomes, especially end outcomes. Other information and other procedures, such as in-depth program evaluation, are needed to identify the extent to which the program contributed to the outcomes. Similarly, outcome information does not indicate what should be done to improve the program, but a well-designed performance measurement system can often provide highly useful clues.

## Analyzing Performance Data

Considerable literature exists on procedures for in-depth, ad hoc program evaluations. However, little guidance currently exists on procedures for examining outcome data obtained from a regular, frequent schedule. Many examinations of performance measurement data by agency personnel appear to be overly quick and casual. The focus in this chapter is on examining outcome information to help agencies determine what changes, what steps toward improvement, if any, should be taken. The focus is on basic steps that all agencies can take, not on more sophisticated, high-powered steps such as extensive statistical analyses and in-depth program evaluations. The following are suggested procedures for systematic examinations:

1. Examine changes over time.
2. Examine the outcome breakouts for each outcome indicator to assess where performance is good, fair, or poor.
3. Compare the program's outcomes to those of similar programs; look for best practices.
4. Use exception reporting—that is, look particularly at indicator values that fall outside the target range.
5. Obtain and examine explanatory information.
6. Determine whether the data on major types of performance indicators are consistent with each other.
7. Focus individual outcome indicators on areas in which the program or agency has particular responsibility or influence.
8. Examine multiple outcomes together to obtain a more comprehensive perspective on overall performance.

9. Use past performance data to trigger trials of new procedures and to help evaluate their success later.

## 1. Examine Changes over Time

After performance information becomes available for more than one reporting period, the latest findings can be compared with findings for prior reporting periods to detect trends and other significant changes. If the data indicate major improvement or deterioration, the agency should identify why it occurred. The following are examples of questions that might be asked to help identify reasons for changes:

- Have external factors significantly affected outcomes?
- Have special events during the reporting period significantly affected outcomes?
- Have resources been reduced (increased) to a degree that affected outcomes?
- Have legislative requirements changed in ways that affected the ability of the program to produce outcomes?
- Have the program staff changed their procedures (strategies) in a way that affected outcomes?

One important use of data collected over time is to detect patterns of deterioration in outcomes. Such patterns alert the agency to consider modifications to the program. For example, if the number of fires and loss of life and property have been increasing for several years, the relevant agency needs to determine the causes and the extent to which they can be prevented, such as by increasing inspections or strengthening fire codes.

*Caution and Suggestion:* Sometimes, performance indicator values can be substantially affected by infrequent events. These cause distortions in the data for a particular reporting period (such as might happen with fire statistics if only one or two major fires occurred during a reporting period). For such indicators, multiyear averages can smooth the data to highlight persistent trends. For example, suppose the fire rate data show 2.6, 9.7, 3.6, 1.5, 18.7, and 3.9 major fires per year, respectively, for six annual reporting periods. A series of three-year running averages, starting with the first three periods, would show rates of 5.3, 4.9, 7.9, and 8.0. This smooths out the effect of outlier values.

*Reminder:* When comparing reporting periods of less than one year, seasonal factors can affect the condition of roads, the amount of crime, the rate of unemployment, and similar outcomes. In such cases, as noted in chapter 9, the program should *compare performance data for a given season* with data for the same season in previous years.

Comparing performance indicator values before new procedures or policies to values afterwards is a way to assess the success of changes.

*Example:* A state legislature might stiffen the requirements for obtaining driver's licenses in the hope of reducing state accident and injury rates. Computing a trend line showing accident rates before the new legislation and afterwards would help assess whether accident rates had improved to a significant extent. If not, the state would need to consider other actions.

Exhibit 10-1 (a variant of exhibit 9-3) shows that average response times for processing loan requests after an automated process was introduced declined from 52.4 to 46.8 days. Whether or not this improvement is worth the investment is a judgment for the agency to make. However, analysis is desirable to assess the likelihood that the difference occurred by chance.

*Caution:* While before-and-after values provide evidence of successful or unsuccessful attempts at improvements, such evidence is weak and should not be relied on exclusively in making agency decisions about change. There are almost always other factors that could have caused the change, and they should be considered before deciding what to do next. In the case of legislation changing driver's license eligibility in order to reduce traffic accidents, alternative explanations for the downward trend in accidents might be stepped-up enforcement of speed limits or higher safety standards in vehicle manufacture.

## EXHIBIT 10-1

**Comparison of Outcomes before and after Process Change**

| | 1997 Quarters | | | | 1998 Quarters | | | | 1999 Quarters | | | | Average Before Change | Average After Change |
|---|---|---|---|---|---|---|---|---|---|---|---|---|---|---|
| | 1st | 2nd | 3rd | 4th | 1st | 2nd | 3rd | 4th | 1st | 2nd | 3rd | 4th | | |
| Average Response Time (Days) | 53 | 51 | 56 | 49 | 53 | 53 | 49 | 47 | 43 | 45 | 44 | N/A | 52.4 | 46.8 |

**Introduction of Automated Process**

## 2. *Examine Outcome Breakouts*

Examine the breakouts for each outcome indicator to assess where performance is good, fair, or poor. Compare the outcomes for various breakouts such as customer characteristics, organizational units, workload difficulty, and type and amount of service. Identify those categories where performance seems to be particularly good or particularly bad.

For subgroups whose performance appears to have been particularly *bad*, the agency should seek out the reasons and take corrective action. (This will be discussed further in the section on exception reporting.)

For subgroups whose performance appears to have been particularly *good*, the agency should seek explanations to help it assess whether these successes can be transferred to other groups. For example, if the outcomes for younger clients are particularly good, the agency should find out why in order to determine whether any program changes are appropriate. The agency might consider actions directed toward improving the outcomes for the elderly, or it might reconsider whether the program is well-suited to helping the elderly in the first place.

Comparing breakouts across organizational units can indicate which units have particularly weak outcomes—and need attention, such as training or technical assistance. This information can also be used as a basis for rewards to persons or organizations with particularly good outcomes or efficiency levels.

To make comparisons more meaningful, and to be fair to the organizational units, the analysis should examine the disaggregation of each unit's outcomes by a variety of relevant breakout characteristics, such as customer demographic characteristics and difficulty of the incoming workload. Exhibit 8-3 illustrated a workload difficulty breakout for a social service organization providing counseling to low-income families. As shown, the units achieved significantly different outcomes for different levels of difficulty. The footnotes in Exhibit 8-3 indicate the type of action a program might take in light of such outcome data.

Statistical analysis can help with this examination by:

- Estimating the likelihood that observed differences occurred by chance rather than being real differences
- Estimating the extent to which outcomes are related to particular service characteristics

Specifically, statistical tests can be used to estimate the likelihood that observed differences in outcomes between *organizational units* or *customer categories* are due to chance rather than to real differences.[1] If the analysis indicates, for example, that an observed difference could have occurred by chance more than 10 times out of every 100, that difference should be interpreted with caution.

The likelihood that an observed difference is a real difference increases as the number of observations grows. If the numbers in each group being compared are in the hundreds, for example, the probability that an observed difference is a real one is high. As the number of observations gets smaller, the chances that an observed difference of a given size is a real difference goes down.

In exhibit 8-3, for example, the number of clients in each box is not given. If the program is large and the number of clients in each category is in the hundreds, observed differences among the units are likely to represent real differences. If the number of clients in each category is small, there may be a substantial likelihood that the differences between the 35 percent improvement rate for clients with minor problems in Unit 2 and the 52 and 56 percent improvement rates for clients in the other two units are due to chance.

Statistical tests can also assess the likelihood that differences in outcomes for *different service approaches* are due to chance, rather than being real differences. If, for example, a program used two different methods to deliver services (such as contracting for part of the service and using agency employees to deliver the remainder of that service), those outcomes can be compared statistically to identify the likelihood that any difference might have occurred by chance.

Statistical analysis can help identify the extent of the relationship between potential causal factors and the outcome observed. For example, if a program has provided a variety of services or service intensities to numerous customers, such analysis can estimate the extent to which the amount of outcome is related to the type and amount of service provided. If the characteristics of the customer population vary, statistical analysis can estimate the extent to which different customer characteristics are associated with differences in outcomes. (As with all outcome data, discerning the *implications* of such relationships for program improvement is a matter of judgment.)

Even the news media get this point on occasion. In a May 1999 article on Maryland school test scores, the *Washington Post* reported:

> Using a statistical technique called multiple regression analysis, the *Post* estimated how closely actual 1997–98 Maryland School Performance Assessment Program scores correlated with student income

and other factors beyond the control of educators. It then used the results of that study to estimate how much higher or lower each school's actual scores were on the MSPAP tests than the schools' "predicted" scores. Schools whose actual scores topped their predicted score by a big margin may well be doing a good job of educating their students—even if the actual raw scores were only average.[2]

In this Maryland example, the outcome data from regular test scores at different schools (breakout data), along with explanatory characteristics (such as the proxy for student income "percent of students eligible for free or reduced-price lunches"), were used to provide fairer and more informative information on school performance. States and their individual school districts can and should use such analysis. Similar analyses can be undertaken by many public and private organizations.

### 3. Compare the Program's Outcomes to Those of Similar Programs

If comparable data are available on any of the performance indicators from other programs, other agencies, other jurisdictions, or the private sector (as discussed in chapter 9), these data should be reviewed. If substantially better outcomes have been achieved elsewhere, ask program staff to assess why. Ask them to justify their lower past performance or performance targets.

The identification and reporting of practices found to have been particularly successful can be a valuable by-product of a performance measurement activity.

### 4. Use Exception Reporting

Under the exception reporting approach, a program establishes target *ranges* (also called *control limits*) within which it expects the values for its indicators to fall and concentrates on indicators whose values fall outside those ranges. This approach is an adaptation from the field of statistical quality control, often used by manufacturing organizations.

Exception reporting has the advantage of enabling the program to focus its subsequent analysis on a relatively small number of indicators for each reporting period, rather than having to review the data on each and every one. In manufacturing, statistical procedures are used to establish the target ranges. For most public and private services, in contrast, these ranges have to be set by staff judgment about what values of a given indicator can be safely ignored.

Once chosen, the target ranges can be programmed into the performance report software so that performance indicator values falling outside them are automatically highlighted for program attention.

The Florida Department of Environmental Protection has used a version of this approach. It put the values for each of its outcome indicators into one of three categories: the first indicating fully satisfactory outcomes, the second calling for closer monitoring, and the third calling for major attention. (This example is described further in chapter 11.)

### 5. Obtain and Examine Explanatory Information

A performance measurement system, whether in government at any level or in the private sector, should explicitly call for explanatory information along with the outcome and efficiency data. This is particularly important in situations where the latest outcome data are considerably worse (or better) than anticipated.

The U.S. Government Performance and Results Act (section 1116 (d)(3)) requires agencies to explain in their program performance reports why goals were not met. New Zealand requires agency heads, as part of their quarterly reports to ministers, to provide explanations for below-standard performance and proposed actions to correct it.[3] But most performance measurement systems to date have underplayed the importance of explanatory information.

Explanatory information can take many forms. At one extreme, it might be *qualitative judgments* provided by program personnel as to why the outcomes were the way they were. Such judgments might be mere rationalizations and excuses, but program personnel should be encouraged to provide substantive information.

At the other end of the spectrum, the agency might have sponsored *in-depth program evaluations* that provide statistically reliable information as to the reasons for the measured outcomes. Such information can help considerably in understanding what the program has achieved and why. These special studies are usually so expensive and time-consuming that they can be done only on a small fraction of an agency's programs in any given reporting period.[4]

Between these two extremes, program personnel should usually be able to provide a variety of information, some quantitative and some qualitative, that will reveal the reasons for problems. Likely reasons include the following, each of which requires a different program response:

• Staff and/or funding changes, such as cutbacks

- Legislation or regulatory requirements that have changed or been found inappropriate
- Poor implementation (for example, inadequate training, inexperience, or motivation of staff)
- External factors over which the program has limited or no control, such as increasingly difficult workload; significant change in the international, national, state, or local economy; unusual weather conditions (e.g., unusually heavy rains can increase runoff, leading to increased pollution of rivers and lakes); new international pressure or competition; new businesses starting up or leaving the jurisdiction (thus affecting outcomes such as employment and earnings); and/or changes in the composition of the relevant population
- Problems in the program's own practices and policies

Another source of explanatory information is the responses to open-ended questions on customer surveys. As noted in chapter 7, when an agency surveys its customers as part of the performance measurement process, the questionnaire should give respondents opportunities to explain the reasons for the ratings they gave (particularly any poor ratings) and to provide suggestions for improving the service. Tabulations of the responses provide clues as to the causes of poorer-than-desired performance and provide suggestions for improvement.

Only a small percentage of respondents (25 percent or less) may provide answers to open-ended questions, and some of their responses may not be understandable or useful. Nevertheless, customer responses can be an important source of explanatory information and ideas for program improvements.

Explanations for lower-than-expected performance might rest in the answers to such questions as: Are procedures being implemented as planned? Is the implementation of high enough quality? Are the procedures the right ones? If the problems identified by the performance data are bad enough, the program may need special investigations to identify causes and to suggest specific improvements.

## 6. Determine Whether the Data on Major Types of Performance Indicators Are Consistent with Each Other

The amount of input (e.g., funds and staffing) should be consistent with the amount of output. This, in turn, should be consistent with the amount of intermediate and end outcomes achieved.

If an agency was not able to produce the amount of output anticipated, the amount of subsequent outcomes that can be achieved is also likely to be less than expected.[5] Similarly, if the expected intermediate outcomes did not occur as hoped, subsequent end outcomes can be expected to suffer as well. These relationships do not always hold, but they sometimes can help explain why measured outcomes were not as expected. For example, one reasonable explanation for a reduced number and percent of successful outcomes is staff cutbacks during the year that resulted in working with fewer clients (thereby producing less output). This subject is discussed at length in chapter 12, on using performance information for budgeting.

### 7. *Focus Individual Outcome Indicators on Areas in Which the Program or Agency Has Particular Responsibility or Influence*

This procedure is best explained with examples. A maternal and child health program may seek to help children jurisdictionwide but its limited resources preclude it from making much of a dent in the outcome values for the whole jurisdiction. Such programs will need to focus on outcome data pertaining to their own customers, such as the percent of low-birthweight babies *of clients that the program actually served.* Clearly, the program can be expected to help those particular women.

Public agencies whose missions cover the entire population may have a responsibility for the whole population in need, even if they do not have sufficient resources to meet that need. If this is the case, the program should track both the outcomes of the customers served (over which it has considerable influence) and the outcomes reflecting jurisdictionwide low-weight births (over which it has much less influence). At least the program can identify for political officials its lack of resources to handle the problem.

As discussed in chapter 8, breakouts should, where possible, identify the incidence of problems over which a program has influence. For example, traffic safety agencies identify the causes of traffic accidents. Performance indicators should identify the total number of accidents and disaggregate the total into categories by cause, allowing the agency to focus on causes it can change. Traffic accidents due primarily to mechanical failure or bad weather, for example, are much less controllable by public agencies than accidents related to problem intersections.

Similarly, questionnaire response categories for customer surveys should be designed to separate reasons for negative responses that can be affected by the program from reasons that cannot. Tabulations of reasons by category can help the program obtain insights as to why poor outcomes happen and what is likely to improve results in the future.

Surveys that seek information on citizen participation rates (such as the use of public transit, libraries, parks, and other services) can give respondents a list of possible reasons why they did not use the service. Such reasons might include:

a. Did not know about the service
b. Service times were inconvenient
c. Service location was inconvenient
d. Heard that the service was not good
e. Had previous bad experiences with the service
f. Don't need the service
g. Don't have time for the service

Responses (a) through (e) refer to things that could be corrected by the program. For example, if a substantial proportion of the respondents indicated that the hours of operation were inconvenient, the agency could consider whether changes in those hours are feasible. (Note that the responses may not indicate what the optimal hours are. To determine that, the program would need to ask questions as to the best times for customers.) The last two categories, *don't need* and *don't have time for the service*, are reasons over which the agency has little or no influence. No action is likely to be appropriate for these categories unless they are by far the most common response, in which case the agency might wish to reconsider its customer base.

Another example is provided by the American Nurses Association, which has suggested indicators related to the care *nurses* provide—as distinct from the health care services *hospitals* provide. Its service quality indicators include the following:[6]

• The rate at which patients admitted to acute care settings develop urinary tract infections (as defined by the federal Centers for Disease Control and Prevention) within 72 hours of admission, assuming the patients showed no evidence of the infection at admission
• The rate at which patients fall and injure themselves during the course of their hospital stay
• The rate at which patients develop skin pressure ulcers—Grade II or higher—72 hours or more after admission
• Patient ratings of
  — care received during their hospital stay

— how well nursing staff managed their pain
— nursing staff efforts to educate them regarding their condition and care requirements

An important characteristic of the above example is the precise way each indicator is defined.

Note that an agency may not be able to take direct action itself but may still want to propose legislation or other actions by others to alleviate identified problems. For example, while vehicle mechanical failures are not within the control of local governments, the federal government, and to some extent state governments, can take action if significant patterns of such failures occur. Agencies should recognize the presence of shared and joint responsibility for indicators, particularly outcome indicators. (Sharing may be with other agencies, other levels of government, and/or with other sectors of the economy.)

The important point here is that by properly designing data-gathering instruments and analyzing the resulting data, the program can obtain important clues as to what the problems are and what the program can do about them.

*Suggestion: Categorize each outcome indicator by the degree of influence the program has and include this information in performance reports.* The degree of influence might be expressed in three categories, such as *little or no influence, modest or some influence,* or *considerable influence.* The agency using such categories should define them as specifically as possible and provide illustrations for each. Such categorization helps users of the information understand the extent to which the agency is likely to be able to affect outcomes. (For an outcome indicator to be included in a program's set, the program should have some influence, even if small.)

Generally, agencies and their programs will be less able to influence end outcomes than intermediate outcomes. Even most intermediate outcomes are not likely to be fully controllable by any agency. This does not absolve agencies from the responsibility to recognize the amount of influence they do have.

### 8. *Examine Multiple Outcomes Together to Obtain a More Comprehensive Perspective on Overall Performance*

Most programs will have more than one performance indicator that they need to track. It is tempting to examine these indicators separately, but programs should also examine the *set of performance indicators,* including key breakouts, together in order to obtain a better understanding of past performance and, thus, what improvements may be needed.

For example, the manager of a traffic safety program might find that an indicator based on trained observer ratings showed traffic signs were in satisfactory condition, while another indicator found that a substantial percentage of citizens had problems with the signs. A third indicator showed increasing traffic accidents. A fourth indicator reported a high percentage of delayed response times to requests to fix traffic sign problems. The agency would need to consider all of these findings (and others) in determining what action, if any, is needed.

A program's performance may improve on some indicators and deteriorate on others. Classic examples are improved road surfaces or lower response times to calls for assistance, combined with growing proportions of customers giving poor ratings for their rides and response times. Program staff need to look for reasons for the apparent conflict. Defects might be found in the program's measurements of customer satisfaction or technical conditions. Examining breakout information might reveal that the program's road maintenance had focused on primary roads and not neighborhood roads or had neglected certain areas of the jurisdiction, where a large amount of dissatisfaction was present. The pattern of reasons for dissatisfaction given by survey respondents might also identify a problem to which the program had not directed much maintenance or measurement attention.

A program sometimes has directly competing objectives. In such cases, the outcomes relating to these multiple objectives need careful examination to achieve a reasonable balance. For example, reducing high school dropouts might lower average test scores because more students with academic difficulties are being tested. Improved water quality might be associated with reduced economic performance in an agricultural industry. Analysts need to examine these competing outcomes together to assess overall program performance.

### 9. Use Past Performance Data to Trigger Trials of New Procedures and to Help Evaluate Their Success

When performance data indicate the presence of problems, the solutions are often not clear. The program can sometimes experiment with new service approaches and use subsequent performance data to assess the results before making a commitment to any particular approach. A program that has an ongoing performance measurement system can use it to help evaluate new or modified procedures or policies, as discussed in chapter 9.

Exhibit 9-4 compares computer to manual processing of eligibility determinations in a program that applied the new process to part of its incoming work. The program then tracked the outcomes separately for an appropriate period and then compared the findings across the different procedures. A simpler but less powerful approach to examining new or modified processes is to only compare outcomes for the old service procedures with outcomes after introduction of the new procedures. (See exhibit 10-1 and associated discussion for this "before versus after" measurement approach.)

These procedures are similar to a variety of standard program evaluation procedures. Exhibit 10-1 is a simple illustration of a pre-post program evaluation. The example in exhibit 8-3 is of a basic comparison-group design. The example in exhibit 9-4 is a simple illustration of a random-assignment controlled experiment. The comparisons of demographic breakout categories discussed in chapters 8 and 9 can provide basic data for comparison-group program evaluations (such as comparing the outcomes for male customers to those for female customers). In all these variations, a full program evaluation would use the outcome data but add such steps as more extensive statistical analysis and an intensive search for explanations for the outcomes.

### Special Analysis Problem for Programs That Need to Combine Outcome Data from Many Sources

Agencies (particularly federal and state agencies) may obtain data for some outcome indicators from other agencies, such as those in another level of government. This situation can also arise for private, nonprofit organizations, such as a local United Way that wants aggregate counts of progress on an indicator from the agencies it supports.

Can the data be combined? If so, how? The problem is that the agencies supplying the data are very likely to have used somewhat different data collection procedures.

An agency wanting to combine data for an outcome indicator can often develop some rough aggregate data but will likely need to accept some differences among data collection procedures. The process might be the following.

1. The data would be obtained from each decentralized site.
2. The data-gathering procedures and specific definitions used would be examined to ascertain whether the coverage of the data from each site is at least roughly comparable. For example, if all states have their own

standardized tests of eighth grade mathematics, the number and percentage of students that scored at a certain percentile in a given year might be provided to the aggregating agency.

3. The aggregation could be in several forms, including the following:
   - A calculation of the percent of *students* who scored at or above the X percentile. This number would be calculated from the number of students that took each state test.
   - The number of *states* in which at least X percent of students scored at the Y percentile or above.

4. The report that presents these data should indicate clearly the limitations of the procedure (in this example, how much the subject matter differed from test to test and whether the same criteria were used to exclude students from testing).

This process, while unpleasant to many analysts and other users of the information, nevertheless seems preferable to the alternative of not doing any aggregation at all.

### Recommendations from Analysis of Performance Data

Based on the findings from procedures such as those discussed above, analysts should be able to recommend one or more of the following types of actions:

- Specific corrective procedures (with provisions that when future outcome data reports become available, these should be assessed to determine whether the actions appear to have resolved the problems)
- An in-depth evaluation to identify causes and what corrective actions should be taken
- An examination of program activities that explanatory information indicated might be causing problems
- An experiment to test a new procedure against the current one
- A wait-and-see strategy in the expectation that the unsatisfactory outcomes are aberrations—the result of a temporary problem rather than a trend—and will correct themselves in the future

## Reporting Performance Information

How the findings are reported can be as important as what is reported. Outcome reports for managers and other officials (and citizens) should summarize the selected performance comparisons undertaken by the program. (See chapter 9 for a discussion of comparison options.) As discussed in chapter 6, a program is likely to find it useful to track a relatively large number of outcome indicators for internal use, but it should select a shorter list for external reporting. The department's highest officials, its budget office, and the relevant legislative body are likely to want a relatively short list of indicators.

The tabular formats described below (which use hypothetical data) can be used for reporting both internally and externally. They are just a sample of the many formats that can be constructed based on the special needs of a program. (Oral reporting techniques are also important but are beyond the scope of this book.)

- *Format 1, exhibit 10-2, compares actual outcomes to targets for both the last and current reporting periods.* It does this for each of a number of outcome indicators. This format is likely to be a key one for most programs.
- *Format 2, exhibit 10-3, is similar to format 1 but shows both report period and cumulative values for the year.* This format is useful for outcome measurement systems that provide data more frequently than once per year (as is usually highly desirable).
- *Format 3, exhibit 10-4, compares the latest outcomes for various geographical locations. This format is useful for making comparisons across any breakout categories identified by the program.* For example, a pro-

---

### EXHIBIT 10-2

**Reporting Format 1: Actual Outcomes versus Targets**

| Outcome Indicator | Last Period | | | This Period | | |
|---|---|---|---|---|---|---|
| | Target | Actual | Difference | Target | Actual | Difference |
| Percent of Children Returned to Home within 12 Months | 35 | 25 | −10 | 35 | 30 | −5 |
| Percent of Children Who Had over Two Placements within the Past 12 Months | 20 | 20 | 0 | 15 | 12 | +3 |
| Percent of Children Whose Adjustment Level Improved during the Past 12 Months | 50 | 30 | −20 | 50 | 35 | −15 |
| Percent of Clients Reporting Satisfaction with Their Living Arrangements | 80 | 70 | −10 | 80 | 85 | +5 |

**Note:** This format compares actual outcomes to targets for both the last and current periods. Plus (+) indicates improvement; minus (−) indicates worsening.

## EXHIBIT 10-3

### Reporting Format 2: Actual Values versus Targets

| Outcome Indicator | Current Period | | Cumulative for Year | | Year's Target (%) |
|---|---|---|---|---|---|
| | Target (%) | Actual (%) | Target (%) | Actual (%) | |
| Percentage of Parents Reporting Knowledge or Awareness of Local Parental Resource Center Activities | 75 | 70 | 70 | 65 | 70 |
| Percentage of Parents Reporting That Parental Resource Centers Led to Their Taking a More Active Role in Their Child's Development or Education | 50 | 65 | 50 | 60 | 50 |

Note: This format shows cumulative values for a year rather than for previous reporting periods. It will only be useful for outcome measurement systems that provide data more than once a year.

## EXHIBIT 10-4

### Reporting Format 3: Outcomes by Geographical Location

| Outcome Indicator | Geographical Location | | | | United States |
|---|---|---|---|---|---|
| | Eastern | Central | Mountain | Pacific | |
| Percentage of K-12 Schools Participating in the Star Schools Program | 30% | 15% | 20% | 35% | 29% |
| Number of Students Enrolled in Star Schools High School Credit, College Preparatory, or AP Courses That Had Not Been Available Previously | 1,500,000 | 600,000 | 850,000 | 1,950,000 | 4,900,000 |
| Percentage of Students Reporting Increased Interest in School Because of Distance-Learning Activities in Their Classes | 65% | 90% | 85% | 75% | 77% |

Note: This format makes comparisons across any breakout categories identified by the program, such as managerial units, individual projects, schools, school districts, or particular student characteristics.

gram may want to illustrate comparisons across managerial units, individual projects, or particular customer characteristics. To do this, the program would change the column labels in exhibit 10-4 to correspond to the relevant breakouts. (Refer to exhibit 8-3 for a breakout by family services unit.)

- *Format 4, exhibit 10-5, displays outcome data for one indicator by organizational unit and workload (customer) difficulty.* This format is a variation of exhibit 8-3. It is likely to be quite useful for internal reports, because it shows how each organizational unit has performed relative to the others. Displaying by difficulty of the incoming workload will make the comparisons considerably fairer and more informative.
- *Format 5, exhibit 10-6, displays on a single page responses from a customer survey, broken out by several demographic or program characteristics for a single outcome indicator.* This is an internal format that enables program staff to identify which respondent characteristics show unusually positive or negative results for a particular outcome indicator. The format can be used to report on any indicator for which data on a variety of customer (or program) characteristics have been obtained.

Displaying the findings on a single page eases the task of spotting unusual findings. For example, the data indicate that considerably poorer usage occurred in the central and northeast regions, for households with incomes below $30,000, for younger adults, and for nonwhite males. These findings suggest that the program should consider giving special attention to households with these characteristics. Data obtained in future years will indicate whether any such special attention improved outcomes for those groups.

The previous formats use *tables* to present the data. Other graphic presentations can be considerably more powerful, especially for external consumption. A picture is often worth 1,000 words (or numbers)![7]

Options include the following:

- *Line graphs.* This presentation of individual outcome indicators is especially good for showing trends—the values of the indicator plotted against time, perhaps by quarter or year. Exhibit 10-7 presents an example. As shown, multiple lines can be used to compare breakout groups or jurisdictions (but avoid overcrowding).
- *Bar charts.* These are an excellent way to show comparisons. Exhibit 10-8 compares county

---

**EXHIBIT 10-5**

**Reporting Format 4: Outcomes by Organizational Unit and Difficulty**

| Difficulty Level | Applications Processed within X Days (%) | | | |
|---|---|---|---|---|
| | Unit 1 | Unit 2 | Unit 3 | Total |
| High | 35 | 30 | 54 | 39 |
| Low | 52 | 35 | 56 | 47 |
| Medium | 58 | 69 | 61 | 63 |
| **Total** | **48** | **44** | **57** | **60** |

**Note:** This format displays outcome data for one indicator broken out by one demographic or customer difficulty characteristic and displayed for each organizational unit. It shows program staff how each unit has performed relative to others. Displaying this information by key characteristics, such as difficulty of incoming workload, will make the comparisons fairer and more informative.

EXHIBIT 10-6

**Reporting Format 5: Breakouts of Responses to a Customer Survey by Demographic or Program Characteristics**

| Respondent Characteristics | Households Reporting Their Frequency of Use of City Buses in the Past 12 Months (%) | | | | |
| --- | --- | --- | --- | --- | --- |
| | Not At All (*N*=50) | A Little (*N*=83) | Somewhat (*N*=429) | Considerably (*N*=63) | Total Responding (*N*=625) |
| **Sex and Race** | | | | | |
| White Male | 7 | 11 | 71 | 10 | 265 |
| White Female | 8 | 13 | 68 | 11 | 284 |
| Nonwhite Male | 11 | 30 | 53 | 6 | 36 |
| Nonwhite Female | 10 | 17 | 65 | 8 | 40 |
| **Age** | | | | | |
| 18–34 | 13 | 16 | 58 | 13 | 272 |
| 35–49 | 6 | 11 | 75 | 8 | 125 |
| 50–64 | 3 | 11 | 80 | 5 | 105 |
| 65 and over | 6 | 11 | 74 | 9 | 123 |
| **Family Income** | | | | | |
| less than 20,000 | 12 | 22 | 55 | 11 | 150 |
| $20,000–29,999 | 15 | 19 | 55 | 11 | 117 |
| $30,000–39,999 | 4 | 16 | 70 | 10 | 100 |
| $40,000–49,999 | 7 | 5 | 78 | 10 | 69 |
| $50,000–74,999 | 2 | 9 | 78 | 11 | 104 |
| $75,000 and over | 3 | 2 | 88 | 7 | 85 |
| **Region** | | | | | |
| Central | 12 | 17 | 60 | 11 | 150 |
| Northeast | 13 | 16 | 59 | 11 | 174 |
| Northwest | 6 | 12 | 74 | 8 | 76 |
| Southeast | 3 | 9 | 77 | 11 | 113 |
| Southwest | 5 | 9 | 71 | 15 | 112 |
| **Total** | **8** | **13** | **69** | **10** | **100** |

**Note:** This format enables program staff to identify what categories of customer show unusually positive or negative results on a particular outcome indicator.

high school dropout rates to statewide rates for a number of years. *Reminder:* When comparing outcomes or expenditures across jurisdictions or programs, it is usually necessary to normalize the data—that is, adjust for differences in size—to make the information meaningful. Another bar chart is shown in exhibit 9-2. There, the normalization is achieved by expressing annual library circulation as *circulation per capita* (i.e., total number of items circulated by the library system divided by

EXHIBIT 10-7

## Illustration of a Line Graph

### Low Birthweight by Ethnicity in King County

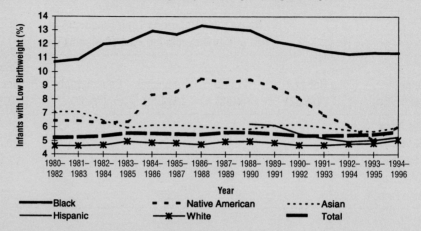

**Source:** *Indicators of Sustainable Community: A Status Report on Long-Term Cultural, Economic, and Environmental Health for Seattle/King County* (Seattle: Sustainable Seattle, 1998).

EXHIBIT 10-8

## Illustration of a Bar Chart

### High School Dropout Rates in Multnomah County and Statewide, 1990–95

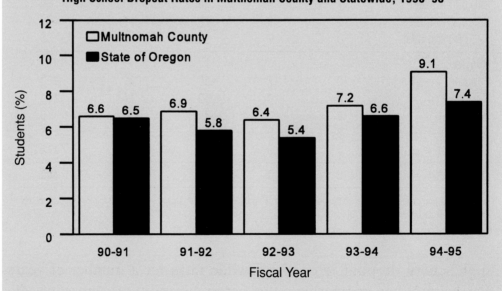

**Source:** Oregon Department of Education, *Dropout Rates in Oregon High Schools* (Salem, 1996).

EXHIBIT 10-9

## Straphangers Campaign Subway Profile

### Straphangers Campaign
### ③ SUBWAY LINE PROFILE

**Straphangers Campaign Line Rating 80¢***

The Straphangers Campaign ranks the 3 line as the 5th best out of 19 subway lines. Our ranking is based on the MTA New York City Transit data below.

**The 3 has an average amount of daytime service, but doesn't run at night.**

scheduled minutes between weekday trains as of September 1997

|  | AM Rush | Noon | PM Rush | Overnight |
|---|---|---|---|---|
| 3 line | 6 | 10 | 6 | - |
| System Average | 6.1 | 9.5 | 6.6 | 20 |

**You're less likely to get a seat on the 3.**

% of passengers with seats at most crowded point during rush hour

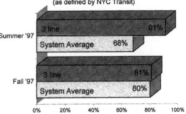

**The 3 arrives with regularity more often than the average line. . .**

% of trains arriving at regular intervals (without gaps in service or train "bunching") between 6 a.m. and 9 p.m.

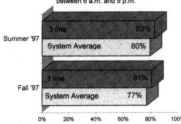

**The 3 is cleaner than average. . .**

% of cars with "light or no interior dirtiness" (as defined by NYC Transit)

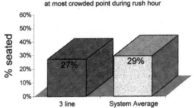

**and breaks down less often than the system average.**

average miles traveled between delays caused by mechanical failures, July to December 1997

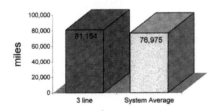

**and performs both above and below average on in-car announcements.**

% of trains with correct announcements (as defined by NYC Transit)

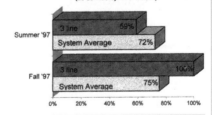

*Straphangers Campaign Line Ratings are based on a formula that gives the most weight to the amount of scheduled service, followed by other performance measures. Under this formula, a line would be rated $1.50 if on average its 1997 scores for the measurements above matched a baseline standard defined in our first "State of the Subways" report. For the last six months of 1997, the best line was the 7, which scored $1.20. The worst line was the N, at 65¢. For more information, call the Straphangers Campaign at (212) 349-6460.

**Suggestions? Complaints? Call the 3 line superintendent at (718) 345-1452.**

**Source:** Straphangers Campaign, *How Does Your Subway Line Rate?* (New York: New York Public Interest Research Group Fund, Inc., June 1998).

the population of the area served). This is why exhibit 10-8 shows dropout *rates* (percentages) and not numbers of dropouts.

Exhibit 10-9 displays a series of bar charts rating a number of outcome indicators on New York City's subway system. Similar ratings were provided for each of the subway system's 19 lines. The published report used color, making the presentation considerably more attractive than this exhibit. (These data were obtained, assembled, and analyzed by a citizens' group, the Straphangers Campaign—see chapter 7).

- *Maps.* These are a dramatic way to present geographical data. The geographical areas might be portions of a county, state, or local jurisdiction, showing the percent of customers who are employed, healthy, satisfied with particular services, have low rates of feeling unsafe walking around their neighborhoods at night, and so on. (See exhibit 7-11 and exhibits 8-4 and 8-5.)

A final suggestion on report formats is that outcome values that warrant attention should be highlighted, such as by circling or coloring those numbers. (See exhibit 8-3 for an example.[8])

### Provide Highlights, Including Explanatory Information, When Reporting

Explanatory information gives the program an opportunity to explain significant outcomes, such as indicator values that were worse or better than expected. Here are some summary suggestions:

1. The information can be qualitative, quantitative, or a combination of the two. Quantitative evidence is most desirable, but program staff judgments can also be presented.
2. Provide explanatory information when any of the comparisons show unexpected differences in outcome values, for example when:
   - The actual value for an outcome indicator deviates substantially from the target value (better or worse) or
   - The outcome values show major differences among operating units, categories of customers, or other workload units
3. Consider both internal and external explanatory factors. Internal factors affecting outcomes might include significant unexpected loss of program personnel (or other resources) during the reporting period. External factors might include unexpected changes in state or federal legislation.
4. Provide a summary of the report's highlights—emphasizing information that particularly warrants attention—to help users focus quickly on the important findings. These highlights should include both "suc-

cess" and "failure" (problem) stories. The summary should be a balanced account to reduce the likelihood that readers will consider the report self-serving.

5. Reports, especially those going outside the program, should also identify any actions the program has taken, or plans to take, to correct problems identified in the outcome report. This step, along with the explanatory information, can help avert, or at least alleviate, unwarranted criticism.

6. Explanatory information should be included as part of the report and should be clear, concise, and to the point.

7. Incorporate the findings from any special evaluations that provide an in-depth examination of the program and its achievements. Such findings may, in fact, supersede the outcome data collected as part of the routine outcome measurement process. At the very least, recent program evaluation findings should be given prominence in the presentation of a program's outcomes. Such studies are likely to provide considerably more information about the impacts of the program than outcome data alone can reveal.

## What Happens If the Performance News Is Bad?

Almost certainly, every performance report will include some indicators showing results significantly below expectations (compared to the targets of the reporting period). Any performance measurement system is in fact intended to surface problems of below-par outcomes so that those who can do something about them are alerted and, after corrective actions are taken, can assess whether the actions have produced the desired results.

Agency and program officials should *include with their performance reports explanations as to why any poor outcomes occurred and identify the steps taken, or being planned, to correct the problem.*

As one city police chief told the Urban Institute team in the 1970s, "If the data looks good, I will take the credit. If the data looks bad, I will ask for more money." This is another approach.

## Additional Suggestions for External Reporting

The following are suggestions for reporting outside the agency, such as to the legislature, other funders, and the public. They are based on principles that in the past, unfortunately, have often been violated.

- Be selective as to which and how many indicators are included. Focus on those most likely to be of interest to the audience (probably not data on outputs or efficiency). Selectivity does *not* mean selecting only those indicators that make the agency look good—reporting needs to be balanced in order to be credible.

- Pay particular attention to making the reports easily understandable. As discussed earlier, use charts and graphs either to supplement tables or to be the main focus. Use color if practical.
- Obtain feedback periodically from major constituencies, such as elected officials, funders, and the public (perhaps obtaining feedback from the public by use of focus groups), regarding the usefulness and readability of the performance reports. Use the feedback to help tailor future performance reports to the particular audience.

## Dissemination of Performance Reports

*Performance reports should be disseminated to everyone on the program's staff as soon as possible after the data become available. Program personnel should be given the opportunity to provide any additional relevant explanatory information.* This will encourage all program members to feel they are part of a team whose purpose is to produce outcomes that are as good as possible. As will be discussed further in chapter 11, the program manager might hold staff meetings on the outcome data to identify any actions that the performance data indicate are needed.

The performance report—including data, explanatory information, and the highlights or summary—should then be provided to offices outside the program. *A key question to consider is how much detail should be given to those outside the program.* Avoid overloading outside readers with detail. Select indicators that are likely to be of most interest to those outside the program. Breakout data also need to be provided, but selectively, to avoid overwhelming readers with too many numbers. The breakouts provided should be those considered most important to report users. Outcomes broken out by customer demographic characteristics, such as race or ethnicity, for example, are often quite important and of considerable interest. More breakout detail can be included in appendixes.

Special news releases, distribution through libraries, special inserts in local newspapers, and the Internet are all ways to disseminate the performance material. Here again, the program will need to decide what detail will be of interest to these groups. Inclusion of explanatory information and statements of corrective actions already taken, or planned, can help defuse negative reactions to data that appear to represent poor performance.

External performance measurement reporting is of special concern to agency officials, who can be expected to be particularly apprehensive of performance reports provided to the news media. The objective should be to provide media representatives with an understanding of what the data tell and what the data's limitations are.

Avoid choosing just data that make the agency look good—tempting as this may be. Over the long run, the media and special interest groups will catch on, and the reports will lose credibility.

Summary annual performance reports can be an effective way to communicate with citizens and increase public credibility, as long as they are user-friendly, timely, and provide a balanced assessment of performance.

---

## References and Notes

1. It is beyond this book's scope to describe the many statistical procedures that can help an agency analyze performance information. For further information, see, for example, Kathryn E. Newcomer, "Using Statistics Appropriately," and Charles S. Reichardt and Carol A. Bormann, "Using Regression Models to Estimate Program Effects," both in *Handbook of Practical Program Evaluation*, ed. Joseph S. Wholey et al. (San Francisco: Jossey-Bass Publishers, 1994).

2. Amy Argetsinger, "Beating Poverty in the Classroom," *Washington Post*, 16 May 1999, p. C5. Agencies will need statistical personnel or consultants to utilize these specialized statistical procedures.

3. The Treasury, Government of New Zealand, *Purchase Agreement Guidelines 1995/96: With Best Practices for Output Performance Measures* (Wellington, April 1995), 20.

4. Description of the procedures for in-depth evaluations is outside the scope of this book. The selected reading list at the back of the book lists a few publications on this topic.

5. Some outputs are closely related to outcomes, such as number of miles of roads maintained and number of clients provided service. Other outputs are not likely to be closely linked to outcomes, such as number of reports completed and number of training programs held.

6. For more details, see American Nurses Association, *Nursing Quality Indicators: Guide for Implementation,* and *Nursing Quality Indicators: Definitions and Implications* (Washington, D.C., 1996). Data collection on these indicators is currently being pilot-tested.

7. Two worthwhile discussions of presenting visual data are Gene Zelazny, *Say It with Charts*, 2nd ed. (Homewood, Ill.: Business One Irwin, 1991) and Edward R. Tufte, *The Visual Display of Quantitative Information* (Cheshire, Colo.: Graphics Press, 1983) (old, but still a classic).

8. When displaying results for use by elected officials and the general public, it may well be worth the added cost of developing special presentation procedures. Many attractive displays can be generated with advanced computer processing and graphics options.

# Major Uses of Performance Information and Incentives for Using It

I t is one thing to describe a good performance measurement process. It's quite another to get the products of that process used effectively. How can and should the information be used? In the past, performance measurement has been most frequently used simply to respond to accountability mandates from higher levels of authority. This is a great waste. Responding to demands for accountability is an important use, but even more important is that managers, staff, and other public officials use performance information to make program improvements that would not have been made in its absence.

This fundamental purpose of performance information has often been neglected. One reason is that such information is new to many managers. They have not received information on outcomes before. They are unfamiliar with the data and what it can do for them. Another major reason is lack of incentives for managers to use the information for program improvement. Concern (unfortunately, realistic) that the performance data will be used by others primarily to cast blame has led programs to select performance indicators that are easier for them to influence (outputs and a few intermediate outcome indicators such as response times).

Exhibit 11-1 lists a number of major uses of performance information. All but the first (increase accountability) and ninth (improve communications with the public) are intended to make program improvements that lead to improved outcomes. All but the second,

**Uses of Performance Information**

1. Respond to elected officials' and the public's demands for accountability.
2. Help formulate and justify budget requests (chapter 12).
3. Help in making operational resource allocation decisions and in raising funds.
4. Trigger in-depth examinations of why performance problems (or successes) exist and what corrections are needed.
5. Help motivate personnel to continue making program improvements.
6. Formulate and monitor the performance of contractors and grantees (performance contracting).
7. Provide data for special, in-depth program evaluations.
8. Support strategic and other long-term planning efforts (by providing baseline information and later tracking progress).
9. Communicate better with the public to build public trust.
10. Above all, help provide better services more effectively.

budget formulation and justification, are discussed in this chapter. Results-based budgeting is covered in chapter 12.

*But first a note on avoiding misuse.* Outcome data tell what progress has been made toward objectives but not why that progress (or lack thereof) occurred. Exhibit 11-2 lists some ways to get this message across and reduce user misunderstanding of what outcome data can and cannot do.

*Reminder*: If the wrong performance indicators are used, or if the data reported are bad (substantially inaccurate or excessively old), performance information can lead to poorer decisions than if no such information were available.

## Respond to Elected Officials' and the Public's Demands for Accountability

Traditionally, accountability has been directed at legal and appropriate use of public funds (that is, avoiding waste, fraud, and abuse). When outcome information becomes available, accountability for producing results also becomes a focus.

Because of the limited influence of public (and private) agencies over many outcomes—especially end outcomes—full accountability is rarely possible. *Realistically, accountability for outcomes is usually shared with other agencies, with other levels of government, with private organizations, and with the customers themselves.* This is true today and will inevitably be true in the future, no matter what measurements are used. Some of the ramifications of this are discussed below, in the section on using performance information in monetary incentive systems.

**Reducing Misunderstanding of What Outcome Data Tell**

- Provide explanatory information with performance reports, including findings from program evaluations and other studies about factors that influence the results.
- Footnote performance reports with data limitations. Remind readers that the data do not tell WHY on the first (if not every) page of every outcome report.
- Categorize each outcome indicator by how much influence the program has over it.
- Take steps to educate upper-level officials, legislators, the press, and the public about the limitations of data.

## Help Formulate and Justify Budget Requests

Tracking outcomes can give potential funders greater confidence that any money they provide will be used beneficially. If a program does not have substantial evidence that it is producing benefits, the program is likely to become more vulnerable to being cut out. (See chapter 12 for a discussion of results-based budgeting.)

However, performance information can be a two-edged sword. If a program's measured outcomes are poor or decline over time, funders may decide that the program should be cut or at least changed in some way. This is also a legitimate use of outcome information.

The use of outcome data to help secure funds applies to both public and private sectors. In the private, nonprofit sector, local United Ways have begun using outcome information in their fundraising campaigns. The presumption is that contributors, especially the business sector, will increase or at least sustain their contributions if they are provided evidence that those contributions have led to beneficial outcomes. The same applies to government agencies: evidence of positive outcomes can be used to help obtain funding.

## Help in Making Operational Resource Allocation Decisions

The budget is but one part of an agency's resource allocation process. Outcome information should enable program personnel to identify where problems do or do not exist, a major step in determining the need to reallocate resources, such as personnel. (If outcomes are extremely low, agencies might choose to reduce program activities or eliminate them altogether.) The following are examples:

- The Occupational Safety and Health Administration (OSHA) traditionally tracked numbers of inspections (an output indicator). Maine's OSHA office added an outcome focus. Worker compensation insurance rates, a readily available set of data, were used as a surrogate outcome indicator of occupational safety. These rates are a good surrogate because they increase as the amount of claims increase. When Maine's OSHA office broke out its inspections data by compensation rates paid by individual companies and industry groups, it found that its inspection patterns bore no relation to the rates. The office reassigned its resources to intensify inspection of companies with high rates. Other organizations were still inspected but less intensively. This example potentially applies not only to occupational safety, but also to environmental protection, food inspections, and other programs regulating compliance. (Florida's Department of Environmental Protection recently began focusing its inspections of shellfish processing plants on plants that had high rates of violations.)

- When the U.S. Coast Guard switched to an outcome focus in its maritime safety program by examining fatality rates by type of industry, it found that commercial towing had the highest rates. Searching for explanatory information, the Coast Guard found that most casualties were deck hands who fell overboard—a problem that did not lend itself to the Coast Guard's off-the-shelf inspection program for tugboats. The Coast Guard formed a partnership with the towing industry to develop nonregulatory solutions to the problem. After three years, the Coast Guard reported that the commercial towing fatality rate dropped from 77 per 100,000 workers to 27.[1]

The principle illustrated by the above examples is that outcome data can be used to identify elements with poorer outcomes so that additional resources can be focused on them. Both examples also illustrate the importance of disaggregating outcome data by key characteristics (OSHA by company, the Coast Guard by industry).

## Trigger In-Depth Examinations of Why Performance Problems (or Successes) Exist

To use performance information to the fullest, program managers need to examine *why* the outcomes are as bad or as good as they are. Calculating the types of breakout information discussed in chapter 8 can provide partial clues to why problems are occurring. In addition, programs can undertake or sponsor in-depth studies. Formal, in-depth program evaluations should be undertaken when time and funds permit, although they are likely to be too costly in both time and effort for small programs. More qualitative, less rigorous special studies can be extremely useful for all programs.

A program might form a special team to investigate why outcomes were low and to suggest corrective actions. The program personnel should examine both the outcome and output data, including the data breakouts, to help pinpoint where the problems were occurring. Discussions with the service delivery personnel and customers often provide valuable insights. (Such input might be obtained using procedures similar to those described in chapter 5.) Once programs have identified plausible reasons for outcome indicators whose values indicate a problem, they should prepare plans that identify corrective actions. The plans themselves should probably set targets for the future values of each pertinent outcome indicator and when those values should be reached. At those times, the program should again review the outcomes to assess the extent to which the actions taken have led to better outcomes. (Chapters 8, 9, and 10 suggest procedures for comparing alternative service delivery approaches.)

If a program compares its outcomes to those of similar programs in other jurisdictions, it should also attempt to identify the practices that led to particularly good outcomes—practices that might be adapted to its own use.

## Help Motivate Personnel to Continue Making Program Improvements

By focusing on results, performance information can motivate program managers and their staffs to identify and implement ways to improve services on a continuing basis. Many public and private employees are motivated by their desire to produce good results. Regular performance information for these employees is likely to provide sufficient incentive to improve. But for many, additional encouragement is useful. Exhibit 11-3 lists a variety of incentives to provide such motivation. Each is discussed below.

A major distinction is nonmonetary versus monetary incentives. Monetary incentives in the public and private, nonprofit sectors are quite controversial (and are discussed in a separate section below). Reward schemes, especially monetary awards, have typically relied on supervisors' opinions, a major source of contention. *Performance measurement systems provide more objective data than previously available. Their use is likely to increase the acceptance of rewards as motivators by employees, elected officials, and the public.* Some subjectivity is inevitable in establishing winners and losers, but it is diminished to the extent that objectively measured performance information is used as the basis for the awards.

EXHIBIT 11-3

**Incentives for High Program Performance Derived from Performance Information**

*Nonmonetary Incentives*

- Using recognition awards
- Providing regular performance reports to program personnel
- Setting performance targets and regularly reviewing achievements in relation to those targets
- Providing performance reviews by higher-level managers and elected officials
- Giving managers more flexibility in exchange for more accountability for performance
- Making performance information an explicit part of the agency's individual performance appraisal process
- Establishing performance agreements between central officials and agency heads

*Monetary Incentives*

- Linking pay to performance
- Allocating discretionary funds to agencies or programs with high performance
- Sanctioning prolonged low performance

Rewards can be given to individual managers of other employees or to groups of employees (such as of specific offices, facilities, or whole agencies). Rewards can be based on one or more of several performance criteria:

- *Absolute level* achieved in a period
- *Relative level* achieved in a period compared to that achieved by others in the same period
- *Improvement* over a period (an often neglected criterion that encourages performers who did not perform well in the past to strive for improvement)

Rewards can also be based on a variety of periods of performance, such as:

- Performance in the most recent measurement period
- Performance over longer periods

Using longer periods as the basis for selecting winners *reduces the temptation to focus on quick returns at the expense of longer-term results.*

## Nonmonetary Incentives

*Using recognition awards.* Nonmonetary incentives have the distinct advantage of being inexpensive. They are probably the most common reward in government today, but they are not generally believed to be strong motivators.

*Providing performance reports to all program personnel.* Providing the latest information on achievement of outcomes (and efficiency) relative to targeted levels promptly after each reporting period will encourage program personnel to make use of the performance information. For example, *post quarterly or monthly performance reports on entrances or on an office bulletin board.* Programs might follow the United Way's format for fundraising campaigns—posting regularly updated progress toward the target in the form of a thermometer registering rising temperatures. (If the program does not set targets for the outcomes, it can still post information on the levels achieved. While probably not as effective, it does encourage personnel to focus on performance.) Calling attention to performance provides motivating feedback to all employees who can affect (even slightly) the performance of their group.

It seems likely that program personnel will be particularly motivated to seek improvement if the feedback relates to service outcomes, including service quality as perceived by customers. *Regular data on outcomes related to customers may make employees' jobs more interesting and personally rewarding.*

*Regular reports comparing outcomes broken out by organizational units delivering similar services to similar categories of customers can be a particularly powerful motivator for poorly performing units* to identify why they are different and help find ways to improve their outcomes. But care must be taken here. How this competition is handled by the organization's management will be an important determinant of whether it is constructive or destructive, resulting in lower morale and performance.

*Setting performance targets and regularly reviewing achievements in relation to those targets.* The process of having program personnel set targets for their performance indicators and relating performance data to them is likely to be particularly effective if:

- reporting periods are frequent,
- targets are set for each reporting period (even if the overall targets are set annually in the budgeting process), and
- the results are available soon after the end of each reporting period.

*Providing performance reviews by higher-level managers and elected officials (or by board members of private, nonprofit organizations).* Setting targets, providing regular feedback on performance, and comparing actual performance against the targets are likely to be considerably more effective if they are accompanied by higher-level reviews throughout the year. Such reviews would take place during managers' meetings with their staffs to discuss progress. These "How Are We Doing?" sessions (see box) should discuss the latest performance report, identify problem areas indicated there, and discuss what might be done to reduce those problems. As long as these reviews are reasonably frequent, they may be among the most powerful motivational factors for employees of public and private, nonprofit agencies.

Nothing is likely to capture agency attention more than legislators or board members pushing for accurate data and demanding to see the outcome implications of their appropriations and program policies. A major stimulus to federal agency performance measurement efforts during the early years of the Government Performance and Results Act implementation (1997 and 1998) was Congress's considerable interest in, and its ratings of, agencies' strategic plans and annual performance plans.

Explicit review and questioning of performance during budget reviews, and other reviews of suggested changes in program or policy directions, are likely to be major incentives for agencies and their programs to take performance measurement seriously.

***Giving managers more flexibility in exchange for more accountability for performance.*** This is a popular approach for some governments. The national governments of the United States, Australia, and New Zealand, in particular, have identified this as a major incentive. Increased flexibility might be granted in:

- use of budgeted funds
- authority to make purchases without going through extensive red tape (such as by raising the dollar level at which a manager has to go through a formal competitive bidding process)
- authority to hire, remove, compensate, and move personnel to other tasks and positions

The principle here is granting greater flexibility to an agency or program after evidence has been presented that past outcomes and efficiency have been at desirable levels. This approach can only be implemented effectively in environments that have basic controls in place to ensure the legal, ethical, and honest use of the added flexibility. Agencies (or countries) without reasonable controls (such as a meaningful internal or external audit process) may not find the granting of much flexibility appropriate.

***Making performance information an explicit part of the agency's individual performance appraisal process.*** Two basic approaches to incorporate performance information into an agency's appraisal process are the following:

- Include comparisons of actual values versus targets for the indicators over which the employee had some control. Achievement of targeted performance might be considered in the appraisals for nonmanagement as well as management employees, especially if the focus is on group performance. All persons in a group would receive the same rating on this particular part of the appraisal. (Other parts of the appraisal would address the individual's own contribution.)
- Identify the extent to which managers have implemented and used performance information. This is much less demanding than the first approach and therefore a weaker motivator.

In the early implementation stages of a performance measurement system, the second approach should probably be the primary one until agency personnel have had sufficient experience with the outcome or service quality data to be responsibly rated on them.

***Establishing performance agreements between central officials and agency heads.*** On occasion, performance contracts have been used by governments (such as the government of New Zealand). Under these performance agreements, agency heads agree to produce specified amounts of products in return for specified budget levels and more management flexibility (as discussed above). As part of this process, agency heads can receive extra or reduced compensation, or even be dismissed, based on actual performance. (If compensation is a major element of an agency's performance agreement process, the process becomes more of a monetary than a nonmonetary incentive.)

The government of Costa Rica, for example, has recently begun to develop contracts between its president and individual ministries, agencies, and public enterprises.[2] The U.S. government experimented with such contracts in the mid-1990s, but as of this writing has not imposed them. Some state governments, including Florida, have also tried them.

## Monetary Incentives

In this type of motivational approach, compensation for individual employees or groups of employees, or altered funding for organizations, is based at least in part on performance data. Pay-for-performance plans are considered a powerful incentive in private business. They are considerably more controversial in public or private nonprofit environments.

Monetary incentives are fraught with pitfalls and have often been counterproductive in public environments.[3] The problem with many monetary incentive systems in government has been the lack of performance criteria perceived to be fair and valid. Almost always, compensation systems linked to pay have ended up relying heavily on the judgment of supervisors. Employee unions abhor such a process. Nonunion employees (including managers) who perceive the rewards as unfair can also be upset by them. If sound performance measurements are used as a major part of the reward criteria and are perceived by employees and public officials (and the public) as reasonably objective, fair, and valid, then the use of performance measurement data in determining monetary awards should reduce their potential negative effects on morale.

It can also be argued that such awards often go to those who would perform well without them. If such is the case, monetary rewards use up substantial resources and provide little motivational value. Including awards for *degree of improvement* is likely to alleviate this problem.

Three types of monetary incentive programs are described below:

***Linking pay to performance.*** A number of governments, including the U.S. government, have considered or introduced financial incentives tied to individual compensation. The U.S. Postal Service, for example, provides year-end bonuses to nonunion employees, both managers and nonmanagers (including secretaries). The size of a bonus is based on a formula that includes whether the employees in a cluster of workers met on-time service delivery standards, customer satisfaction targets, and budget targets. The unionized employees have thus far decided against bonuses, in part because bonuses are not added to base pay and do not add to retirement benefits.

A major dilemma here is that external factors can play major roles in affecting outcomes, efficiency, and even outputs. *A desirable condition for monetary incentives is that the employees, elected officials, and the public all explicitly accept that employees will be rewarded if outcomes improve, regardless of the extent to which the employees have actually contributed to the improved outcomes.* Conversely, they should recognize that employees will not be rewarded, despite their efforts and contributions, if performance levels do not meet expectations. (In effect, this is what is done in the private sector, where senior executives receive bonuses based on the performance of their companies, such as sales, profits, and market share.)

*Allocating discretionary funds to agencies or programs with high performance.* A less controversial monetary incentive rewards an agency or individual for good performance with funds that can be used only for organizational purposes, such as for employee training or improving workplace conditions. An example is a teacher incentive system in which high-performing individual teachers receive awards in the form of special equipment or other physical enhancements for their classrooms.

These incentives are likely to be better received by officials and the public, because little additional funding is needed and that funding is used for organization-enhancing purposes.

The most common application in the past has been in situations where a group's cost savings (say half) are returned to the group for discretionary use. These are sometimes called shared savings or gain-sharing programs. Usually, the funds are restricted to organizational activities undertaken by the group as a whole.

High performance on outcome indicators does not usually involve monetary savings. Thus, additional funds need to be added to the organization's budget for such rewards. Agencies can propose that an imputed amount be provided, based on estimates of the added expenditures that would have been needed to achieve the added outcomes levels, a calculation that can be difficult.

Any time a public or private agency links monetary incentives to outcome indicator values, the agency also needs to include indicators that track undesirable negative effects. It is tempting for personnel to focus on outcomes linked to rewards at the expense of other outcomes. For example, if monetary rewards are linked solely to cost per unit of output, employees are likely to focus on producing more output— even at the expense of the quality of that output. Classic examples include focusing on number of arrests, prosecutions, tax collections, or child support payment collections without also including such indicators as the incidence of harassment complaints. The U.S. Internal Revenue Service came under considerable scrutiny in 1998 because its tax collection efforts were perceived as encouraging inappropriate activities by IRS agents.

> If incentives, especially monetary incentives, are linked to performance results, be sure to include performance indicators that can identify potential negative side effects.

In another example, the *Washington Post* reported in April 1999 that a federal law enacted in 1997 promised, among other things, to pay states $4,000 to $6,000 for every child adopted over a baseline number. This created a substantial financial incentive for the states. The newspaper noted concerns by child advocacy groups that caseworkers would be pressured to seek adoptions before the children or families were ready or to place children with inappropriate families. For example, the family might not be told the extent of the abuse that the adoptive child had suffered, and might subsequently find itself unable to cope with the child.[4]

To reduce this danger, agencies should strive to make their performance measurement system comprehensive. It should cover potentially important negative effects linked to program activities, such as number of validated complaints and employee misbehavior.

*Monetary incentives for many programs should also depend on whether the outcomes lasted for a reasonable amount of time.* For example, in the case of the adoption program mentioned above, the monetary inventive should depend on the extent to which the placements were troublefree after a reasonable period of time had elapsed, say 12 months after the adoption. In such cases, some of the payments would need to be delayed for that period of time, but the delay would probably ensure that the incentives encouraged successful adoptions.

***Sanctions for prolonged low performance.*** The most dramatic and threatening monetary sanctions are salary reduction, demotion, and discharge. As outcome data become more widespread, they are also likely to be increasingly used by public officials as a basis for such sanctions. Clearly, special care is needed when using outcome data for these types of "incentives." On one hand, outcome performance will be readily observable and based on relatively objective findings. On the other hand, outcomes are seldom fully controllable by public managers. *Continued* low performance, rather than performance during one period, should normally be a major element in such decisions.

Another form of monetary sanction is for a funding organization to reduce or withhold the funding of agencies or programs that have not met expected performance levels or have not provided adequate information to assess performance. Such sanctions have to be very carefully designed so that they do not penalize customers of poorly performing programs. Again, such sanctions are probably best applied to programs where poor performance has continued over a substantial period of time. If customers show no signs of deriving significant benefit from the program, consideration should be given to discontinuing it altogether.

***Examples of monetary incentives.*** The use of financial incentives based on outcome information appears to be growing. Maryland and North Carolina have been using reward systems for individual schools that show marked improvement on student test scores and other performance indicators. In 1998, the Maryland Department of Education awarded almost $3 million in cash awards to 83 public elementary and middle schools that showed significant improvement on such measures. Another 200 schools that did not receive cash bonuses were given recognition awards for significant progress. Awarding on the basis of improvement means that both schools with initially high scores and schools with initially low scores have incentives to improve their performance. Schools received bonuses ranging from $16,000 to $65,000, with the size of the bonus based on the size of the school. Because the awards are one-time grants, schools cannot use them to hire staff. They typically use them to train teachers or to buy computer equipment or classroom supplies.[5]

North Carolina's state board of education developed the ABCs of Public Education program in 1996. It provides monetary awards to individual schools based on student achievement on end-of-course tests in various subjects in a number of grades. In addition, nonmonetary recognition awards were provided to schools with somewhat less improvement but with at least 80 percent of students performing at or above grade level. Schools identified as low-performing (such as those in which a majority of students performed below grade level) were assigned school improvement teams of three to five full-time persons for a year. In the first year (1997–98), all 15 schools with these assistance teams substantially improved their results.

Virginia recently proposed using negative incentives. The proposal would require a local school district to pay the cost of any remedial classes that students had to take as college freshmen. This would be a strong incentive for local school districts to do a better job of preparing students for college-level work, but it might be a hardship for school districts with high proportions of students with learning disabilities.

## A Possible Model for Interagency Motivational Programs

The North Carolina Department of Health and Human Services' Division of Maternal and Child Health worked with the state's Association of Local Health Directors to develop a set of outcome indicators on which each county health department has to provide data annually to the state. The division then generates data comparing the outcomes of the county agencies. The counties are grouped into four categories: urban (the 10 largest), western, central, and eastern. Within each category, counties are ranked annually on each set of indicators. For the family planning program, for example, each county was ranked on four indicators: adolescent (age 10–17) pregnancy rate; percentage of repeat teen pregnancies (age 10–17); percentage of women who had two births within 12 months; and rate of live births to unmarried women.

For each of these four indicators, the counties are ranked on two measures: the most recent three-year county rate and the amount of improvement from the previous to the most recent three-year period. The division expects to identify a few counties in each grouping at the top and the bottom of the ratings. It plans to meet with the low-ranking counties to identify needed improvements, perhaps asking the top-ranking counties to help. Counties that receive very low program rankings for two consecutive years are subject to increased state involvement. As long as a county makes a good-faith effort, the division does not plan to assess any financial penalty. However, if corrections are not made, the division may exercise its option to transfer funds from the county agency to other agencies that can provide the service. Fiscal year 1996–97 was the first year of implementation.

This use of outcome information motivates service providers in a constructive way. Assistance is made available to offices that are having problems in achieving outcomes that other, similar offices have achieved.

The same approach can be adapted to agencies that have multiple offices within the same level of government, as long as the offices provide essentially the same services to the same types of clients. Similarly, for private, nonprofit service agencies, comparative data can motivate those with lower outcomes to improve, perhaps by seeking ideas from agencies with higher levels of achievement.

Exhibit 11-4 summarizes the components of this model. Because of the constructive interaction between state and local agencies, this approach is a good example of a performance partnership.

## Formulate and Monitor the Performance of Contractors and Grantees (Performance Contracting)

If the agency contracts or provides grants to other organizations for services to customers, it can include outcome-based performance targets in the agreements and then compare outcomes against those targets. This is called outcome-based performance contracting, and interest in it has been growing.

If targets are included in a contract or grant agreement, they need to be carefully developed by the agency and should be compatible with the indicators in the program's performance measurement system. The indicators should be included in requests for proposals (RFPs). In some instances, the targets for each indicator might also be included in the RFP. In other instances, targets are negotiated ahead of time or are part of con-

**Intergovernment Performance Partnership**

1. The central agency and representatives of local agencies jointly select a set of outcome indicators, such as rate of low-weight births.
2. The local agencies provide quarterly information on each data element to the central agency.
3. The central agency tabulates the data for each agency.
4. The central agency provides each local agency with summary data for each outcome indicator and with comparisons among the local agencies.
5. Technical assistance is provided to poorly performing local agencies—perhaps by high-performing agencies.
6. The central agency and representatives of local agencies sponsor an effort to identify exemplary practices and disseminate them to all local agencies.

Adapted from procedures being used by human services agencies in North Carolina and Minnesota.

tract or grant competitions, with organizations that promise higher levels of outcomes being given higher ratings.

A combination of rewards and penalties can be included in these agreements, such as:

- Rewards for meeting or exceeding targets
- Reduced fees for failing to meet targets

Most service contracts include termination options for nonperformance, but these generally apply to extreme circumstances (usually only vaguely defined) and do not appear to provide much incentive for improving performance. An additional motivator for good performance is to *make past performance an explicit criterion for future awards*, as long as this option is legal for the agency's procurement system. For example, the United Ways of Minneapolis, New Orleans, and Rochester have begun to require that the service providers they support provide outcome data and expect to consider outcome attainment as a factor in their future funding decisions (but only after they feel comfortable with the data).[6] United Way of Minneapolis is beginning to use multiyear contracts with its service providers, at least in part because some end outcomes can take more than one year to achieve.

Outcome-based performance contracting is particularly attractive (at least to contractors) in situations where greater accountability can be exchanged for more flexibility in how the work is performed. Thus, if the contract holds the contractor accountable for results, it probably would contain fewer specifications as to how the work should be performed.

Performance contracting with incentives has been tried with a number of services in the United States, including payments based on the number of vehicles requiring additional work after initial repairs, success in drug treatment, missed garbage collections, the number of persons placed in employment, and the amount of child support payments secured.

## Example of Performance Contracting

Oklahoma's Department of Rehabilitation Services (DRS) has established the Milestone System—an outcome-based payment system for contractors that provide employment services to severely disabled clients of the state's vocational rehabilitation services.[7] At various outcome milestones for each client, contractors are paid a percentage of their "average total cost per successful case closure," as specified in their initial bid. For example, the contractor receives a preestablished percentage after the client's initial placement, an additional percentage if the client is still in the job after four weeks, and another installment if the client is still in the job after 10 weeks. The jobs must meet specific DRS guidelines for employment, such as minimum weekly hours of work and the minimum wage.

United Way of Central Indiana has used a similar arrangement for welfare-to-work projects stressing services for hard-to-place clients. In outcome-based performance contracts, payments are made at the following client milestones: (1) when emergency needs have been met; (2) when an individual employment plan has been developed; (3) when clients are placed in a job; (4) when clients have remained in the job for 90 days; (5) when clients have remained in the job for 180 days; (6) when clients have remained in the job for 360 days; and (7) when clients achieve an advancement in responsibility and/or pay.[8]

The National Science Foundation (NSF) Comprehensive Partnerships for Mathematics and Science Achievement program has used a form of performance contracting in grants aimed at getting more minority students interested in mathematics and science. For example, the program's 1995 five-year, $1.6 million cooperative agreement with the Surry County (VA) Public Schools contains a number of performance targets. These include, for each of the five years, the number of minority students (in specified grades) who successfully complete (grade C or better) specific mathematics and science courses. The grantee is required to provide annual reports containing data on its progress in reaching these goals. Moreover, the agreement specifies that continued NSF support will depend on an annual review of achievements.

**If you can give them money, why can't you expect results?**

The District of Columbia's 1998 contract to overhaul and maintain 15,000 parking meters specified financial penalties for the contractor if fewer than 97 percent of the meters, on average, were operational.

## Issues in Considering Performance Contracting

When monetary bonuses or penalties are included in contracts or grants, an agency will need to work out incentive provisions that are fair both to the public and to the contractor or grantee. Development of these provisions will require considerable skill and cooperation from the program and contract offices.

To make performance contracting effective, an agency also needs a strong contract oversight function that either collects the performance data itself (e.g., as part of the agency's performance measurement system) or regularly checks the quality of performance data provided by the contractor. In the latter case, if the contractor is serving its own clients, direct follow-up of clients by the funding agency might be impossible, given the contractor's need to preserve client confidentiality. In such a case, the agency's oversight should probably focus on reviewing the data collection procedures used by the contractor.

The most feasible approach in many cases is to encourage and help grantees and contractors maintain their own outcome measurement processes but require them to allow the funding organization to undertake periodic quality control audits of the data systems. This might include checking a sample of the actual data. (Suggestions for quality control of performance are provided in chapter 13.)

Timing is important in setting performance payment schedules. For some services, important outcomes cannot be assessed for a considerable time after the contractor's services have been completed. In these cases, the performance agreement may need to provide for postservice measurement before final payments are determined. In the Oklahoma rehabilitation service contracts described above, the primary service is job placement. The final installment is not paid to the contractor until the client has been on the job for 10 weeks. Final payments for drug and alcohol treatment program contracts might be based on the client's situation 12 months after completion of treatments. In such cases, final payments will need to be delayed until after the service period.

Incentive provisions are typically more readily accepted for contracts with private, for-profit contractors than private, nonprofit agencies. However, as some of the above examples indicate, their inclusion in grants to nonprofits seems reasonable for some, if not most, services. Though monetary

EXHIBIT 11–5

**Outcome-Based Performance Contracting Questions**

- To what extent should contractors be involved in the selection of performance indicators?
- What incentives should be included in contracts?
- How should the size of penalties and positive incentives be related to outcomes?
- Should initial performance contracts include a hold-harmless clause?
- What role should the contractor play in data collection?
- How should external factors be considered when determining rewards and sanctions (e.g., escape clauses)?
- How can outcome incentives be used to encourage contractor innovation?
- Should performance on past contracts help determine future contract awards?

incentives are likely to be less important to nonprofit organizations than to public agencies, they do seem likely to stimulate motivation.

Exhibit 11-5 lists a number of key questions an agency needs to answer when establishing outcome-based performance contracting.

## Provide Data for Special, In-Depth Program Evaluations

An agency's performance measurement system can often provide an excellent starting point for special evaluation efforts. Its regularly collected data can often substitute for some of the data the evaluators would otherwise have to collect, saving considerable time. Even when the system does not reduce the amount of data the evaluation will have to collect, it can shed light on the issues addressed by the evaluation and even lead to the framing of new hypotheses.

Such information should also provide the basic data needed for performance audits (which can be considered a form of program evaluation) and can be very useful in identifying program areas that need explanation and attention in the agency's annual program evaluation agenda.

The usefulness of the performance measurement system to the program evaluators will be considerably enhanced if its regular reports provide breakouts (chapter 8) and explanatory information (chapters 10 and 11).

In cases of service changes, the performance measurement system will also supply before-and-after data, thereby providing at least a preliminary impact estimate.

Strategic plans usually include a mission statement, a statement of long-term objectives, and a formulation of strategies for achieving those objectives. They should also consider alternative means of service delivery, including the costs, likely impacts, and major implementation hurdles of each option. They should include outcome indicators that are explicitly related to the objectives identified in the plan and that can be used to track progress toward meeting these objectives. Finally, they should include recent baseline values for each of the outcome indicators to show where the program currently stands in regard to key strategic objectives and to provide the starting point for the plan.

*Thus, the agency's performance measurement system is needed for three purposes in strategic planning:*

- To provide baseline values for each of the plan's performance indicators, and thus establish the extent of action needed
- To provide historical data on each indicator so that outcomes can be projected for each of the options examined
- To provide data on key outcome indicators that can be used in regular reports on progress toward meeting strategic plan objectives

Two distinctions between the data contained in the agency's strategic plan and the data yielded by its performance measurement system need to be highlighted. First, *the indicators contained in the strategic plan will inevitably be only a subset of the indicators an agency tracks in its performance measurement system.* For example, a strategic plan relating to child health might include a long-term target on infant mortality. The performance measurement system should track infant mortality as one of its outcome indicators, but it should also track indicators covering key intermediate outcomes, such as improving nutrition, avoiding drugs, and other steps that expectant mothers can take to improve an infant's chances of surviving. The agency's performance measurement system should also break out end and intermediate outcomes for various demographic groups, such as mother's age and race or ethnicity, and the cause of the infant's death. Some of these breakouts might be included in the strategic plan, but others might not.

Second, *strategic plans almost always cover only selected segments of the agency.* For example, the statewide indicators in Oregon's benchmark plan did not cover the state's road maintenance activities, even though maintenance is a major expenditure. An agency's performance measurement system, on the other hand, should be comprehensive enough to provide regular feedback on results covering all, or all but the very smallest, programs.

A major temptation of strategic plans is to set targets at high, politically attractive levels without considering the cost and feasibility of achieving them. Unrealistic targets draw down criticism on the agency when they are not met. Data from the agency's performance measurement system, along with cost data, can be used to help make plausible estimates of what can be achieved, and at what expense. Such information should be provided to agency officials, even if the politics of the situation subsequently mandate setting official outcome targets that are not in line with likely funding or capability.

The performance measurement system and the strategic planning process should be closely related. The strategic planning process may identify indicators that the agency's performance measurement process has neglected, perhaps because some objectives were overlooked. Similarly, the indicators contained in the agency's existing performance measurement system may suggest objectives and related progress indicators that the strategic plan should include.

*Caution:* Projecting numbers into the future is an art form that requires not only historical data and statistical estimation techniques, but also qualitative judgment formed from experience.

## Communicate Better with the Public to Build Trust

A performance measurement system opens up a number of ways to communicate with the public and, over the long run, to increase the public's trust and confidence in the program. Other chapters have identified roles citizens can and should play in developing and sustaining a performance measurement process. The following are three areas in which agencies should seek citizens' help:

1. Identifying the service outcomes the agency should track. The use of customer focus groups to provide such input is described in chapter 5. In this case, the agency and its programs should note in performance reports that customers were included in the determination of what outcomes would be tracked.
2. Providing feedback on the outcomes and quality of services. Chapter 7 points out the importance of customer surveys to obtain such feedback on a regular basis as part of the performance measurement process.

3. Using the performance information. Summaries of annual performance reports should be made available to citizens. Those reports should not only contain information that describes the agency's activities and its physical outputs, but also focus on service outcomes and quality. *The key is to make the information readily available to citizens.* Normally, the main avenue for getting information to the public is through the press. *Annual performance reports should be available at libraries. The internet and public TV station programs are also mechanisms for getting the material out.* Significant effort should be made to let people know that the information is readily available and how the material can be obtained.

Agencies need to help citizens understand the performance information, such as what the data tell and do not tell. (Data do not tell, for example, "who is to blame.") This is basic to enabling citizens to use the data properly. Most citizens will be interested only in data showing major problems, such as high crime rates and poor children's test scores. Citizen interest groups will focus on data relevant to their special interests; for example, environmental groups will be interested in air and water pollution reports. And, citizens will be considerably more interested in data about their own geographical area than about the nation or jurisdiction as a whole.

In all cases, to build trust, performance reports need to be clear and perceived as honest, accurate, and complete—showing the bad as well as the good. Otherwise, performance reporting will damage the agency's reputation.

## Help Provide Better Services More Efficiently

Helping to provide better services more efficiently, in order to maintain and improve the quality of life, is the goal of performance measurement.

Here are a few special ways to encourage improvements:

- Use performance data to identify organizational units with disappointing outcomes.
- Require those units to develop implementation plans.
- Provide them with technical assistance.
- Require more frequent and more intense reporting of the program's outcome indicators to monitor improvement.
- After changes have been implemented and sufficient time has elapsed to expect improved outcomes, use data to help determine whether improvements have indeed occurred.

Florida's Department of Environmental Protection (DEP) (described in chapter 10) provides an example of this procedure with its shellfish-processing inspection program.[9] Deteriorating compliance rates caused the department to require the program to submit a corrective action plan. The program administrator drafted a plan after meeting with members of the regulated community to discuss causes and solutions. DEP then started using targeted inspections of plants suspected of noncompliance rather than fully random inspections. (This resulted initially in a further decline in compliance, as might be expected since state inspections were targeted primarily at at-risk businesses. To assess long-term results, the department will need to undertake random inspections to compare pre- and post-implementation noncompliance rates.)

All the ways of using performance information discussed in this chapter should help reach this fundamental goal of improving services to the public. If a performance measurement effort does not do this, it will have been largely wasted.

---

### References and Notes

1. Rick Kowalewski, *Using Outcome Information to Redirect Programs: A Case of the Coast Guard's Pilot Project under the Government Performance and Results Act*, American Society for Public Administration Case Study F3 (Washington, D.C.: American Society for Public Administration, April 1996).

2. For example, see Government of Costa Rica and the World Bank, *Guidelines for Drafting Compromiso de Resultados* (San Jose, Costa Rica, February 2, 1996).

3. See Harry P. Hatry, John M. Greiner, and Brenda G. Ashford, *Issues and Case Studies in Teacher Incentive Plans*, 2nd ed. (Washington, D.C.: Urban Institute Press, 1994). Also see John M. Greiner et al., *Productivity and Motivation: A Review of State and Local Government Initiatives* (Washington, D.C.: Urban Institute Press, 1981).

4. Barbara Vobejda, "Revamping of Foster Care Brings Surge in Adoptions," *Washington Post*, 13 April 1999, p. A3.

5. Amy Argetsinger, "Improved Test Scores Pay Off for Maryland Schools," *Washington Post*, 19 November 1998, p. B6.

6. Telephone interviews, August 21, 1998.

7. See, for example, Daniel O'Brien and Rebecca Cook, "Oklahoma Milestone Payment System" in *Invitation to Change: 1997 Better Government Competition Winners*, eds. Charles D. Chieppo and Kathryn Ciffolillo (Boston, Mass.: Pioneer Institute for Public Policy Research, 1997).

8. United Way of America, *Workbook from United Way of America's Forum on Outcomes II* (Alexandria, Va.: United Way of America, December 3, 1997).

9. Meetings with Department of Environmental Protection officials, March 1999.

# Results-Based Budgeting

Budgeting is the annual (sometimes biennial) process by which organizations estimate their resource needs and allocations for the future. The focus of this chapter is on how performance measurement information, particularly outcome data, can be used to assist budget formulation and review.

For many governments, making the budget process more results-based has been the primary motivation for legislating performance measurement. A budget process should encourage, if not demand, a performance orientation.[1]

## Results-Based Budgeting: A New and Evolving Concept

Results-based budgeting can be said to be new because of the central attention it gives to outcomes and its attempt to link resource allocation explicitly to outcomes. It is also new in that it emphasizes the importance of the entire management process in supporting and demanding better results—including planning, budget execution, auditing, and reporting. Unfortunately, not much is known about what results-based budgeting is or how to do it! The suggestions in this chapter are intended to provide a start for defining it and for developing procedures for doing it. Individual agencies will need to devote much time to refining the process.

Results-oriented performance measurement provides basic information to those formulating, and subsequently justifying, a budget. The information helps indicate where problems and successes exist that may need additional or reduced resources. *The key element of results-based budgeting is that it attempts to consider, if only roughly, the future values of performance indicators—the amount of outcomes expected from proposed budgeted resources—and projected outputs.*

Agencies preparing performance budgets make projections for each performance indicator for the forthcoming year(s). Projections of outputs and outcomes are intended to reflect the estimated consequences of the resources budgeted. These projections represent what the agency is buying for its money. *The data from an agency's performance measurement system should provide basic information for developing budget proposals and help justify the budget proposals that have already been developed.* This information is likely to have even greater weight if linked to strategic plans.

By focusing systematically on the results sought, results-based budgeting should better enable decisionmakers to achieve the following:

- *Identify poorly performing programs*, thereby signaling the need to make changes. (Other information is needed to determine which changes to make.)
- *Identify programs that are performing well* and presumably need no significant changes. (Even here, other information is needed to determine what, if any, changes may be desirable.)
- *Examine the value of existing programs* on the basis of their outcomes rather than solely on their costs, outputs, and general statements as to their value.
- *Assess new programs* for what they are specifically expected to accomplish, not just their costs or general statements of their expected value. (Some governments, such as the state of North Carolina, have asked for outcome information in budget requests only on new or expansion requests.[2])
- *Compare different proposed options* on their expected outcomes and costs.
- *Help identify agency activities that have similar outcome indicators and are thus candidates for coordination and perhaps revision, reduction, or deletion.*
- *Justify the budget choices more effectively* to agency and elected officials—and the public.
- *Link, even if only roughly, the proposed budget size (funds and personnel) to the amount of outcome expected.*
- *Provide the basis for greater agency accountability,* to the extent that reasonable performance targets are set for the budget year and achieved values are subsequently compared to targets.

The first three points are discussed at length in chapter 10—primarily in the context of analyzing performance information for changing programs and policies during the budget year. Here the focus is on using the same information for establishing and examining budgets.

Results-based budgeting is intended to support an overall agency focus on outcomes. Here is an example of its use in helping justify budgets:

> The Massachusetts Department of Environmental Protection sought to obtain funding from the state legislature to line unlined landfills. It justified the expenditure by reporting the product of the expenditure as *the number of acres expected to be lined.* This did not move the legislature, which turned down the request. The department then switched to a more outcome-based approach and justified the request in terms of *gallons of leachate prevented.* Legislators asked for a definition of leachate. When they found that it referred to potential pollutants leaked into the groundwater and water supply, they approved the funding request.[3]

In a performance-based budgeting system, agencies need to select targets (make projections) for the budget year for each output, outcome, and efficiency indicator, as well as for expenditures.[4]

*A key problem for results-based budgeting, especially at the state and federal levels, is to persuade legislators and legislative staffs to switch from primary dependence on line-item budgeting to an outcomes focus.* At the very least, legislators and their staffs need to address outcomes during appropriation hearings. The executive branch is responsible for providing meaningful, reliable, important outcome information to its legislators—in a user-friendly format. A major problem in some state governments in their initial results-based budgeting efforts has been loading legislators with large numbers of indicators, and data, presented in an unattractive fashion—which discourages their use.

This book is not intended to cover budgeting in general. Instead, it addresses the new dimension of outcome information. The key issues in results-based budgeting are listed in exhibit 12-1 and discussed later in this chapter—after a bit of history.

## A Bit of History

Performance budgeting has been around at least since the 1960s. At that time it focused primarily on the relationship between inputs and outputs. Some communities (such as Milwaukee, WI, and Nassau County, NY) produced budgets that contained hundreds of unit-cost measurements that

EXHIBIT 12-1

**Key Issues in Results-Based Budgeting**

1. The appropriateness of budgeting based on outcomes rather than outputs
2. Limitations in the value of performance measurement for results-based budgeting
3. The time frame that should be covered by results-based budgeting, especially considering that outcomes will often occur years after the one in which the funds were budgeted
4. The extent to which proposed inputs can be linked to outputs and outcomes
5. The role of efficiency indicators
6. Setting performance targets in budgets
7. The use of explanatory information
8. The extent of program influence over future outcomes
9. Steps for using performance information in formulating and examining budget requests
10. Applying results-based budgeting to internal support services
11. Using results-based budgeting for capital budgeting
12. "Budgeting-by-objectives"
13. The use of special analytical techniques
14. The role of qualitative outcome information in results-based budgeting

linked costs or employee-hours to outputs. Sunnyvale (CA) has used such measurements since the early 1970s, converting unit-costs into productivity indices focusing on outputs. These indices permit comparisons across services and across years. More recently, Sunnyvale has begun focusing on outcomes.

A typical output-based performance indicator would be, for example, "the cost (or number of employee-hours) per ton of asphalt laid." In some cases, these output-based indicator reports were dropped because the number of unit-cost indicators overwhelmed the external users of the information. Nevertheless, such unit-cost information can be useful to managers and supervisors (and elected officials, if they wish) for tracking the technical efficiency of their activities.

*The major new dimension is to relate outcomes to budget requests.* The term *results-based budgeting* reflects this new focus.[5] At both the federal and state levels, recent legislation has emphasized the concept that budget decisions should be made not on the basis of dollars alone, nor on physical outputs, but in relation to outcomes.

Of the many recent performance measurement systems that have been initiated primarily with the intent of providing some form of results-based budgeting, the Government Performance and Results Act (GPRA) of 1993 is a prime example. This federal budget action is unique in (a) having support from both political parties and both the executive and legislative branches and (b) being explicitly embodied in legislation, unlike earlier approaches such as the Planning-Programming-Budgeting-System (PPBS), Zero-Based Budgeting (ZBB), and Management by Objectives (MBO).

## Key Issues in Results-Based Budgeting

### 1. The Appropriateness of Budgeting Based on Outcomes Rather Than Outputs

Using outcome information for budgeting seems quite sensible on the surface, but in fact, its use in budgeting for agency operations is controversial. It has, for example, been the major subject of debates comparing the New Zealand to the Australian and U.S. approaches to budgeting at the federal level. New Zealand's approach has been to hold its operating departments responsible for outputs but not outcomes—and to use performance agreements with department heads (described in chapter 11) to hold them accountable for outputs. New Zealand's rationale is that agencies control outputs, but too many other factors beyond the control of the operating departments affect outcomes. Only ministers are held responsible for outcomes.

The difference in approach is not as great as it seems at first glance, however, because in New Zealand outputs include service quality—such as accuracy, timeliness, accessibility, and customer satisfaction—attributes that in this book (and elsewhere) are often categorized as outcomes.[6]

The counterargument to the view that agencies should only be held responsible for producing outputs is that outcomes are the fundamental reasons for establishing an agency in the first place. The activities of operating agencies clearly contribute to program outcomes, even if no single group of persons, whether operating personnel or the policymakers themselves, fully controls them. Take as an example income maintenance and public assistance programs. Who is eligible for assistance and what level of payments are to be provided are primarily policy issues. They are decided by the legislature and the upper echelon of the executive branch of government. However, if the policy is not implemented well—if program personnel do not execute the policy properly and/or get the correct checks to the right people or mail them out quickly—the desired outcomes will be compromised, and program personnel can be at least partly responsible for the failure.

Encouraging agency personnel to work to improve service outcomes seems a much better way to go. *Many, if not most, outcomes are produced by many agencies and sectors of the economy, and responsibility is thus inherently shared.* This is the implicit philosophy of the Australian and U.S. governments.

As suggested in chapter 10, agencies can rate the extent of their influence over individual performance indicators in their performance reports. This alerts users to the inherent limitations of outcome information while accepting a degree of responsibility.

The controversy over output versus outcome responsibilities has been less an issue at lower levels of government (especially at the local level) and in private agencies.

## 2. Limitations in the Value of Performance Measurement for Results-Based Budgeting

Performance measurement looks *backward*. It attempts to provide the best possible data on what happened in the past. Past outcome data provide important information for projections, *but making estimates about future outcomes is radically different from assessing past performance*. Past trends are only one among many influences on future outcomes. The future effects of those other influences are inevitably a matter of uncertainty, particularly in cases where little is known about the *quantitative* relationship between inputs and outcomes.

*Suggestion:* For outcome forecasts that are particularly uncertain, provide a range of values instead of a single value. This is likely to be more realistic and informative.

## 3. The Time Frame to Be Covered by Results-Based Budgeting

Typically, budgets only present data for the current budget year(s), especially at the state and local levels of government and in the private sector. Some central governments, such as those of the United States and Australia, now include out-year funding estimates (perhaps for three additional years). Including out-year forecasts is important for three reasons:

- It reduces the temptation for agencies and their programs to focus all their efforts on the short term.
- For some programs, achievement of the hoped-for outcomes will require funds not only from the current year's budget but from future budgets as well.
- If the program is requesting resources whose effects on outcomes will not occur until after the budget period, the outcome targets for the budget year will not reflect the intended effects; therefore, budget proposals, especially those of the higher levels of government, should include out-year estimates for some outcomes.

The key assumption is that organizations will make better resource allocation decisions when they explicitly consider expected costs and outcomes for at least a few out-years. For example, the results of funding a new federal or state program to reduce alcohol abuse might not be apparent for two or more years. Time will be needed to gain acceptance by localities, train staff members in the program, publicize and run the program, make sure clients receive the program's services, and then measure the outcomes. Even for intermediate outcome indicators, measurable effects may not be expected until after the budget year. Another example: Road construction can reduce accidents and congestion over several years. Should not estimates of the magnitude of these future improvements be included in the budget justification?

*The solution is to build into the budget process the outcomes expected to result in years beyond those covered by the proposed budget.* To make budget decisions, programs might be asked to provide estimates of the value of each outcome indicator for each out-year the budget is expected to affect. This introduction of outcome projections into the budget development process is likely to encourage agencies to plan beyond the current budget year.

For some programs this can be done readily. For example, funds may be proposed for rehabilitating the homes of 100 families. The years in which those rehabs will occur can be predicted relatively accurately, and estimating the number of households whose homes will be rehabilitated in particular out-years should also be reasonably straightforward. A program that provides drug treatment will find it more difficult to estimate the number of clients who will become drugfree and in which years. Performance measurement data on past success rates will likely help those preparing or reviewing the budget to estimate such outcomes.

A less demanding option is to ask for estimated future outcomes without requiring that they be distributed by year.

The need to consider future outcomes of the current year's budget is less frequent for local than for federal and state programs. But even at the local level, some programs, such as school and health programs, will have long-term outcome goals.

The problem of long-term outcomes has not been addressed by most governments. A partial exception is that some state governments separate expansion requests (including new programs) from requests for programs needing funding continuation. For the expansion requests, these governments require out-year projections of future outcomes.

### 4. The Extent to Which Proposed Inputs Can Be Linked to Outputs and Outcomes

In analyzing performance information, a critical step is to link information on inputs to associated past outputs and outcomes. Results-based budgeting, and similar resource allocation efforts (including strategic planning), enter into a new dimension—*estimating the link between inputs and expected future results.* Such estimates are usually subject to considerable uncertainty.

Part of the uncertainty relates to lack of good historical cost information. This problem is potentially curable. More difficult is estimating *future* costs, especially estimating the effects on support and overhead costs of new program investments. Even more difficult is estimating the amount of expenditures needed to increase outcomes, especially end outcomes, by specific amounts. Typically, programs do not know with any certainty how much more (or less) funding or staffing is needed to increase (or reduce) an end outcome by a certain amount. As programs gain experience with their outcome data, they should be able to make better estimates of this relationship, although it will never be as predictable as the relationship between funding or personnel and output indicators.

> **Estimating the amount of future outcomes that will occur given specific amounts of inputs, even for only one year into the future, is much more difficult than tracking past performance.**

Making accurate projections becomes increasingly difficult and uncertain as one moves from linking inputs to outputs, to linking inputs to intermediate outcomes, and, finally, to linking inputs or outputs to end outcomes. The following sections discuss the linkages between inputs, outputs, intermediate outcomes, and end outcomes. Little past work has examined these latter relationships.

*Linking inputs to outputs.* The amount of output expected in the budget year can be used to estimate the associated costs and personnel requirements or vice versa. If the amounts of dollars and personnel are the starting point for the budget, the amount of output achievable can be estimated.[7] Many, if not most, programs can estimate somewhat accurately how much output is likely, given particular amounts of staff and funds. Programs will likely have reasonably accurate counts of past outputs and the direct costs of employee time. If they do not currently record such information, they can obtain it.[8]

If funding needs are developed from estimates of the workload, estimates of future expenditures of employee time and money will be affected by the program's ability to estimate accurately the magnitude and character of the budget year workload and the effects of any new service procedures or technology. For example, school systems try to estimate the next year's school population in order to make decisions about school buildings, classrooms, teachers, and purchases of books and other teaching materials. Inaccurate projections have been known to embarrass school officials.

Performance measurement information from earlier years normally provides the basis for projecting the relationship between inputs and outputs for the current budget year. However, if the *complexity of the workload* during the forthcoming budget year is likely to differ substantially from that in previous years, this change needs to be considered when developing the budget. For example, the Internal Revenue Service can tabulate the number and complexity of tax returns that come in each year. However, many factors—such as revisions to the tax code—can alter the future mix of tax-return difficulty.

*External factors* can also affect future workload. For example, at the state and local levels, expected future weather conditions (e.g., long-term projections of freeze-thaw conditions for the budget year) can alter estimates of future road work and costs, as can changes in the estimated amount of future traffic. The number and characteristics of incoming clients, such as their need for employment, health, and social service programs, can be highly unpredictable because they are affected by many economic and social factors—and projections based on past data are by no means certain. For some programs, agencies can use reasonably reliable estimates of population, but these are also subject to uncertainties, such as increased immigration from countries in crisis.

*Linking inputs to intermediate outcomes.* Developing precise relationships between past input data and past intermediate outcome data can be accomplished for some outcome indicators. Even so, past relationships between the intermediate outcomes and inputs will usually provide only rough indications of what will happen in the budget year. For example, federal agencies such as the Departments of Education, Housing and Urban Development, Health and Human Services, and Labor and the Environmental Protection Agency provide much of their assistance to state and local agencies rather than to the ultimate customers. If these state and local agencies undertake promising steps that the federal department has encouraged, the steps are intermediate outcomes for that department. Data on the past relationship between the amounts of federal funds and assistance, on the one hand, and the extent to which the state and local governments undertook promising initiatives, on the other, are likely to be useful. But the past relationship provides only a rough estimate of what state and local agencies will do in the budget year.

Some intermediate outcomes can be estimated relatively accurately. For example, agencies can make fairly accurate estimates of intermediate outcomes such as future response times, given particular amounts of staff and dollar resources.[9] Even here, however, a number of outside factors over which the program has little control can intervene. For example, an unexpectedly large number of requests for service or changes in the proportion of complex requests can have major effects on response times.

Examples of difficult-to-predict intermediate outcomes:

- Number of businesses (or households) that alter their handling of waste so as to be more environmentally prudent after receiving assistance from state or local programs
- Number and percentage of parents who take special parenting classes and then alter their behavior in ways that encourage learning by their children in school
- Customer satisfaction

All of these are driven not only by agency efforts to seek certain customer behaviors and perceptions but also by many aspects of the behavior and circumstances of the customers themselves, as well as outside factors.

The bottom line is that agencies should expect historical data on costs and intermediate outcomes to be useful in preparing cost and intermediate outcome information for budgets. In many cases, however, they will be able to make only rough projections as to the future relationship between costs and intermediate outcomes.

*Linking inputs to end outcomes.* As a general rule, agencies should not expect to have solid, known relationships between inputs and end outcomes, no matter how good the historical data are. (In economic terms, little information is available about the production function that relates the inputs to the end outcomes.) Nevertheless, these relationships are extremely important and need to be considered, *at least qualitatively*, in any budget process.

Some end outcomes are easier to relate to inputs than others. For example, *the number and percent of a state or local jurisdiction's roads that are in satisfactory condition* can be considered an end outcome indicator for road maintenance services. These numbers are closely related to the funds that the agency applies to road maintenance and repair. Past data on this relationship can be used to estimate the expenditures needed in order to achieve a certain value for this outcome indicator (or conversely, to estimate the percent of road miles in satisfactory condition given a particular funding level). But the

Performance Measurement: Getting Results

extent to which a client's condition is improved by expenditures of particular amounts of federal, state, local, or private funds to reduce substance abuse or to enhance elementary education is considerably more difficult to estimate.

Projecting the extent to which budgeted resources will achieve *prevention* (whether of crime, disease, family problems, etc.) is extremely difficult. At best, the historical data will provide very rough clues about the relationship between resources and prevention. In-depth studies can provide evidence, but some decisionmakers may need to rely more heavily on qualitative information and subjective judgments as to the prevention outcomes to be expected from a particular level of budgeted resources.

In general, the more direct the influence a program has over outcome, the greater its ability to develop numerical relationships between inputs and outcomes. Local governments and private agencies generally have more direct influence on end outcomes than state or federal agencies; therefore, the relationships between their inputs and outcomes (both intermediate and end) are likely to be clearer. Nevertheless, for many end outcome indicators, the relationship will inevitably be very imprecise. How many more resources would be needed to increase the percentage of customers satisfied with their recreation experiences by 5 percentage points (such as from 65 percent to 70 percent)? The answers to questions like this usually can be estimated only very roughly, at best.

If identifying the quantitative (or even qualitative) relationships between size and type of input, type of intervention, and amount of outcomes achieved is crucial, an in-depth program evaluation should be sought. Even if little is known about these relationships, budget determinations and justifications should explicitly address outcome expectations, even if only qualitatively.

*Linking outputs to outcomes.* Outcomes flow from outputs. For example, the number of calls answered is an output for a service (whether these calls relate to police, fire, sewage backups, travel information, or any other service request). This output leads to outcomes, such as whether the requests were fulfilled to the satisfaction of the customers and what resulted. Some outcome indicators explicitly relate outputs to outcomes, such as "the percent of those to whom services were provided (an output) who had successful outcomes."

Persons preparing or reviewing budget proposals should examine the amount of output expected in the budget year and assess what outcomes can be expected from that number—and when. If $X$ customers are expected to be served during the budget year (an output), how many customers can be expected to be helped to achieve the desired outcomes that year and in future years (an outcome)? For example:

- How many persons are expected to find employment after receiving training services and when?
- What percentage of babies born to low-income women who received prenatal care will be healthy?

Those preparing the budget request and those subsequently examining it should *ascertain that the outcome numbers make sense relative to the amount of output.* For services that have lengthy lag times between the timing of outputs and outcomes, the outcome numbers for the budget year need to be compared to output numbers *in the relevant previous years.*

*Linking intermediate outcomes to end outcomes.* It can be difficult to provide quantitative relationships between intermediate and end outcomes, but it is often easier than directly estimating the relationships between input and end outcomes. For example, a state agency might provide funds or technical assistance to a local agency to undertake environmental protection regulation designed to lead to cleaner air. The relationship between the local agency's successful implementation of its regulatory efforts (an intermediate outcome for the state agency) and the extent to which cleaner air results (an end outcome for both agencies) is likely to be quite uncertain. Some relationships are better understood, such as the extent to which increased percentages of children vaccinated against a disease can be expected to lead to reduced incidence of the disease among the vaccinated population.

*How to make these linkages?* Knowledge about most of the above linkages, for most programs, is lacking. Historical data from the performance measurement process, even if it has been implemented for only one or two years, can provide clues. (See the discussion of special analytical techniques below.) But there will almost always be considerable uncertainty about projections of outcomes, especially end outcomes, for given budget levels for the budget and later years. The key is to be able to make *plausible* connections between the amount of budgeted funds and the outcomes projected. These connections can be based on past performance, as modified by information on changes expected in the budget year in either internal or external factors.

## 5. The Role of Efficiency Indicators

Efficiency is an important consideration in the budget process. As noted earlier, efficiency has traditionally been measured as the *ratio of inputs to outputs.* The new element added in results-based budgeting is *ratios of inputs to outcomes.* An example of this is *cost per person served whose condition improved significantly after receiving the service.* The more traditional, output-based efficiency indicator is cost per person served.

When reasonably solid numerical relationships exist between outputs or outcomes and the associated inputs, past data can be used to develop historical unit-cost figures, such as the *cost per lane-mile of road maintained* or the *cost per lane-mile rated as being in good condition.* These figures can then be used to make estimates for the budget year. Likely future factors need to be factored in. For example, road maintenance budget estimates should consider any planned price changes, any new technologies that might be used and their cost, and any indications that repairs will be more extensive or more complex than in past years.

Some outcomes, such as *road condition*, can reasonably be numerically related to outputs, such as the number of lane-miles expected to be repaired during the budget year for a given dollar allocation. Budget preparers and reviewers can then examine various levels of the number of lane-miles to be repaired for various levels of expenditures and then estimate the number of lane-miles that will be in satisfactory condition for each expenditure option. This range of estimates will inform decisionmakers of the trade-offs between costs and outcomes, so they can select their preferred combination.

In police investigative work, the number of cases cleared per police dollar or per investigation hour is an outcome-based efficiency indicator. Past data on clearances can be used in making estimates for the forthcoming budget. However, the number and percent of crimes cleared in the budget year will also depend to a significant extent on the number of crimes reported, the types of crimes (for example, burglaries have substantially lower clearance rates than robberies), and the amount of evidence available at the scene. Factors largely outside the control of the police department (such as case difficulty) as well as internal factors (such as the amount of investigator turnover and the quality and quantity of investigative effort) can significantly affect clearance rates. Trends in such factors should be considered when projecting clearance rates from past efficiency data.

The use of unit-costs in which the units are *outputs* is common in budgeting. However, the use of unit-costs in which the units are *outcomes* is rare. One reason for this is that outcome data have not commonly been part of the budget preparation process. This is changing. In the future, the primary reason for limited use of costs per unit of outcome will be not lack of outcome data but rather lack of solid numerical relationships between inputs and outcomes.

## 6. Setting Performance Targets in Budgets

Key numbers in a results-based budget submission are the projected values of individual outcome indicators. In view of the considerable uncertainty surrounding future conditions and the links between agency resources and indicator values, how should agencies go about projecting these targets? Suggested steps are listed in exhibit 12-2. The specific factors to be considered in step 3 are listed in exhibit 12-3.[10]

Two special target-setting options exist for programs that have major uncertainties about the future values of one or more outcome indicators: variable targets and target ranges.

The *variable target option* applies to outcome indicators whose values are highly dependent on characteristics of the incoming workload *and* where major uncertainty exists about these characteristics. In this procedure, the expected relationship between the characteristics and outcomes is first identified. The final outcome target is determined *after the fact*, depending on the workload characteristics that actually occurred in the budget year.

*Example:* If an outcome is expected to be highly sensitive to the mix of workload (e.g., customers) coming in, and the mix for the budget

---

**EXHIBIT 12-2**

**Suggested Steps in Developing Outcome Targets**

1. Examine the agency's strategic plan (if one exists). Targets contained in the budget should be compatible with targets in the strategic plan.
2. Analyze the historical relationships between inputs (expenditures and staffing), outputs, and outcomes. Examine any explanatory information that accompanied the historical data. Use that combination of information to provide an initial estimate of targets compatible with the amount of resources being considered for the program's proposed budget.
3. Consider each of the factors listed in exhibit 12-3 (such as outside resources, environmental factors, changes in legislation or requirements, and expected program delivery changes) and adjust the targets accordingly.
4. Consider the level of outcomes achieved by similar organizations or under various conditions (as discussed in chapter 9). For example, the outcomes achieved by better-performing offices or facilities that provide similar services provide benchmarks the program may want to emulate.
5. Review the findings and recommendations from any recent program evaluations to identify past performance levels and past problems. Consider their implications for the coming years.
6. Use program analysis, cost-effectiveness analysis, and/or cost-benefit analysis to estimate the future effects of the program.

EXHIBIT 12-3

## Factors to Consider When Selecting Specific Outcome Targets

- *Past outcome levels.* The most recent outcomes and time trends provide a starting point for setting the outcome targets. (For example, recent trends may indicate that the values for a particular outcome indicator have been increasing annually by 10 percent in recent years; this would suggest the next year's number should be increased by a similar percentage.)
- *Amount of dollar and personnel resources expected to be available through the target period.* If staff and funds are being reduced or increased, how will this affect the program's ability to produce desired outcomes?
- *Amount of outside resources expected to supplement the program's resources.* Potential sources include other agencies, foundations, volunteers, and the business community. If such resources can play a significant role in producing the outcomes sought by the program, and the program has indications that these are being significantly increased, how is this likely to affect the outcomes?
- *Factors likely to be present in the wider environment through the target period.* These include such factors as the economy, population demographics, weather, major changes in industries in the area (such as major new industries scheduled to begin or depart), and major changes in international competition.
- *Recent or pending changes in legislation and other requirements of higher level governments.* To what extent are they likely to increase or decrease the ability of the program to produce favorable outcomes?
- *Changes planned by the program in policies, procedures, technology, and so on.* It is important to consider lead times to implement such changes.
- *Likely lag times from the time budgets are approved until the outcomes are expected to occur.* This applies both to the effects of past years' expenditures on the outcome values targeted for the budget year and to the likely timing of outcomes produced with the funds allocated in the budget year. (For some outcome indicators, effects will be expected in the budget year, but for others, effects will occur primarily in years after the budget year.)
- *Political concerns.* Politics may at times push for reporting outcome targets that exceed feasible levels. (Even so, the program and budget analysts should provide those selecting the targets with estimates of the likely achievable levels of outcomes.)

year is subject to considerable uncertainty, the program can set targets for *each category* of workload without making assumptions about the workload mix. The *aggregate target* is determined after the budget year closes and the mix is known.

For the indicator "percent of persons who leave welfare for work," the program might set separate targets for groups of welfare families defined by their amount of formal education. Suppose the program estimated that 75 percent of those coming in with at least a high school diploma would find jobs and get off welfare in the budget year, but only 30 percent of persons with less than a high school education would do so. These would be the targets presented in the budget. The aggregate percent that might also be included would be based on the program's estimate of the likely mix of clients.

At the end of the year, the aggregate target for the year would be calculated for the actual education mix and compared to the actual aggregate percent. If during the year, 420 persons who had not completed high school and 180 persons who had completed high school were on welfare, the aggregate target for the overall percentage of these persons that would leave welfare for work would be 44 percent—30 percent of 420 (126), plus 75 percent of 180 (135), equaling 261. Dividing 261 by the total number on welfare that year (600) yields the aggregate target for the share expected to go off welfare, 44 percent.

The target might also be linked to the national unemployment rate. For example, the program target might be 15 percent off welfare if the national unemployment rate turned out to be over 5.4 percent and 25 percent off welfare if the national unemployment rate turned out to be less than 5.0 percent. A formula might also be used that relates expected outcome to the value of the external factor—in this example, a formula that relates the expected percentage off welfare to the national unemployment rate.

The *target range option* applies to any outcome indicator for which major uncertainties exist as to future values. Many programs might benefit from this approach, especially for their end outcomes. A range of values, rather than one number, is given as the target for the indicator. For example:

- The customer satisfaction level is expected to be in the range of 80 percent to 87 percent.
- The percentage of clients who will be off illegal drugs 12 months after program completion is expected to be between 40 and 50 percent.

***The danger of gaming and ways to alleviate it.*** As the targets in budget documents begin to be taken seriously by higher level administrators as well as elected officials, the temptation to game targets will inevitably grow. Such gaming can occur at any level. Program managers and upper-level officials might set targets so that their projected outcomes will look good. (This is an argument for legislators to ask independent audit offices to review and comment on proposed budget targets, especially at the state and federal levels.) Elected officials might manipulate targets for a variety of political purposes.

Setting targets that are extremely easy to achieve will be tempting to those whose funding or individual compensation is based to any significant extent on achieving targets. The opposite—setting very optimistic, if not impossible, targets—is tempting to those seeking support for high budgets.

The following are some ways to alleviate gaming:

- Establish a multilevel review process in which executive personnel check targets to identify values that are overly optimistic or overly conservative on their face.
- Use one of the special target-setting options noted above to avoid a single-number target. These ranges can still be gamed, but the effects of gaming should be reduced.
- Explicitly identify in performance reports any future outcomes that are particularly difficult to estimate. Budget documents should also identify outcome indicators that are new, pointing out that setting targets for them is particularly difficult because there is no experience on which to base estimates.
- Ask programs to provide explanations for unusual-looking targets.
- Avoid major incentives linking funding or salary compensation to target achievement. However, pressure to link compensation to target achievement is likely to increase as agencies switch to outcome-based target-setting procedures; in such cases, an in-depth examination of the reasons for highly successful or highly unsuccessful outcomes should be undertaken before final funding or salary decisions are made.
- Examine the past relationships between inputs, outputs, and outcomes to see if the proposed targets are consistent with those relationships.

In some instances, executives and elected officials will prefer unclear, fuzzy goals. For example, school districts have debated whether they should include precise student test improvement objectives (such as increasing the overall scores by two percentage points or reducing the difference in performance between the minority and majority student population by three percentage points during the year). These officials might be willing to accept a target range (discussed above).

*Note:* Agency personnel are often reluctant to provide targets that are lower than the previous year's targets, even if budget-year resources are lower in real terms (i.e., after allowing for cost increases). They fear this will make them look bad. Even so, it is important that agencies and their individual programs realistically estimate the consequences of reduced resources. Agencies should encourage such reporting if it can be justified. Not being able to do everything they did in the previous year is not a basis for applying blame to programs if resources are cut. Upper management may believe that productivity improvements can make up for the reduced resources (and this may be true—up to a point). If political pressure requires that a program establish published targets that are higher than the program believes are achievable, the distinction should at least be made clear internally.

Setting performance targets is an excellent management tool for agencies, particularly if the targets are provided and progress is examined periodically during the year, such as monthly or quarterly. An agency can choose to retain an internal outcome-targeting process even if it does not use outcome targets in its budget process.

## 7. The Use of Explanatory Information

As discussed in chapter 10, agency programs should be encouraged to provide explanatory information along with their past performance measurement data when developing and submitting budget requests.

Persons preparing budgets should examine such information for insights into why the program performed well or poorly and for any suggestions as to what is needed to improve it. This information can also help identify program changes likely to have an effect on cost and outcome estimates.

As already noted, the results of any relevant program evaluations should be part of budget preparation and review. The findings on outcomes and the extent to which the program has been instrumental in producing the outcomes are likely to be important for judging the value of the current program. Persons who review the program's proposed budget can use later performance data to assess whether the proposed budget reflects the changes suggested by the evaluation. *Program evaluation findings should typically take precedence over findings from the agency's performance measurement system.*[11]

### A Special Concern with Targets

*Will reporting outcome targets increase liability for not achieving them?* In some situations, agencies may be concerned that reporting targets may increase their liability if the targets are not met, particularly when a standard is built into the indicator. Consider, for example, the outcome indicator "percent of time that responses to calls for emergency medical services exceeded X minutes." Does such an indicator increase the responsibility, and thus the liability, of an agency when the standard is not met? Can families successfully sue an agency if the response to their request exceeded the standard and the patient appeared to have added health complications as a result? These are legal questions an agency needs to address. It would not be surprising if liability litigation began to occur in such situations.

Nevertheless, for most performance indicators, liability does not seem likely to become an issue. It appears fairly clear that these targets are *projections* based on a variety of conditions and factors that can affect achievement of outcomes. Moreover, the target data in budgets are *grouped data*, not data for specific individuals or households. In any case, even if there is no formal performance measurement system, an agency can be subject to litigation if evidence exists that agency personnel performed irresponsibly in a case where serious damage resulted.

*Agency programs should also be encouraged to provide explanations for their targets, especially on key outcome indicators whose values deviate substantially from past results.* Such information should identify the basic assumptions used to develop the outcome projections and identify important external factors expected to cause the outcome value to deviate from past performance levels.

Explanatory information on past performance, including any available findings from recent program evaluations, can help identify the reasons for success or lack of it—that is, program strengths and weaknesses. Budget preparers and reviewers can then assess the extent to which steps have been taken, or are needed, to correct problems.

## 8. The Extent of Program Influence over Future Outcomes

Agency managers are usually quite apprehensive about including outcome indicators as a part of their performance measurements. As discussed in previous chapters, those managers often have only partial control over outcomes, especially end outcomes.

To alleviate this concern and give users of performance information a better perspective on the data's meaning, *a performance measurement system should consider categorizing each outcome indicator by the extent of the agency's influence over it* (see chapter 10). This will identify the extent to which the agency can affect each indicator relative to outside factors likely to have a major impact on the program's outcomes.[12] Note that *agencies and their programs may be able to have more influence than they think. Innovative approaches to their missions might well, in many instances, influence outcomes in meaningful ways, including making recommendations for legislative changes.*

Indicators need to be slotted into only a small number of broad categories, such as considerable influence, some influence, or little influence. (If the program has no influence over the value of a performance indicator, it should not be considered a performance indicator. For budget examination purposes, however, programs should be asked to identify the reasons why they think they have no influence.)

*Lack of influence may indicate that the program is not doing the right things, perhaps requiring major program changes.*

## 9. Steps for Using Performance Information in Formulating and Examining Budget Requests

The budget preparation and review process is intended to help ensure that needed resources are budgeted for the most cost-effective purpose.

The availability of data on past inputs, outputs, outcomes, and efficiency, as well as explanatory information, allows analysts to formulate and examine program budget proposals in a much more comprehensive and meaningful way than in the past. Outcome information, even if relatively crude and partial, enables analysts to consider both resource needs and results—and under what conditions results have been good or bad. This adds much more substance to a budget process. Chapter 10 described how to analyze *past* performance. Similar approaches are useful in results-based budgeting.

Some basic steps for developing and examining budget requests are listed in exhibit 12-4 and discussed below. Together, these steps represent a heavy workload for those reviewing or developing budget requests; however, they can be used selectively. The steps are also likely to be appropriate at any time during the year when a program seeks additional resources.

*A. Examine the budget submission to ascertain that it provides the latest information and targets on the amounts of workload, output, intermediate outcomes, and end outcomes—as well as the amounts of funds and personnel resources requested.* The budget submission should include past data on each indicator, the latest available outcome data for the current budget year, and the targets for the fiscal year(s) for which the budget is being submitted. If an indicator is too new for data or targets to be available, the submission should note this and indicate when data will be available (both actual data and targets).

If the program does not believe it can obtain numerical values for important indicators, the program should explain why and provide qualitative information on past and expected future progress.

*B. Assess whether the outcome indicators and targets are consistent with the mission of, and strategies proposed by, the program and provide adequate coverage of that mission.* If the agency's programs do not have explicit mission statements that adequately define their major objectives (such as those included in strategic plans) or descriptions of the strategies the programs propose to use to achieve the objectives, the reviewers will need to construct these—discussing them with program personnel as necessary.

For example, federal, state, or local litigation offices in their formal mission statements may have emphasized *deterrence of future criminal behavior*. Litigation programs, however, do not usually include indicators that explicitly address deterrence. The outcome indicators tracked will probably focus on bringing offenders to justice. From the program's viewpoint this is reasonable, but reviewers should consider whether it is feasible to track deterrence using counts of nondeterrence as a surrogate (i.e.,

EXHIBIT 12-4

## Steps for Examining Performance Information in Budget Requests

A.  Examine the budget submission to ascertain that it provides the latest information and targets on the amount of workload, output, intermediate outcomes, and end outcomes—as well as the amounts of funds and personnel resources requested.

B.  Assess whether the outcome indicators and targets are consistent with the mission of, and strategies proposed by, the program and provide adequate coverage of that mission.

C.  If the program is seeking an increase in resources, assess whether adequate information is provided on the amount by which each output and outcome indicator is expected to change over recent levels.

D.  Examine the projections for the program's budget year workload, outputs, intermediate outcomes, and end outcomes, as well as the amounts of funds and personnel. Make sure these numbers are consistent with one another (e.g., that the amount of output is consistent with the projected workload). Determine whether the program has included data on the results expected from the outputs it has identified.

E.  Compare *past data* on the amount of workload, output, intermediate outcomes, and end outcomes with the proposed budget targets. Identify unusually high or low projected outputs or outcomes.

F.  Examine the explanatory information provided by each program, especially for outcome indicators whose past values fell significantly below expectations and for any performance targets that appear unusually high or low.

G.  For programs likely to have delays or backlogs that might represent substantial problems in service delivery, be sure the data adequately cover the extent of delays, backlogs, and lack of coverage.

H.  For regulatory programs, be sure that adequate coverage is provided for compliance outcomes (not merely number of inspections).

I.  Ascertain that sufficient consideration has been given to possible changes in the program's workload that are likely to affect outcomes (such as higher or lower proportions of difficult workload).

J.  If recent outcomes for a program have been substantially worse than expected, make sure the program has included in its budget proposal the steps it plans to take toward improvement.

K.  Examine findings from any program evaluations or other special studies completed during the reporting period. Assess whether these have been adequately incorporated into the budget proposals.

L.  Determine whether the program has developed and used information on the relationship between resource requirements, outputs, and outcomes (e.g., the added number of dollars estimated to be needed to increase the number of successfully completed cases by a specified amount).

M.  Identify indicators for which significantly *reduced* outputs or outcomes are projected for the budget year (compared to recent performance data) without any decrease in funding (adjusted for projected price increases), staffing or output. Identify and assess the program's rationale for these.

N.  Identify outcome indicators for which significantly improved outcomes are projected by the program for the budget year (compared to recent performance data) without any increase in staffing, funding (adjusted for projected price increases), or output. Identify and assess the program's reasons for these.

O.  Identify what, if any, significant outcomes from the budgeted funds are expected to occur in years beyond the budget year. Assess whether they have been adequately identified and support the budget request.

P.  Identify any external factors not considered in the budget request that might significantly affect the funds needed or the outcomes projected. Make needed adjustments.

Q.  Compare the latest program performance data to those from any other programs with similar objectives for which similar past performance data are available. Assess whether projected performance is compatible with that achieved by similar programs.

R.  Identify any overarching outcome indicators that can provide a more meaningful and comprehensive perspective on results. Consider coordinating with other programs, other agencies, and other levels of government.

the amount of reported criminal behavior) or be content to seek qualitative information. (Note: measuring deterrence directly is usually best done, if done at all, through in-depth studies and not through a performance measurement process.) Reviewers might also decide that the litigation program does not in fact have the responsibility or the capacity for estimating prevention. They might determine that the mission statement was overstated and that the program's focus on number of offenders brought to justice is appropriate.

*C. If the program is seeking an increase in resources, assess whether adequate information is provided on the amount by which each output and outcome indicator is expected to change over recent levels.* The changes might be expressed as a special table showing pluses or minuses for each affected indicator. Programs need to make clear what effects their special proposals are expected to have on outputs and outcomes—not merely on funding and personnel resources.

*D. Examine the projections for the program's budget year workload, outputs, intermediate outcomes, and end outcomes, as well as the amount of funds and personnel. Make sure these numbers are consistent with each other (e.g., that the amount of output is consistent with the projected workload). Determine whether the program has included data on the results expected from the outputs it has identified.* Use steps such as those listed in exhibit 12-3 to develop and examine the targets. Output indicators normally should be included in the budget submission for each major category of workload. (Note: *outputs* represent completed work. *Workload* includes items that are pending but not yet begun and work in process.) Intermediate outcomes should be consistent with outputs and end outcomes with intermediate outcomes. If such information has not been included, the program can be asked to provide the needed data.

Those reviewing the proposed budget should assess the extent to which data on outcomes have been provided and appear reasonable. The data on outputs and outcomes should be checked for consistency with each other. For example, do the number of successes for a reporting period exceed the number of cases completed during that period?

Note, however, that substantial time lags can occur between the time a customer comes in for service and the outcomes. For example, the outcome indicator "percent of cases that were successful" should be derived by dividing the number of cases expected to be *successfully* completed during the budget year by the number of cases completed during the year, regardless of the year in which the case was initiated, not by the number of cases worked on or started during the budget year. Another example: The estimate for the outcome indicator "percent of child adoption cases in which the child was placed with adoptive parents within 24 months of the child's entry into the system" needs to be based on the number of children that came into the child welfare system two years before the budget year. Where appropriate outcome indicators and/or outcome data have not been provided, ask the program to provide them.

Two reminders:

- Outcomes can result from activities undertaken prior to the budget year. Also, some outcomes that originate in the budget year's funds take place after the budget year. The budget submission should identify such situations.
- In the initial years of introduction of the performance measurement system, programs may not be able to provide data on some outcome indicators.

E. *Compare* past data *on the amount of workload, output, intermediate outcomes, and end outcomes with the proposed budget targets. Identify unusually high or low projected outputs or outcomes.* This can be done in at least two ways:

- Compare the latest data on actual performance to those for previous reporting periods and to the proposed budget targets.
- Compare historical data on individual outcome indicators to the past targets set for those indicators to assess the program's accuracy in setting targets. In light of this past experience, assess the program's proposed targets. Some agencies may have a pattern of being highly optimistic about their ability to achieve outcomes; others may have a pattern of overly conservative targets. Budget analysts should take this into account as they interpret target achievement. Ideally, targets should be set at a level that encourages high, but achievable, performance. (The budget analysis office should keep track of the proclivities of individual program managers to set their targets overly high or low.)

Where projected performance values differ considerably from past values, or appear otherwise unusual, seek explanations as to why. Has the program provided any other information that explains this? If not, ask for explanations. For example, if a program has the same targets it had last year, and it fell far short of those targets, ask what has changed to make the targets more achievable this year. If the program is requesting a considerable increase in funds without increasing outcome targets over previous years' actual results, ask why the added funds are needed.

Lower projected values for outputs or outcomes may indicate reduced workload (check the related workload indicators), reduced resources (check the related expenditure and staffing amounts), unusually difficult or complex workload (check any evidence provided by the program), or reduced efficiency or effectiveness in delivering the service.

*F. Examine the explanatory information provided by each program, especially for outcome indicators whose past values fell significantly below expectations and for any performance targets that appear unusually high or low.* This step should be given special attention when any of the earlier steps indicate that the performance levels projected need further examination. Explanatory information should be examined before any conclusions are drawn as to the performance of the program and its resource implications.

Explanations can be substantive or be merely rationalizations or excuses. To assess the value of the explanations, the analysts may need to follow up with the program to clarify and/or obtain more information.

*G. For programs likely to have delays or backlogs that might represent substantial problems in program services, be sure the data adequately cover the extent of delays, backlogs, and lack of coverage.* Buildups of such problems can be a major justification for added resources. The size of any delays or backlogs, and the extent to which these may be growing, can be important customer-focused, quality-of-service performance indicators for social, health, welfare, loan, licensing, and many other programs. For legal prosecutions and court cases, "justice delayed is justice denied."

Conversely, if a program's indicators show no evidence of significant delays, this is evidence that existing resource levels are adequate for the future—unless the program provides evidence that a significant buildup of its future workload is likely. If the program can systematically categorize its incoming caseload by level of difficulty or complexity (as agencies should encourage all their programs to do—see chapter 8), it should also project the size of its caseload by difficulty or complexity as a factor in determining its proposed budget. *Is there any evidence that the program is now getting or expects to get more complex and/or more difficult cases?* If so, this would provide justification for additional resources.

Indicators that programs can be asked to provide include:

- Counts of the number of cases pending and projected at the end of each year (tracked over time, this will indicate buildups)
- Indicators of the time it has taken and is expected to take, given proposed budget resources, to complete various activities
- Estimates of the number of cases that will have to be turned away (for programs that have the discretion to turn them away)

*H. For regulatory programs, be sure that adequate coverage is provided for compliance outcomes (not merely numbers of inspections).* Examples include environmental regulations, civil rights programs, and regulatory boards. The analysts should ascertain that the outputs and outcomes of compliance-monitoring activities are identified. For example, do the indicators report on outputs (such as the number of needed inspections that are actually expected to be done), and the intervals at which they are expected to be done? Do the indicators report on such outcomes as the percent of organizations found in the past to be in compliance as a percent of those monitored, or those scheduled to be monitored during the budget year that will be found to be in noncompliance? Do the monitoring resources proposed in the budget appear too little or too large compared to the expected outcomes?

*I. Ascertain that sufficient consideration has been given to possible changes in the program's workload that are likely to affect outcomes (such as higher or lower proportions of difficult workload).* Programs may not report such breakouts in their budget submissions, but they are often able to supply such information. (Note that programs should be encouraged, *for their own data analyses,* to break out their outcome data by various work and customer characteristics, such as type of case, its difficulty, and different locations or facilities.) For example, federal and state correctional facilities will probably have internal reports on individual facilities and facility categories, such as security level and type of prisoner. Health and human services programs can probably provide some service data on individual facilities or offices and on various demographic groupings of clients.

Examine whether the outcomes are substantially different for some service characteristics (such as some facilities or regions) than for others. If so, examine why. This information can be very helpful in interpreting a program's projected outcome data. For example, certain types of locations or cases may be considerably more difficult to handle than others, suggesting that lower than desired projected performance is due to an increase in the proportion of difficult cases and thus providing a supportable case for lower outcomes. Budget reviewers should look for evidence that more difficult cases are likely to come in during the budget year.

Comparing outcomes among demographic groups is also important in assessing equity and fairness. Are some groups being underserved? Should additional resources be applied to those groups? Even though identifying who loses and who gains can be a political hazard, the information is basic to resource allocation. It needs to be addressed.

*J. If recent outcomes for a program have been substantially worse than expected, make sure the program has included in its budget proposal the steps it plans to take toward improvement.* If the program projects improved performance, are the resources and planned steps commensurate? If not, why not? (For example, substantial time may be needed between the time that funding is approved, implementation, and the consequences of the funded activities for achievement of certain outcomes.)

*K. Examine findings from any program evaluations or other special studies completed during the reporting period. Assess whether these have been adequately incorporated into the budget proposals.* This includes studies that might have been produced by other organizations. Such information may provide added support for the activities and budget proposed by the program, or it may contradict the findings produced by the program to support its proposed activities and budget.

*L. Determine whether the program has developed and used information on the relationship between resource requirements, outputs, and outcomes (e.g., the added number of dollars estimated to be needed to increase the number of successfully completed cases by a specified amount).* Assess that information for plausibility. Few programs are likely to have undertaken much systematic analysis of this relationship. Programs should be encouraged to do so to help substantiate future budget requests.

Relating expenditures and resources to outcomes (both intermediate and end outcomes) is usually difficult and uncertain. However, to the extent that additional dollars and staff enable the program to take on more work (more customers, more investigations, more road repairs, more inspections, etc.), the program can probably estimate roughly how much additional work it can handle based on past performance information. For example, a program may be able to estimate the percent of cases or incidents it might not be able to handle (such as identifying illegal immigrants) without the added funding requested.

Many, if not most, programs will be highly reluctant to make the cost-to-output and cost-to-outcome relationships that underlie their budget requests explicit. They may even believe it cannot be done. However, these relationships are at the heart of resource allocation decisions, implicitly if not explicitly, and the program should be pushed to be as explicit as possible about them. *After all, the projected targets the program sets each year on the basis of its outcome indicators by definition imply such relationships, however rough the estimates may be.*

A program seeking additional resources will tend to be overly optimistic about the outcomes that will result. Budget analysts should look for supportable estimates of the relationships between resource requirements (dollars and personnel) and at least approximate values for each outcome indicator.

Over the long run, programs should be encouraged to develop information about these relationships. The analysis needed for such studies usually requires special background, however, which is not likely to be in place in most programs. Analytical staffs, whether attached to each program or to a central analysis office, need to be developed for the purpose.

**M. Identify indicators for which significantly reduced outputs or outcomes are projected for the budget year (compared to recent performance data) without any decrease in funding (adjusted for projected price increases) or staffing. Identify and assess the program's rationale for these.** Reduced funding or staffing projections are obviously plausible rationales for reduced outcome projections, as is a more difficult or complex workload in the new year. If the program has been systematically categorizing its incoming caseload by level of difficulty or complexity, it should be able to provide evidence supporting a reduction. The program might already have in its pipeline many especially difficult cases. For example, litigation or investigation programs may be working on a number of cases that are highly complex and require considerable additional program resources.

Other possible reasons for lower outcome targets include (a) an unexpected jump in workload during the budget year without an accompanying increase in resources, leading to reductions in the percent of cases for which the program can produce successful outcomes; (b) new legislative or agency policies that add complications or restrictions, reducing the probability of successful outcomes in certain categories of cases; and (c) external events that would impair outcomes, such as the expected departure of key industries from a community, affecting local employment and income.

**N. Identify outcome indicators for which significantly improved outcomes are projected by the program for the budget year (compared to recent**

*performance data) without any increase in staffing, funding (adjusted for projected price increases), or output. Identify and assess the program's reasons for these.* Budget reviewers should ask the program how it expects to achieve the improved performance—to check the plausibility of the higher targets. Such improvements might occur if the program plans to improve the efficiency of its operations. Another reasonable rationale is that the program expects its workload to be easier or less complex. The program may already have in its pipeline cases that it expects to be successful in the budget year.

*O. Identify what, if any, significant outcomes from the budgeted funds are expected to occur in years beyond the budget year. Assess whether they have been adequately identified and support the budget request.* As noted earlier, many programs and their activities affect outcomes in years beyond the budget year (particularly federal and state programs that work through other levels of government and any investment programs). To justify expenditures for such activities, programs should project these expenditures' effects on the various outcomes for years beyond the budget year. The program should also provide rationales for such projections. Budget analysts should review these rationales for plausibility. This point was discussed further in the section on linking inputs to outputs and outcomes.

*P. Identify any external factors not considered in the budget request that might significantly affect the funds needed or the outcomes projected. Make needed adjustments.* The persons examining the budget request may be privy to information not available to those preparing it. For example, newly proposed or passed legislation or recently released economic forecasts can have major effects on the outcome projections.

*Q. Compare the latest program performance data to those from any other programs with similar objectives for which similar past performance data are available. Assess whether projected performance is compatible with that achieved by similar programs.* This point and the next are resource allocation issues that cross program lines. Agency budget analysts should consider the performance experience of other, similar programs even if the programs are in another agency. Are the program's past accomplishments poor relative to similar programs? If so, work with program personnel to determine why and identify what can be done to improve future performance. Make any resource judgments that such future actions might entail. Does the program complement or overlap other programs' efforts? If they are complementary, check whether the data are consistent among the programs. If they overlap, consider whether altered resource allocations might be appropriate to reduce the overlap.

**R.** *Identify any overarching outcome indicators that can provide a more meaningful and comprehensive perspective on results. Consider coordinating with other programs, other agencies, and other levels of government.* Few programs produce outcomes alone, especially end outcomes. This is a core concern in performance measurement. Programs related to employment, youth development, substance abuse, crime, and so on generally involve scores of other programs that also influence the desired ends. For example, crime control involves investigation, apprehension, adjudication, punishment, and probably a variety of social services. Each component is critical to final success, and each is handled by different programs and agencies.

Analysts should attempt to derive some consolidated outcome indicators for programs within an agency. *The agency should also coordinate and collaborate with other agencies—at the same level, at other levels of government, and in the private sector—in measuring progress and in determining the roles and responsibilities of each in achieving jointly targeted outcomes.*

> *Example:* Reduced drug and alcohol abuse involves many different programs, agencies, and sectors. Each agency with a substantial role in helping reduce substance abuse should track the overall incidence and prevalence (but one agency would normally be responsible for data collection)—recognizing that theirs is a shared responsibility. Each program is likely to have its own intermediate outcome indicators and to focus on but one part of the overall problem (such as on reducing drug abuse by one age group).[13]

## 10. Applying Results-Based Budgeting to Internal Support Services

Governments at all levels and private agencies support a variety of administrative functions, such as building maintenance, facilities maintenance, information technology, human resources, risk management, purchasing, and accounting. The linkage between the products of such activities and public service outcomes is distant and usually extremely difficult or impossible to determine, even roughly.[14]

These activities are nonetheless important in providing needed support for operating programs. Good management requires that administrative services track their own intermediate outcomes (such as the quality of their services to other agency offices). The principles and procedures described in earlier chapters can be readily adapted to administrative services. For example, the types of data collection described in chapter 7—agency records, customer surveys, and trained observer ratings—can be used to obtain data on service quality.

### 11. Using Results-Based Budgeting for Capital Budgeting

Many state and local governments prepare separate capital budgets. Sometimes these take the form of multiyear capital improvement programs, but typically, they list proposed projects and the estimated capital funds required for each in the budget year. Multiyear plans usually contain such information for each out-year. These plans may include general statements as to the purposes of the expenditures *but seldom contain information about their expected effects on outcomes.*

There is no reason why results-based budgeting should not apply to capital budgets. The agency should gain experience with result-based budgeting and then call for the explicit estimation of the effects of major capital expenditures on outcomes. For example, planned capital expenditures for road rehabilitation might be justified in terms of their expected effects on future road conditions, such as added rideability and safety, compared to the conditions that would occur without the capital expenditures. Similarly, funds for water and sewer purposes should be related to projected improvements in water quality and health protection. For capital projects that primarily benefit particular segments of the community, estimates should be provided as to who is expected to benefit.

Many agencies are also faced periodically with the need to make investments in information technology. These investments should be assessed not only on the basis of their effects on future expenditures but also on their expected benefits. For example, to what extent does the proposed technology reduce response times to customers or change the accuracy of service delivery?

Some capital expenditures, such as those for administrative services, do not lend themselves well to linkage with end outcomes. New construction of office buildings is a good example. For this construction, a performance measurement system might track such internal outcomes as being completed on time, being completed within budget, and user ratings of the quality of the facilities built.

The purpose here is not to expect exact numbers but to obtain rough, yet supportable figures. Decisionmakers and the public should not be expected to make capital investment decisions without information on the benefits expected from these expenditures.

## 12. "Budgeting-by-Objectives"

Conceptually, it makes sense for a department to submit budgets with proposed funding grouped by major objectives.[15] For example, child abuse prevention, alcohol abuse reduction, unemployment assistance, and traffic accident reduction might be major sections. All activities related to the particular objective would be included, regardless of which program or agency is involved. Budgeting-by-objectives was a characteristic of the original program budgeting and PPBS (Planning-Programming-Budgeting-System) in the late 1960s and 1970s. However, this approach has yet to be seen outside the Department of Defense.

The major question that confronts departments if they try this approach is how to sort out objectives and programs. Most programs have multiple objectives, and their personnel and other resources simultaneously affect more than one objective. The crosswalk between objectives and programs or agencies can be quite cumbersome. If some activities simultaneously affect more than one objective, how should costs be split between them, or should they be split at all? For example, transportation programs can influence multiple objectives across a wide range of the policy spectrum, including (a) making transportation quick and convenient; (b) enhancing health and safety; and (c) protecting the environment.

At this point, it is by no means clear whether budgeting-by-objectives can be made practical. Providing crosswalks linking activities to each outcome, however, does seem a reasonable approach for modern information technology (as has been done by the state of North Carolina). Agency programs that contribute to several outcomes can be coded to identify which programs contribute to which outcomes.[16]

## 13. The Use of Special Analytical Techniques

Estimating future costs, and especially future outcomes, can be very difficult, as already emphasized. Program analysis (sometimes called cost-effectiveness analysis) and cost-benefit analysis are techniques that can help agencies select program variations that should be budgeted and help estimate the outcomes from them. These techniques have been around for many years, but their use in budget preparation and review is not common.

This book will not detail these techniques, but the following brief review identifies the major features of each that can help in results-based budgeting.[17]

***Program analysis.*** This term is applied to *special quantitative analyses used to estimate the future costs and effectiveness of alternative ways to deliver* *a service.* While program evaluation is retrospective, program analysis is prospective. The Department of Defense is one of the few agencies in the country that have designated personnel to undertake regular program analysis. Otherwise, systematic program analysis has not taken hold in the public sector or in nongovernmental organizations. The Department of Health, Education, and Welfare (now the Department of Health and Human Services) and the state of Pennsylvania had special offices with such expertise in the 1960s, when these were fashionable as part of PPBS efforts, but later discontinued them. While some agencies currently have policy analysis shops, these are usually heavily qualitative. Program evaluation offices may sometimes take on this role, since some of the same technical skills are involved. Program evaluations are of value when findings are used to help make decisions about the future.

For results-based budgeting, program analysis is particularly helpful when an agency proposes to introduce a new service delivery approach or a significant variation of an existing approach. Unless the delivery approach being proposed closely resembles an approach for which relevant past data are available, projecting costs and outcomes from past data is not terribly useful.

Agencies can consider doing pilot tests or experiments (as discussed in chapter 9), using the performance measurement system to provide data on the old and the new service approaches and then using that information as the basis for estimating outcomes and costs. These procedures are worthwhile if the agency can wait to make its final decision until the test has been completed and the findings have become available. If not, program analysis techniques can be considered.

As the use of performance measurement, and particularly results-based budgeting, grows, the need to project outcomes systematically will also grow. The field of program analysis may then stage a comeback.

*Cost-benefit analysis.* Cost-benefit analysis goes one step further than program analysis. It is used to provide a *monetary estimate of the value of a program.* (Cost-benefit analysis can also be used to help evaluate the value of a program's past performance.) Its key characteristic is that it translates nonmonetary outcomes into monetary ones, which are then combined and compared to the program's expenditures—allowing calculation of cost-benefit ratios and estimates of the difference in the monetary values of the costs and benefits. Before the calculations into monetary values can be done, the basic outcome values (usually measured in nonmonetary units) are needed. That is, program analysis needs to be done first. Cost-benefit analysis adds an additional, usually difficult, step to the process.

The monetary value of many outcomes has to be *imputed* in some way. For example, an estimate that X number of traffic accidents could be avoided by a particular activity needs to be converted into monetary estimates of the costs of those accidents, including damage repair, hospital and other health care, time lost from work, and the economic value of any lives lost. The costs of the activity being considered would then be compared to these dollar valuations and a cost-benefit ratio calculated.

Sound cost-benefit analysis, whether of past program accomplishments or projected program value, can provide major backup information for program budget requests. Such calculations can also appeal to public and private officials, because most outcomes are converted into dollars and summarized in one number (the cost-benefit ratio), which can be interpreted as the value of the program. One summary number is much easier for decisionmakers to handle. The usual application of this approach is to compare options within a single service area, but it could also be used to compare programs across services.

Cost-benefit analysis has a number of drawbacks. The calculations of monetary value usually require numerous assumptions that can be quite controversial. For example, how should the value of lost work time or of deaths be determined? (The value of lives lost has sometimes been estimated based on the economic potential of persons at particular ages. This sounds like a reasonable approach, but giving elderly persons little or no value in the calculations implies that it is all right to "knock off" elderly persons.) Another problem is that the monetary values often accrue to different populations from the populations that pay the costs. For example, revenues for most government expenditures are raised by taxes from the general public and businesses, but the benefits often accrue primarily to particular groups.

If carefully done and carefully used, cost-benefit calculations can provide insights as to the expected value of the proposed budget for a program. However, cost-benefit analysis reports should *always* spell out the value assumptions used so that readers can better understand the basis for the findings.

Cost-benefit analysis tends to be time-consuming and expensive, and it can be used only very selectively. Its primary user has been the federal government. The Army Corps of Engineers has undertaken many such studies when selecting major water and other construction projects. Cost-benefit analysis has also been used, and sometimes mandated, for federal regulatory programs.

### 14. The Role of Qualitative Outcome Information in Results-Based Budgeting

As discussed in chapter 6, not all outcomes can be adequately measured in quantitative terms. An agency's budget process should at least *qualitatively* consider the implications of the budget for desired (and undesired) outcomes. Explicitly including the consideration of outcomes in the budget, and in the political debate over amounts and allocations, even if outcomes can only be expressed qualitatively, can help improve decisions on expenditures.

## Summary of the Relationship between Performance Measurement and Results-Based Budgeting

The primary uses of performance data in budgeting are to help formulate the budget and to make a more convincing case for the budget recommendations. Performance information, especially if it includes credible outcome data, should lead to better choices and more convincing choices than are possible in its absence. Outcome targets for the budget year also establish a baseline for accountability (encouraging reviews of actual accomplishments throughout the year and at year's end).

Performance measurement of outputs, outcomes, and efficiency for past years is important for budget allocation decisions. First, the performance information provides baseline data on outcomes, which is fundamental for making decisions. *If you do not know where you are, you will have difficulty determining where you need to go.* Second, historical data are usually a primary *basis* for budget projections of future accomplishments.

Making projections for the budget year and beyond is considerably more difficult and is subject to *much* more uncertainty than measuring past performance. The future is very hard to predict, even if for only one or two years, because of the many external factors beyond the control of agencies that can affect results. This problem becomes particularly troublesome if the program is suggesting significantly new program variations or new programs to tackle its mission. Then past data will be a much less adequate guide to the future.

However uncertain the data, addressing the relationship of inputs to outcomes should be a major issue in making resource allocation decisions and budget justifications in any budgeting system. *Even if such discussions are heavily qualitative and judgmental, they are far better than nothing, because they encourage those making budget decisions to focus on what is most important to achieve.*

The budget review effort should be viewed as an opportunity for both the program and the agency's budget review staff to develop the best possible budget, to make the best possible case for budget requests, and to focus attention on maximizing outcomes for a given amount of resources. The inherent tension between budget analysts who perceive their primary job as keeping costs to a minimum and program personnel (who want to obtain as many resources as they can) will inevitably pose problems. The two groups will find the process much less difficult and less contentious if they work to make it as much of a partnership as possible. The interests of both groups are best served if the final resource allocation decisions forwarded to higher levels are presented as effectively as possible. These days, that means proposals need to be justified, at least in part, on the basis of outcomes—the potential benefits to the public.

## References and Notes

1. This is discussed at length in The International Bank for Reconstruction and Development, *Public Expenditure Management Handbook* (Washington, D.C.: The World Bank, 1998).
2. North Carolina Office of State Budget and Management, *Instructions for Preparation of the 1999–2001 Recommended State Budget and the Biennial State Plan* (Raleigh, April 1998).
3. Personal communication, David Strauhs, Commissioner of Massachusetts Department of Environmental Protection, December 4, 1997.
4. Note on terminology: The word *target* is not always used. The Government Performance and Results Act of 1993 uses the term *annual goals*. Another terminology problem arises for programs, such as law enforcement, in which the word *targets* for some outputs or intermediate outcomes might be interpreted as establishing quotas, such as on the number of arrests, prosecutions, or collections. For this reason, programs whose missions are investigative, such as criminal investigation activities, might use another, more neutral, label, such as *projections*.
5. The terms *performance-based budgeting* and *budgeting-for-results* are also used.
6. See, for example, The Treasury, Government of New Zealand, *Purchase Agreement Guidelines 1995/96: With Best Practices for Output Performance Measures* (Wellington, April 1995). For more on the New Zealand effort, see Allen Schick, *The Spirit of Reform: Managing the New Zealand State Sector in a Time of Change* (Wellington: State Services Commission, 1996).
7. This book does not address the many issues involved in developing comprehensive cost estimates for particular programs, such as how to handle indirect or capital costs. For many public and private agencies, cost accounting is deficient. Efforts such as activity-based costing may help, but they still have substantial limitations for projecting future costs. More important for budget formulation is for agencies to have good cost *analysis* capability—that is, to be able to make estimates of the likely *additional*

expenditures that will be incurred to produce particular outcome levels. One approach to cost analysis is contained in David H. Greenberg and Ute Appenzeller, *Cost Analysis Step by Step: A How-to Guide for Planners and Providers of Welfare-to-Work and Other Employment Training Programs* (New York: Manpower Demonstration Research Corporation, October 1998).

8. This, however, can be a major problem for developing countries that have not yet established reasonably accurate procedures for keeping track of expenditures and outputs.

9. Those readers who do not believe that response times to requests for services should be labeled an outcome might prefer a label such as *quality-of-output* indicator.

10. For the application of performance targeting in other countries, see Sylvie Trosa, "Public Sector Reform Strategy: A Giant Leap or a Small Step?" in *Monitoring Performance in the Public Sector: Future Directions from International Experience*, ed. John Mayne and Eduardo Zapico-Goni (New Brunswick, N.J.: Translation Publishers, 1997).

11. Preferably, an agency would sponsor in-depth program evaluations for each of its major programs, say, once every few years. New programs might be required to provide an evaluation strategy. Unfortunately, in-depth evaluations are expensive and time-consuming. Agencies and programs with highly limited resources might instead schedule periodic, but less comprehensive, reviews of each of their programs to learn more about how well they are working and why.

12. Degree of influence does not refer to the ability of an agency or program to *manipulate* the data to its own advantage. That is a quality control issue, discussed in chapter 13.

13. The U.S. Office of Drug Control Policy has been a leading agency in attempting to work out such cooperative efforts among federal, state, local, and foreign governments. See Office of National Drug Control Policy, *Performance Measures of Effectiveness: A System for Assessing the Performance of the National Drug Control Strategy*, Report no. NCJ 168953 (Washington, D.C.: Office of National Drug Control Policy, 1998).

14. The costs of support services, however, need to be considered when analyzing the total costs of a program and comparing its costs to its benefits.

15. This approach is discussed in Mark Friedman, *A Guide to Developing and Using Performance Measures in Results-Based Budgeting* (Washington, D.C.: The Finance Project, May 1997).

16. An example of this is the crosswalk developed by the Oregon Progress Board and the Department of Administrative Services, *1999 Benchmark Blue Books: Linking Oregon Benchmarks and State Government Programs* (Salem, May 1999).

17. See Selected Readings for readings on these topics.

# Other Performance Measurement Issues

Joseph S. Wholey

# Chapter 13

"In God We Trust. Everyone else we audit!"
"Nothing increases your golf score like witnesses."

# Quality Control: Assessing the Accuracy and Usefulness of Performance Measurement Systems

As more performance measurement systems have been implemented, policymakers, managers, auditors, and evaluators have begun to focus on quality control issues—those related to assessing the accuracy and usefulness of performance measurement systems. Usually, quality control does not get much attention in the early stages of developing and implementing a performance measurement system. Only after performance data are reviewed do potential users begin raising questions about the information's validity, reliability, relevance, and usefulness. *It is preferable to consider ways to ensure reasonable quality of the performance measurement process from the beginning*—to help build accuracy and usefulness into the design of the measurement system and into the training of personnel.

This chapter presents criteria for judging the quality of a performance measurement system and suggests ways they can be applied and by whom. The chapter ends by applying the criteria to two performance measurement systems judged to be of good quality.

One approach to judge quality is to focus mainly on technical quality—the extent to which performance data provide a clear, accurate picture of agency

The author of this chapter is affiliated with the University of Southern California (USC) and the U.S. General Accounting Office (GAO). The views and opinions expressed are his own and should not be construed to be the policy or position of USC or GAO.

and program performance. Another approach is to focus mainly on agency use of performance measures in management and reporting. The assumption underlying reliance on the second approach is that, if agencies are really *using* performance measures, most of the other criteria will be met.

Both are legitimate perspectives. Clearly, the technical quality of performance measurement systems is important, but its usefulness is at least as important. Performance information is intended to be used by managers, policymakers, and others affected by or interested in agency or program activities to (a) improve agency and program management and performance, (b) increase accountability to key stakeholders and the public, and (c) support resource allocation and other policy decisionmaking. If performance measures are inaccurate (invalid or unreliable), performance measurement can be expected to lead to poor decisions. Use of performance information by program managers, higher-level officials, and legislators should therefore encourage agencies to be concerned about data quality.

*Note on system cost:* The cost of performance measurement is always a significant issue. Whether the primary purpose of a performance measurement system is improvement of performance, accountability, or support for decisionmaking, agencies must balance the cost of performance data against the value added. Finding the appropriate balance is the key. Costs of performance measurement systems include management, staff, and other stakeholders' time used in designing the measurement systems; management and staff time required to collect, analyze, and use performance data; costs of any contracts for data collection and analysis; the burden imposed on reporting entities; and other political and bureaucratic costs. In assessing performance measurement systems, therefore, the ultimate questions are: Are the performance data sufficiently accurate and useful to justify the cost of the performance measurement system? Would changes in the performance measurement system make the performance data less costly, more accurate, or more useful?

Concern with the cost of performance measurement is a subsidiary theme in this chapter. Its central focus is on the criteria and processes that managers, auditors, evaluators, and others can use to assess the accuracy and usefulness of performance measurement systems.

## Criteria for Assessing Quality

Exhibit 13-1 displays suggested criteria for assessing performance measurement systems. These criteria are drawn from the Government Performance and Results Act, technical quality standards, expert opinion, and the

**Criteria for Assessing Performance Measurement Systems**

**A. Are the Prerequisites for Useful Performance Measurement in Place?**

*Criterion 1: Agreed-on goals and strategies are in place.* There is a reasonable level of agreement among senior officials, managers, staff, and other key stakeholders on agency or program goals (including outcome-related goals) and on the resources, activities, and processes required to achieve the goals.

*Criterion 2: The performance measurement system is of sufficient technical quality* to assess and report on performance in terms of the agreed-on goals. The system provides data that are sufficiently complete, accurate, and consistent to document performance and support decisionmaking (see exhibit 13-2).

**B. Is the Performance Information Used?**

*Criterion 3: Performance information is used in managing the agency or program* to achieve performance goals: for example, by creating intangible or tangible incentives for improved program performance, reallocating resources to improve performance, or redirecting program activities to improve performance (see exhibit 13-5).

*Criterion 4: A reasonable degree of accountability is provided.* Performance information is used to document the extent of progress toward agency or program goals. Performance information is used to communicate the value of agency or program activities to key stakeholders and the public.

*Criterion 5: More effective or improved performance is demonstrated*, indicating that agreed-on goals have been met or that current performance exceeds prior performance.

*Criterion 6: Performance information supports resource allocation or other policy decisionmaking.* Policymakers within or above the agency use performance information in resource allocation; development of legislation, regulations, or guidelines; and other policy decisionmaking.

experiences of leading public sector organizations. In this exhibit and the discussion that follows, the criteria are grouped under two overarching questions: (a) Are the prerequisites for useful performance measurement in place (*criteria* 1 and 2)? (b) Is the performance information used (*criteria* 3–6)?

## *Are the Prerequisites for Useful Performance Measurement in Place?*

Two prerequisites are needed for useful performance measurement systems: (a) that within the department or agency and among its key stakeholders there is a reasonable level of agreement on goals and strategies for achieving the goals and (b) that the measurement system is technically capable of documenting performance in a way that supports decisionmaking.

*Criterion 1: Agreed-on goals and strategies are in place.* In order to assess the quality and usefulness of a performance measurement system, one must first have a basic understanding of what is to be assessed. There must be a reasonable level of agreement among senior officials, managers, staff, and other key stakeholders on strategic or performance goals (performance targets) and on the resources, activities, and processes required to meet those goals. As discussed in chapter 4, though differences will always exist, agencies can often agree broadly on goals and strategies through planning processes that include broad consultation with (a) managers and staff, (b) those who influence the allocation of needed resources, (c) those who make other policy decisions affecting the agency or program, and (d) other key stakeholders affected by or interested in agency or program activities.

Agencies should define performance broadly enough to cover the dimensions that are important to the primary intended users of performance information. To meet concerns raised by Radin[1] and others, the definition should be extended to include minimizing or controlling important unintended outcomes of agency or program activities, such as corruption, creaming, other failures to provide fair treatment, or costs incurred by individuals or organizations as they respond to agency or program activities. Managers and staff can use logic models to ensure that they have identified relevant elements of the program design: key program inputs, activities, outputs, intermediate outcomes, end outcomes, assumed causal linkages, and key external factors that could significantly affect performance (see chapter 5). If agency or program managers have not developed appropriate logic models, auditors or evaluators can develop such models for them.

Rarely will a single performance measurement system meet the information needs of all key stakeholders. Different performance measurement systems often pull managers and staff in different directions. *The usefulness of performance measurement will increase to the extent that the measurement systems reflect and relate to a coherent set of goals and strategies covering major agency programs and activities.* Those reviewing performance measurement systems for quality control need to assess the extent to which the agency has achieved reasonable agreement on defining performance. As the U.S. General Accounting Office (GAO) puts it, results-oriented organizations:

- Involve their stakeholders
- Assess their internal and external environments
- Align their activities, core processes, and resources to support mission-related outcomes.[2]

*Criterion 2: The performance measurement system is of sufficient technical quality.* As agencies implement performance measurement systems, they should balance the costs of data collection against the need to ensure that the data are sufficiently complete, accurate, and consistent to document performance and support decisionmaking at various organizational levels. In particular, the data must be sufficiently free of bias and other significant errors that would affect conclusions about the extent to which program goals have been achieved.

A particular source of potential bias that needs to be guarded against is the incentive for employees to game the system by manipulating indicator values to make their performance look good. A classic example of such ingenuity in circumventing quality control procedures took place in West Virginia. The Postal Service has for many years funded a contractor to mail letters quarterly from various locations to assess delivery times. (This is a form of the trained observer rating procedures discussed in chapter 7.) A window clerk in a West Virginia post office somehow became alerted that a particular batch of letters were part of this test mailing and notified other post offices around the state about the addresses involved. Post offices in the state gave special attention to those letters to ensure quick delivery times.[3]

---

**EXHIBIT 13-2**

**Dimensions of Technical Quality in Performance Measurement Systems**

*A. Demonstrate results:* Performance indicators should tell each organizational level how well it is achieving its goals, for example, those related to intermediate outcomes, end outcomes, or productivity.

*B. Cover a few vital indicators:* The number of performance indicators for each goal at a given organizational level should be limited to the vital few. These indicators should cover the key performance dimensions that will enable an organization to assess accomplishments, make decisions, realign processes, and assign accountability.

*C. Respond to multiple priorities:* Performance measurement systems at each organizational level should take into account factors such as quality, cost, customer satisfaction, and stakeholder concerns—and create incentives for managers to strike the difficult balance among competing demands. These systems should cover the performance dimensions—the outputs and outcomes—that are important to the primary intended users of the performance information.

*D. Link to responsible programs:* Performance indicators should be linked to program offices that have responsibility for making programs work.

*E. Be complete, accurate, and consistent:* Performance data should meet reasonable tests of validity, reliability, and timeliness. As agencies implement performance measurement systems, they should balance the costs of data collection against the need to ensure that data meet these tests. Agencies should periodically review data collection procedures and the completeness, accuracy, and consistency of at least a sample of the data.

**Sources:** Adapted from U.S. General Accounting Office, *Executive Guide: Effectively Implementing the Government Performance and Results Act* (Washington, D.C., 1996) and Harry P. Hatry, working paper (Washington, D.C.: Urban Institute, 1997).

---

To meet criterion 2, the technical quality of the system and the data it produces must be assessed along a number of dimensions (exhibit 13-2). Tension among the various quality dimensions and between quality dimensions and cost are inevitable. To the extent that performance measurement systems focus on results or outcomes (*dimension A*), for example, performance measurement will tend to be more costly and it may be more difficult to ensure that performance data are sufficiently accurate (*dimension E*). Similarly, *dimension B* encourages the limitation of performance measurement systems to a small number of key performance indicators for each goal at each organizational level, whereas *dimension C* encourages greater comprehensiveness and tends to increase the costs of performance measurement.

Whatever the data source on which a performance measurement system is based—agency or program records, records of other agencies, surveys, or ratings by experts or trained observers—technical quality issues can arise. Exhibit 13-3 presents questions for use in assessing a system's technical quality.

Though managers typically have more ongoing contextual information than policymakers, both groups need formal assurance that agencies and programs have in place reasonable quality control processes that review data collection procedures and test the validity and reliability of at least a sample of data periodically.

An example of a process for ensuring technical quality is the Department of Education's strategy for strengthening the quality of its performance data. The department's plans, listed in exhibit 13-4, include developing departmentwide standards for performance measurement; training employees in the application of the standards; standardizing definitions of key variables; coordinating data collection across information systems; having managers, as part of their performance agreements, attest to the reliability and validity of their program performance data or submit plans for data improvement; and using audits and evaluation studies to strengthen the quality of performance data. The department's draft includes data quality standards for accuracy, comparability, editing, calculations, timeliness, and reporting.

## Is the Performance Information Used?

Performance measurement systems are intended to be useful to managers, policymakers, and other key stakeholders affected by or interested in the program. These systems should, therefore, cover the key performance dimensions that are important to all major intended users of the information. When the quality control reviewers are satisfied about the technical quality of the performance measurement system, they then need to explore how the information the system produces is actually used.

EXHIBIT 13-3

**Questions for Use in Assessing the Technical Quality of Performance Measurement Systems**

### I. Validity

1. *Completeness:* Do the performance indicators cover the performance dimensions that are important to the intended users of the information? Are the data timely?
2. *Accuracy:* Do the performance indicators measure what they purport to measure? Are samples representative? Are there sufficient staff for data collection? Are response rates sufficiently large? Are planned observations completed? May managers or staff be manipulating performance data to serve their own interests?

### II. Reliability

3. *Consistency:* Are samples large enough to yield reliable data? Do repeated measurements yield the same results? Do measurements by different staff members yield the same results? Are data from different offices, projects, or organizations based on similar definitions of data elements and data collection procedures?

### III. Validity and Reliability

4. *Data Collection Procedures:* Are there flaws or errors in collecting, recording, or transcribing data? Are performance data analyzed for inconsistencies or unusually high or low values?
5. *Data Maintenance Procedures:* Are there adequate procedures for maintaining data? May records be altered, lost, or incorrectly transferred?
6. *Data Analysis Procedures:* Are data analyses done correctly? Are correct formulas used in analyzing and summarizing information?

### IV. Other

7. Do staff have the training required to collect sufficiently complete, consistent, and accurate data?
8. Does the agency have procedures for ensuring that performance data are free of significant error and that bias is not introduced?
9. Do the agency's procedures provide for periodic review of data collection, maintenance, and processing procedures to ensure that they are consistently applied?
10. Do the agency's procedures provide for periodic sampling and review of performance data to ensure that they are sufficiently complete, accurate, and consistent?
11. Do the agency's procedures call for formal assessments of performance data by external parties?
12. Do the agency's procedures address known problems in data quality?
13. Does the agency certify the accuracy and completeness of its data and identify any limitations?

**Sources:** Adapted from Martha Taylor Greenway and Harry P. Hatry, *Focusing on Program Outcomes: Summary Guide* (Alexandria, Va.: United Way of America, 1996); Harry P. Hatry et. al., *Customer Surveys for Agency Managers: What Managers Need to Know* (Washington, D.C.: Urban Institute Press, 1998), and U.S. General Accounting Office, *The Results Act: An Evaluator's Guide to Assessing Agency Annual Performance Plans* (Washington, D.C., 1998).

*Criterion 3: Performance information is used in managing the agency or program.* Performance measurement systems should be used primarily in managing agencies and programs to achieve performance goals. This criterion addresses the quality of internal reporting in improving management for results. As discussed in chapter 11 (and listed in exhibit 13-5), performance-based management practices include delegating authority and flexibility in return for accountability for results, creating incentives

EXHIBIT 13-4

**Strategies and Approaches for Strengthening the Quality of Performance Data Strategies**

*Strategies*

1. Develop departmentwide standards for performance measurement.
2. Train employees in the application of those standards to data on performance.
3. Monitor data quality. The department is developing a formal process of rating data quality against data quality standards. It will also use program evaluations for data validation. In addition, the department is working closely with its Office of Inspector General to achieve independent monitoring of the reliability of its data quality in high-priority areas.
4. Have managers attest to the reliability and validity of their performance indicators or submit plans for data improvement. Managers attesting to the quality of their data coupled with periodic external validation of their assertions is a powerful new incentive to improve program performance information.

*Planned Approaches*

1. Identify indicators in the department's strategic plans and program plans that are essential to evaluating the performance of state grantees against program goals and objectives.
2. Identify which indicators are appropriate to collect at the national level and which ones should be reported at the state level.
3. Determine the best indicators available within an appropriate range of costs and data collection burden.
4. Align state performance reporting to indicators, including exploring electronic means of data transmission.
5. Agree to standards for data reliability and validity.
6. Coordinate data collections across different information sources, including state performance reports and general-purpose statistical collections. The latter can serve as an independent check on self-reported performance information.
7. Standardize definitions of key variables, avoiding duplicate data requests and increasing the level of communication between the major users and providers of performance data.
8. Use evaluation methods and findings to provide a more accurate and complete picture of the activities and the outcomes of the programs.
9. Continue or expand interagency coordination of data matches to help improve accuracy and reduce the burden on respondents.
10. Establish industrywide standards for data exchanges to stabilize data requirements, improve data integrity, and reduce costly errors.
11. Strengthen indicators of customer satisfaction to provide early warning of possible delivery system problems.
12. Ensure the quality of performance information on internal management systems. A priority area will be evaluation of the quality of performance data, including data for customer surveys, performance contracting, and employee performance ratings and awards.

**Source:** U.S. Department of Education, *FY 1999 Annual Plan* (Washington, D.C., 1998), 87–90.

for improved program performance, redesigning management systems to focus on performance, reallocating resources or redirecting program activities to improve performance, and developing partnerships designed to improve performance. Those assessing performance measurement systems' quality can assess whether and to what extent the uses listed in exhibit 13-5 have actually occurred over, say, the past year.

EXHIBIT 13-5

**Managing for Results: Performance-Based Management Practices**

- Delegate greater authority and flexibility in return for greater accountability for results—for example, by simplifying the rules for budgeting, human resource management, or financial management.
- Create intangible incentives for improved program performance—for example, through performance agreements setting challenging but realistic performance goals for agencies or programs, through quarterly or more frequent performance measurement and reporting, through meetings focusing on performance issues, through publicity about relative performance levels or changes in performance, or by delegating greater authority and flexibility in human resource management or financial management to higher-performing organizations.
- Create financial incentives for effective organizational performance—for example, by introducing competition among service providers, reallocating resources to higher performing or most-improved service providers, or giving bonuses to managers and staff of higher-performing or most-improved organizations.
- Provide training and technical assistance to build expertise in strategic planning, performance measurement, and management use of performance information.
- Redesign central management systems (budgeting, human resource management, information management, procurement, grants management, financial management) to focus on performance.
- Incorporate goals, performance indicators, and performance incentives into contracts and grant programs.
- Reallocate resources to improve performance.
- Redirect program activities to improve performance.
- Develop partnerships designed to improve performance—for example, among public agencies, among nonprofit organizations, or between public sector agencies and nonprofit organizations or private firms.

*Criterion 4: A reasonable degree of accountability is provided.* This criterion focuses on reporting outside the agency. Those assessing performance measurement systems will need to examine the extent to which the performance data included in outside reports to the chief executive, the legislative body (or board of directors), other key stakeholders, and the public adequately covers the agency's mission and goals. Do agency reports provide an accurate perspective on agency or program performance?

*Criterion 5: More effective or improved performance is demonstrated.* Do performance reports provide credible information demonstrating that performance targets have been met or that current performance represents improvement over past performance?

*Criterion 6: Performance information supports resource allocation or other policy decisionmaking.* What evidence is there that performance information has been used by higher-level managers, budget analysts, or legislators in their resource allocation or other policy decisions? Have policymakers made appropriate use of performance information? To obtain such information, those assessing the quality of a performance measurement system will probably need to interview a sample of relevant personnel.

## Who Should Assess Performance Measurement Systems?

Managers should be accountable for data quality, but the performance measurement system should also be subject to periodic assessment by independent organizations.

Agency and program managers bear the primary responsibility both for collecting performance data and for quality control of the performance measurement process. Thus, managers should be responsible for periodically reviewing their performance measurement systems to ensure that the measurement systems provide data that are sufficiently complete, accurate, and consistent to document performance and support decisionmaking. Assessment of data quality will also be less costly if agency or program managers and their staffs do their part. Managers might be asked to attest formally to the quality of the data they provide (as in the Department of Education example in exhibit 13-4).

When performance measurement systems are used for accountability to higher levels or to the public, however, there is a natural fear that the data might be manipulated or otherwise misleading. This is why independent efforts are needed periodically to ensure the accuracy and credibility of the performance data. Independent assessment of the quality of the performance data or the measurement process can be requested from internal or external auditors, evaluators, statistical agencies, or others with the required expertise.

## What Process Might Be Used to Assess the Accuracy and Usefulness of Performance Measurement Systems?

Exhibit 13-6 outlines a five-step process for assessing the accuracy and usefulness of performance measurement systems according to the criteria proposed in exhibits 13-1 and 13-2.

*Step 1. Assess the extent of agreement on goals and strategies for achieving them.* Agency missions, multiyear goals, and strategies for achieving the goals will typically be presented in agency strategic plans or

**Suggested Process for Assessing Performance Measurement Systems**

**Step 1.** Assess the extent of agreement on goals and strategies for achieving them.

**Step 2.** Clarify how each goal is to be achieved. Use logic models to identify relevant inputs, activities, processes, outputs, intermediate outcomes, intended results, important unintended outcomes, assumed causal linkages, and key external factors that could significantly affect achievement of the goals.

**Step 3.** Identify the performance measurement systems in use in the agency or program.

**Step 4.** Assess the technical quality of the performance measurement systems.

**Step 5.** Assess the extent to which performance information is used in systems for managing the agency or program to achieve performance goals, in accountability to key stakeholders and the public, in demonstrating effective or improved performance, and in resource allocation or other policy decisionmaking (see exhibit 13-1, *criteria 3-6*).

business plans. Annual performance targets for agency programs will typically be presented in performance plans, performance reports, grant applications, or budget requests. They may also appear in strategic plans, business plans, and similar documents. Information on the extent of agreement or disagreement on agency goals and strategies is often found in legislation, hearings, committee reports, and audit and evaluation reports—but may have to be acquired through interviews, focus groups, or surveys of managers, staff members, and other key stakeholders.

*Step 2. Clarify how each goal is to be achieved.* This involves identifying the chain of inputs, program activities, processes, outputs, and intermediate outcomes needed to achieve agency or program goals and key external factors that could significantly affect achievement of the intended results. Some information on strategies for achieving goals may be found in agency plans and other documents. Additional information on strategies for achieving goals may have to be acquired through interviews with managers and other key stakeholders. As noted earlier, logic models can be a very useful way to help identify relevant performance indicators by highlighting inputs, activities, outputs, intermediate outcomes, end outcomes, important unintended outcomes, assumed causal linkages, and key external factors that could significantly affect achievement of intended results (see chapter 5).

*Step 3. Identify the performance measurement systems in use.* Agencies may have many performance measurement systems, including measurement systems for individual programs and subprograms. Information about these can be extracted from agency plans, management systems, audits, evaluations, and performance reports.

*Step 4. Assess the technical quality of the agency's performance measurement systems.* This should be done in terms of the quality dimensions listed in exhibit 13-2 and should be applied to the agency's performance measurement, evaluation, and reporting systems. It is especially useful to compare the agency's systems with the performance measurement, evaluation, and reporting systems of other agencies. Depending on the scope of the assessment, the review might either examine whether the agency has quality control systems in place or test the completeness, accuracy, and consistency of performance information by performing additional measurements or analyses.

It is important for the assessment process to respect the fact that no performance measurement system is—or ever will be—perfect. The most important question is whether the performance data are sufficiently complete, accurate, and consistent to document performance and support decisionmaking at various organizational levels. If the answer to this is positive, the system can be considered adequate.

*Step 5. Assess the extent to which the performance information is used.* The final and most important step in the suggested quality assessment process is for managers, auditors, or evaluators to identify whether and how the performance measurement system is used: in agency or program management systems, in providing accountability to key stakeholders and the public, in demonstrating effective or improved performance, or in supporting resource allocation or other policy decisionmaking. The assessment process should respect the reality that many factors influence management, agency and program performance, and policy decisionmaking. Judgments will be needed as to whether use of performance information is sufficient.

Agency documents, audit reports, evaluation reports, interviews, focus groups, or surveys of managers and staff can help determine whether performance information is used in systems for managing agencies or programs to achieve performance goals. To assess the status of implementation of the Government Performance and Results Act and to identify significant challenges confronting agencies in their efforts to become more results-oriented, for example, the GAO sent a survey to a representative sample of mid- and upper-level managers in 24 federal agencies. GAO's questionnaire asked managers about their perceptions on such topics as the use of performance information now and three years ago, hindrances to measuring and using performance information, and improvements seen or expected as a result of implementation of the act.[4]

To determine whether performance information is used in outside accountability to key stakeholders and the public, in demonstrating effective or improved performance, or in supporting resource allocation or other policy decisionmaking, quality reviewers need to consult budget justifications, other agency documents, audit and evaluation reports, hearings, or interviews; conduct focus groups; survey key stakeholders; and observe the decisionmaking process.

Exhibit 13-7 summarizes the information sources likely to be relevant in assessing agency progress in terms of each of the criteria proposed in exhibit 13-1. Those assessing the quality and usefulness of performance measurement systems will find relevant information in agency plans and reports; agency management systems; grant applications, budget requests, or justifications for requested appropriations; management systems of other agencies; audit and evaluation reports; hearings and committee reports; and the professional literature. In some cases it may be important to supplement such documentation with interviews, focus groups, or surveys designed to elicit the opinions of agency managers and staff, committee staff, budget examiners, internal or external auditors and evaluators, or other key stakeholders affected by or interested in agency or program activities.

---

## Examples of Performance Measurement Systems That Are of Sufficient Technical Quality and Usefulness

This section describes two agencies whose performance measurement systems are of good quality, as assessed by the criteria in exhibit 13-1.[5]

### Chesapeake Bay Program

The Chesapeake Bay Program is an intergovernmental partnership among the U.S. Environmental Protection Agency (EPA); the states of Maryland, Virginia, and Pennsylvania; and the District of Columbia, "built on top of the national and state environmental regulatory programs." EPA's Chesapeake Bay Program Office manages approximately $21 million per year in federal funds and influences the allocation of substantially more federal and state resources.

*Criterion 1: Agreed-on goals and strategies are in place.* In 1987, working with stakeholders, the Chesapeake Bay Program set the core program goal of 40 percent nutrient reduction by the year 2000, reflecting the participants' commitment to efforts that would limit pollution from sources like wastewater treatment plants and fertilizer runoff from farmland. In the 1990s, participants agreed on the program's three primary restoration

EXHIBIT 13-7

## Sources of Information That May Be Relevant in Assessing Performance Measurement Systems

### For criterion 1: Agreed-on goals and strategies are in place.

- Agency strategic plans, business plans, performance plans, and performance reports; grant applications, budget requests, and appropriations justifications; and other agency documents
- Agency management systems
- Audit and evaluation reports
- Legislation, hearings, and committee reports
- The opinions of key stakeholders on the extent of agreement—or lack of any strong disagreement—on performance goals, including outcome-oriented goals*

### For criterion 2: The performance measurement system is of sufficient technical quality.

- Systems for assessing and reporting on agency and program performance
- Strategic plans, business plans, performance plans, performance reports, and other agency and bureau documents related to systems for assessing and reporting on agency and program performance
- Grant applications, budget requests, and appropriations justifications
- The performance measurement, evaluation, and reporting systems of other agencies and programs
- Audit and evaluation reports
- The professional literature

### For criterion 3: Performance information is used in managing the agency or program.

- Agency plans; agency management systems, including informal or formal incentive systems designed to stimulate effective performance in terms of performance goals; audits, evaluations, and other performance reports
- Memoranda proposing or approving program changes
- Use of performance information in the management systems of other agencies and programs
- The opinions of key stakeholders on the extent to which there exist systems for managing the agency or program to achieve performance goals*

### For criterion 4: A reasonable degree of accountability is provided.

- Information from performance measurement and reporting systems, statistical programs, audits, evaluations, and other analyses related to performance in terms of agreed-on goals and performance indicators
- Budget documents, annual reports, and other publications describing the program
- Speeches, press releases, and press coverage
- The opinions of key stakeholders on the extent to which performance information has been used to communicate agency or program performance or changes in performance to key stakeholders or the public*

### For criterion 5: More effective or improved performance is demonstrated.

- Information from performance measurement and reporting systems, statistical programs, audits, evaluations, and other analyses related to performance in terms of agreed-on goals and performance indicators
- Budget documents and annual reports
- The opinions of key stakeholders on the extent to which effective or improved performance has been demonstrated*
- The professional literature

### For criterion 6: Performance information supports resource allocation or other policy decisionmaking.

- Budget documents
- Documents related to use of performance information in decisionmaking by agency policymakers, those who influence the allocation of needed resources, and other key stakeholders interested in agency activities*
- Committee reports and other documents related to legislative use of performance information
- The opinions of key stakeholders on the types and extent of use of performance information in resource allocation and other policy decisionmaking*
- The professional literature

*Key stakeholders may include program managers and staff; those served by an agency or program; senior agency officials; authorizing, appropriations, and oversight committee staff; budget examiners; auditors and evaluators; and others affected by or interested in agency or program activities.

objectives—reduction of nutrient enrichment effects, protection and enhancement of living resources, and reduction of adverse toxic impacts—and on goals stated in terms of key performance indicators. The EPA reported that:

> Environmental indicators/outcome measures have supported goal setting for the Bay Program, both in the longer-term Strategic Implementation Plan and for annual planning and budgeting. . . . The Bay Program has over 25 measurable goals in place at this time and several more under active consideration.[6]

Among the environmental performance indicators used were stream miles opened for migratory fish, acres of bay grasses, nitrogen loads delivered to the bay, phosphorus loads delivered to the bay, striped bass spawning stock, industry-reported transfers of chemical contaminants, and kepone in finfish tissue. The program measured performance in terms of outputs (administrative actions by the EPA and state regulatory agencies) and five outcomes: actions by sources (e.g., installing pollution control equipment); emissions and discharge qualities of pollutants; concentrations of pollutants in the water; uptake or concentration of pollutants in plant or animal tissue; and health or ecological effects (see exhibit 13-8).

## EXHIBIT 13-8

**Chesapeake Bay Program Hierarchy of Indicators**

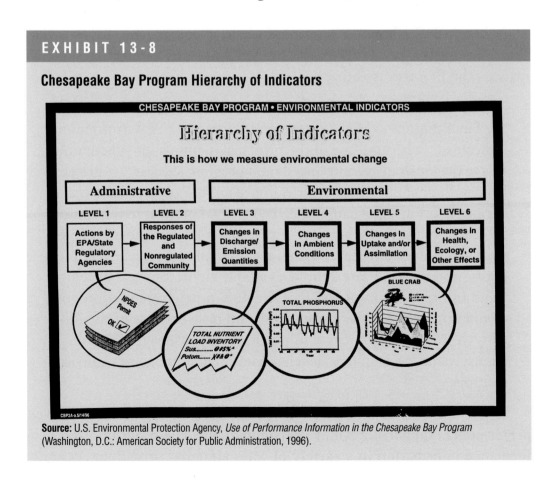

**Source:** U.S. Environmental Protection Agency, *Use of Performance Information in the Chesapeake Bay Program* (Washington, D.C.: American Society for Public Administration, 1996).

---

Quality Control: Assessing the Accuracy and Usefulness of Performance Measurement Systems

*Criterion 2: The performance measurement system is of sufficient technical quality.* Program staff put special emphasis on establishing high-quality systems for monitoring programs in the bay area. The EPA reported that:

> The Chesapeake Bay is one of the most carefully monitored bodies of water in the world. . . . Consistent and comparable data on all traditional water parameters has been taken at over 130 sites in the watershed and the open Bay since 1984. The trends data available from this monitoring program are some of the best in America. . . . [In 1991] the Bay Program Office began to develop a set of environmental indicators, or outcome measures, to support goal-setting and to serve as targets and endpoints for the water restoration effort. . . . Workshops were subsequently held in 1994 and 1995 to build stakeholder involvement in the design and refinement of the measures and the communications products.
>
> The Chesapeake Bay Program is based on good science and high quality data, and data collection and analysis expenses are considerable. About $2.5 million per year of federal funds supports the monitoring costs for air, water, living resources, and submerged aquatic vegetation.[7]

*Criterion 3: Performance information is used in managing the program.* The Chesapeake Bay Program redirected activities to improve performance. The EPA reported that:

> The availability of accepted environmental indicators has enabled the Bay Program to better target its resources. . . . Environmental indicators . . . became one of the principal methods for subcommittees to demonstrate resource needs and program success. . . . Projects from all subcommittees with nonmeasurable objectives are at a decided disadvantage against outcome-oriented projects in the contest for scarce financial resources. . . . Environmental indicators/outcome measures are used to develop and evaluate the effectiveness of program strategies. . . For example, available environmental outcome trend information indicates that the 40% nutrient reduction goal would not be met at the current program pace because of the difficulty in controlling sources of nitrogen. In response to these findings, Pennsylvania has begun to develop additional point source nutrient controls. . . .[8]

*Criteria 4-6: Accountability, demonstrating effective or improved performance, supporting policy decisionmaking.* The program used performance information in a variety of ways aimed at providing accountability to key stakeholders and the public and supporting policy decision-making. The EPA reported that:

> Experience has shown that public support of the program, and financial investment in the program, have been associated with the development and communication of bottom line goals. . . . Coincident with vigorous efforts to develop goals and environmental indicators, federal funds for the Chesapeake Bay Program increased from approximately $13 million in FY 1991 to $21 million in FY 1996. Other leveraged federal agency resources were estimated at an additional $17 million in FY 1994. Bay Program staff estimate that state governments have contributed about $100 million per year for the last several years. The state and local expenditures to implement tributary-specific reduction strategies will be about $400 million per year through the year 2000. Little information is available on local government and private contributions, but staff believe they are substantial. Bay Program Office staff believe that the increased support given to the program in recent years reflects the enthusiasm for supporting effective Federal-state-local partnerships to address problems. . . . [I]mprovements in the environmental indicators have facilitated goal-setting, thus better defining intended program outcomes and improving accountability to the public.[9]

In sum, the Chesapeake Bay Program Office has put in place the prerequisites for useful performance measurement, and the system is being appropriately used. The agency developed reasonable agreement on an integrated set of output and outcome goals for reducing pollution and improving water quality—and it developed reasonable agreement on the resources, activities, and processes required to achieve the goals. The program developed performance measurement systems of sufficient quality that were used in management systems, in accountability to key stakeholders and the public, and in supporting policy decisionmaking.

## Traffic Safety Program

The National Highway Traffic Safety Administration (NHTSA) is an agency within the Department of Transportation. In FY 1996 it had approximately 600 staff and a budget of approximately $277 million.

*Criterion 1: Agreed-on goals and strategies are in place.* The NHTSA had been engaged in strategic planning since 1992, when it published a notice in the *Federal Register* that resulted in over 100 comments from stakeholders and partners on mission, issues, and future directions for the agency. There was widespread agreement among stakeholders on the agency's mission, which is to save lives, prevent injuries, and reduce traffic-related health care and other economic costs. In 1994, the agency called its partners and stakeholders in for a series of discussions on a draft strategic plan and to obtain input for the development of a five-year strategic execution plan that identified milestones and performance measures for achieving the strategic plan goals and objectives. Implementation of the Government Performance and Results Act led NHTSA to develop a consistent structure of outcome goals, intermediate outcome goals, and performance indicators (see exhibit 13-9).

Though NHTSA's FY 1994 performance plan had been based on its then-current organizational structure, beginning with its FY 1995 performance plan NHTSA defined its performance indicators from the perspective of what intermediate results were critical to achieving its ultimate goals. The agency's FY 1996 performance plan included five end outcome indicators, such as fatalities, injuries, and crashes per 100 million vehicle miles traveled (VMT); six intermediate outcome indicators, such as alcohol-related fatalities and safety belt usage rates; and several output indicators, such as crashworthiness rule-makings, average duration of safety defect investigations, and product recalls.

*Criterion 2: The performance measurement system is of sufficient technical quality.* The NHTSA measured performance primarily in terms of crash rates, injury rates, and fatality rates. The investment in NHTSA's highway safety data systems (approximately $15 million per year) produced outcome data for fatality and injury rates, crash involvement and crash consequence rates, alcohol involvement, and safety belt use, among other indicators. The agency used data from state and local records in some of its performance measurement systems; it used data from federal and state surveys in others.

The agency's Fatal Accident Reporting System, for example, contained data from a census of fatal crashes obtained from state records. As GAO reported:

> According to NHTSA documents, throughout the states, Puerto Rico, and the District of Columbia, trained state employees gather and transmit these data to NHTSA's central computer database in a standard format. State employees obtain data solely from the state's existing documents—including police accident reports, vehicle registration files, and vital statistics records—and then enter them into a central computer database. NHTSA analysts periodically review a sample of the cases.[10]

Data on injuries were drawn from a nationally representative sample of all police-reported accidents. As GAO reported:

EXHIBIT 13-9

## National Highway Traffic Safety Administration Goals and Performance Measures

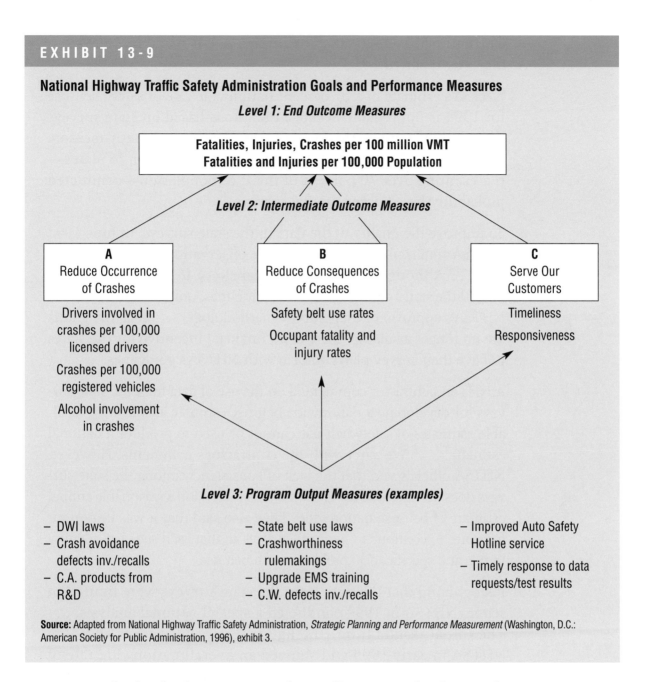

*Level 1: End Outcome Measures*

Fatalities, Injuries, Crashes per 100 million VMT
Fatalities and Injuries per 100,000 Population

*Level 2: Intermediate Outcome Measures*

**A**
Reduce Occurrence
of Crashes

Drivers involved in
crashes per 100,000
licensed drivers

Crashes per 100,000
registered vehicles

Alcohol involvement
in crashes

**B**
Reduce Consequences
of Crashes

Safety belt use rates

Occupant fatality and
injury rates

**C**
Serve Our
Customers

Timeliness

Responsiveness

*Level 3: Program Output Measures (examples)*

– DWI laws
– Crash avoidance
 defects inv./recalls
– C.A. products from
 R&D

– State belt use laws
– Crashworthiness
 rulemakings
– Upgrade EMS training
– C.W. defects inv./recalls

– Improved Auto Safety
 Hotline service
– Timely response to data
 requests/test results

**Source:** Adapted from National Highway Traffic Safety Administration, *Strategic Planning and Performance Measurement* (Washington, D.C.: American Society for Public Administration, 1996), exhibit 3.

To compile the database, NHTSA data collectors randomly sample about 48,000 reports each year from approximately 400 police jurisdictions in 60 sites across the country, according to NHTSA documents. NHTSA staff then interpret and code the data directly from the reports into a central electronic data file. The data are checked for consistency during both coding and subsequent processing.[11]

NHTSA has recognized that its data have limitations. For example, the General Estimates System is based on police reports, but various sources suggest that about half of all the motor vehicle crashes are not reported to police.

The national average safety belt usage rate is based on state surveys. As the GAO reported:

> NHTSA's estimate of a 67 percent nationwide rate of safety belt use for 1994 is not reliable because the rate is based on state surveys that used different methodologies that do not consistently measure belt use. . . . However, NHTSA has pointed out that 28 states—representing over 70 percent of the U.S. population—conducted probability-based observational surveys.

> To improve the quality of the data in the state surveys, in June 1992 NHTSA finalized guidelines for state observational surveys of belt use. . . . Although the guidelines were very flexible and NHTSA helped the states conform with the guidelines, only 28 states received NHTSA's approval of their survey methodology. . . . Since the grants are no longer available, there is no financial incentive for the states to have their survey plan conform with NHTSA's guidelines. . . .

> A NHTSA contractor commented on the use of data from the state surveys for developing a nationwide belt use estimate as follows: "Available estimates of safety belt use cannot be used to produce a national estimate. . . ." We agree with the contractor's comments. However, NHTSA officials said that the lack of consistency among the state surveys does not preclude using the surveys to develop a reasonable annual estimate of belt use nationwide. They also said that it was important for states to continue to perform surveys so that each state can identify trends and specific local problems with belt use.

> Recognizing that the data from the state surveys were limited in scope, NHTSA in 1994 conducted a special national analysis. . . . The initial results from [the national survey] were released by NHTSA in early 1995 and showed an overall nationwide rate of safety belt use of 58 percent for 1994. . . . NHTSA plans to conduct another [national] survey if funds become available, but the agency plans to continue using the state surveys to annually estimate the nationwide rate of belt use.[12]

*Criterion 3: Performance information is used in managing the program.* The NHTSA's budget was driven by its strategic execution plan and its annual performance plan under the Results Act. Beginning with the FY 1998 budget, program offices were required to demonstrate linkages to outcomes in cases where their program budget used an output indicator rather than an outcome indicator.

The agency also involved the states as partners in efforts to improve highway safety and safety data—and redirected program activities to achieve improved performance. The agency reported:

> Assessment of performance measures, such as the involvement of alcohol in fatal crashes, has indicated that there has been some slippage in progress. This has led to increased activities to address the problems identified. For example, measurements indicating a slowing down of increases in safety belt use and recent legislative changes that may increase average speed in crashes [have] led to increased NHTSA and Departmental commitments to increasing the number of states with primary enforcement safety belt laws.[13]

*Criteria 4-6: Accountability, demonstrating effective or improved performance, supporting policy decisionmaking.* The agency used performance information in accountability to key stakeholders and the public—and demonstrated improved performance in terms of its highway safety goals.

> The Fatal Accident Reporting System has enabled NHTSA to document that the rate for one of its desired outcomes—reduction in the fatality rate—decreased from 2.3 to an estimated 1.7 per million vehicle miles of travel from 1988 to 1995. Also, NHTSA has used data from its General Estimates System to document another one of its desired outcomes—a reduction in injury rates—from 169 to an estimated 138 injuries per 100 million vehicle miles of travel from 1988 to 1995.[14]

NHTSA has put in place the prerequisites for useful performance measurement. The agency developed a reasonable level of agreement on an integrated set of output and outcome goals for reduction of highway crashes, injuries, and fatalities—and developed a reasonable level of agreement on the resources, activities, and processes required to achieve the goals. The agency developed performance measurement systems of sufficient quality that were used in management systems, in accountability to key stakeholders and the public, and in supporting policy decisionmaking.

## Implications for Managers, Auditors, and Evaluators

Policymakers, managers, auditors, and evaluators are all moving toward closer involvement in performance measurement. For the foreseeable future, a wide variety of performance-based management initiatives is likely to affect public management, the intergovernmental system, and the nonprofit sector. In coming years, there will be a premium on managers, auditors, and evaluators with the knowledge, skills, and abilities to assess the quality of performance measurement systems and help ensure that performance information is sufficiently complete, accurate, and consistent to document performance and reliably support decisionmaking.

This chapter proposes criteria for assessing performance measurement systems and suggests how to approach the task of assessing the quality and usefulness of performance measurement systems. The suggested process explores the extent to which an agency has achieved agreement on defining performance in terms of agency or program goals and strategies for achieving those goals; the extent to which the performance measurement system is of sufficient technical quality to document performance and support decisionmaking; and the extent to which performance information is used in managing the agency or program, in accountability to key stakeholders and the public, and in supporting policy decisionmaking.

Assessment of the quality and usefulness of performance measurement systems is an important, emerging issue. Such assessments will be increasingly important as public and nonprofit organizations start regularly reporting performance information and using such information to make resource allocation decisions. Both the proposed assessment criteria and the suggested assessment process are still being developed. Refinements are needed in this emerging public management arena.

---

## References and Notes

1. Beryl A. Radin, "Performance-Based Management and Its Training Implications" (Paper prepared for the International Symposium on Performance-Based Management and Its Training Implications, Caserta, Italy, September 24–26, 1997).
2. U.S. General Accounting Office (GAO), *Executive Guide: Effectively Implementing the Government Performance and Results Act* (Washington, D.C., 1996), 13.
3. *Washington Post*, 10 January 1998, A7.
4. U.S. General Accounting Office, *The Government Performance and Results Act: 1997 Government-Wide Implementation Will Be Uneven* (Washington, D.C., 1997), 34–38 and 98–110.
5. The information presented is drawn primarily from case studies published by the American Society for Public Administration and available in electronic form at http://www.npr.gov/initiati/mfr.
6. U.S. Environmental Protection Agency (EPA), *Use of Performance Information in the Chesapeake Bay Program* (Washington, D.C.: American Society for Public Administration, 1996), 8.
7. EPA, *Use of Performance Information*, 3–5, 10.
8. Ibid., 8–9.

9. Ibid.

10. GAO, *Executive Guide*, 28.

11. Ibid.

12. U.S. General Accounting Office, *Motor Vehicle Safety: Comprehensive State Programs Offer Best Opportunity for Increasing Use of Safety Belts* (Washington, D.C., 1996), 20–23.

13. National Highway Traffic Safety Administration, *Strategic Planning and Performance Measurement* (Washington, D.C.: American Society for Public Administration, 1996), 11.

14. GAO, *Executive Guide*, 28.

# Other Performance Measurement Issues

Agency and program managers should expect to face numerous problems as they attempt to implement and sustain an outcome measurement process. This chapter alerts them to the types of problems they are likely to run into and suggests ways of dealing with them. Problem areas include:

- Personnel training needs
- Overall system cost and feasibility
- Changes in legislative and agency priorities
- Maintaining indicator stability over time
- Documentation of the outcome measurement process
- Fear and resistance from program managers
- Participation by other levels of government and the private sector
- Aggregation of outcomes across projects, programs, or sites
- Communitywide versus program-specific outcomes
- Legislative support
- Politics

## Personnel Training Needs

Most managers and staff have had little exposure to, or training in, outcome measurement; however, some training is needed for program personnel at all levels. Managers do not need much technical detail, but they do need to understand what the performance information can and cannot tell them and how such information can be appropriately used. Those who will be responsible for data collection need some technical detail. Agencies should consider including at least a small module on managing-for-results in each of their management courses and in most specialized training courses. (For example, staff training on new program procedures should include a discussion of the procedures' effects on service quality and outcomes.) Nonmanagement personnel need to be informed of their program's objectives, how progress is measured, and what their own roles are in helping meet those objectives.

Escalating this need for training is the inevitable turnover of personnel in any organization and the introduction of new measurement techniques. This means that training needs to be continual, not done merely when an agency first implements a performance measurement process.

Small programs, in particular, may have trouble finding funds and/or persons who can provide the necessary training. Agencies will probably need to obtain assistance, whether from analytical offices within the agency or from outside consultants or universities.

## Overall System Cost and Feasibility

To the extent that new data are needed (from customer surveys, trained observer procedures, and the like), implementing and sustaining data collection is likely to require added resources. Initial development and start-up costs can be considerable; however, once the procedures become routine, the annual costs usually shrink.

It certainly can be argued that tracking results-focused performance information is just a basic requirement of good management and that resources for it should be budgeted as part of normal agency operations. But special data collection activities, such as customer surveys and trained observer rating procedures, are quite visible, and their costs will inevitably be particularly vulnerable to budget cuts when funds are very tight. (Chapter 7 includes a number of cost reduction options for customer surveys, some of which also apply to trained observer rating procedures.)

As important a concern as monetary cost is feasibility. Organizations that do not have and cannot afford to obtain personnel with the specialized technical skills needed for some of these data collection procedures face a major impediment to implementing regular in-house data collection.

A serious problem for many agencies, especially small ones, is the administration of surveys, whether by mail, telephone, or in person. *Organizations that want to encourage agencies, programs, grantees, or contractors to track customer outcomes regularly through customer surveys might use an "incubator" approach.* In such an approach, the organization selects one or more organizations with survey capability (such as universities and survey research firms) and subsidizes the cost of their services (e.g., a 50 percent share of the full cost). An agency covered by this arrangement can then contract with one of the approved survey organizations (paying *its share* of the total cost of the surveys), thus considerably reducing costs and effort. The organization's arrangement with the survey organizations can be open-ended, but it should have an upper limit. The organization might also develop model survey contracts to further ease the administrative burden of covered agencies.

Private, nonprofit agencies may be able to obtain volunteer assistance to help their programs with the special technical requirements of surveys, trained observer ratings, and associated data processing.

## Changes in Legislative and Agency Priorities

Periodic changes in priorities (perhaps driven by changes in elected or appointed officials), including funding uncertainties, are inevitable but need not discourage development of a stable performance measurement process. This is because priorities most often do not substantially change the mission of a program but rather focus on the means to accomplish the mission. A well-constructed outcome measurement process should be able to provide much, if not most, of the information required by such changes as part of its regular tracking function. Changes are most likely to be restricted to intermediate outcome indicators, since these are most directly affected by changes in service approach. However, to the extent that decisions about priorities change an agency's mission, the agency's outcomes and outcome indicators will need to be modified.

## Maintaining Indicator Stability over Time

Since a major use of performance information is to examine changes over time, performance indicators need to be reasonably stable to avoid comparing, as the saying goes, apples with oranges. As discussed in chapter 9, comparing current performance with the previous period's performance is common and usually given considerable attention. Examination of outcome data over several years is also useful to programs for examining what is happening, such as whether actions taken are having the desired effects. The stability concern is not so much with adding new indicators as with dropping or substantially modifying old ones. Changing either performance indicators or the data collection procedures associated with them can destroy, or at least reduce, comparability with previous reporting periods. Some continuing improvement of the performance measurement process is obviously desirable. The trick is to keep such changes small. From an external perspective, a program that makes frequent changes may even be looked on with suspicion: Is the program manipulating the performance indicators so that only those with favorable outcomes that year are reported?

Obviously, for good government and good management, indicators should not be deleted because they bring bad news. This tactic may be advantageous in the short term, but it will hurt long-term credibility. Equally obviously, past data collection procedures that turn out to be invalid should be changed. A pragmatic solution for the comparability problem is to retain the older, less satisfactory indicators and data collection procedures, introduce the new approach, and then phase out the less satisfactory procedures.

## Documentation of the Outcome Measurement Process

The outcome measurement process should be documented so that the persons responsible for data collection, and the users of the data, know what is supposed to be done. Documentation is particularly helpful in alleviating problems due to staff turnover. The program may find it useful to *prepare outcome indicator specification sheets for each outcome indicator* so that program personnel and any other users have a description of each indicator. Exhibit 14-1 illustrates a format for such documentation.

| EXHIBIT 14-1 |
|---|
| **Outcome Indicator Specification Sheet**<br><br>Program: _____  Date: _____<br><br>1. Outcome<br><br>2. Outcome indicator<br><br>3. Category of indicator (e.g., intermediate or end outcome)<br><br>4. Data source and collection procedures<br><br>5. Breakouts of the outcome indicator that are needed<br><br>6. Frequency of collection and reporting<br><br>7. Who is responsible for data collection and its quality |

A useful form of summary documentation is to group outcome indicators by data source. One such list would consist of all the indicators that came from agency records. Another would group the indicators measured by trained observer ratings. Yet other lists would group indicators by customer category (such as surveys of students, parents, or school administrators). An important use for these lists of indicators by data source is to provide a basis for developing (and later modifying) data collection instruments, whether they be forms, survey questionnaires, or rating guides.

## Fear and Resistance from Program Managers

Program managers are usually less than enthusiastic about imposed requirements to identify, collect, and report outcome data. Since such mandates from higher levels seek more accountability and justification of budget proposals, the requirements will more often than not be perceived as a threat to the managers and to the program's budgets. Managers will worry that they will be blamed for less-than-expected results over which they have only limited control.

This is a legitimate concern, as we have noted in previous chapters, but agencies can alleviate managers' fear and resistance in several ways:

- Make sure that program managers have a major role in selecting the performance indicators. (See chapter 3.)
- Provide adequate training and technical assistance to program managers (as discussed above), so that they fully understand the performance measurement process and the uses to which they can put performance information (such as those internal uses discussed in chapter 11).
- Make explicit provision for, and encourage the use of, *explanatory information* in performance measurement reports so that program managers have an opportunity to account for less-than-expected results. (See chapters 10 and 12 for a more detailed discussion.)
- Make sure that program managers see the performance measurement results *before* they are sent to higher levels (or outside the agency) to give them an opportunity to provide explanations where needed.
- Use the performance measurement report information constructively and nonpunitively, at least until it becomes fully clear that punitive action is appropriate.

Even if all these steps are taken, the fears of program managers may be justified when performance measurement information is transmitted to higher administrative or policy levels and to the media. Opponents of a program, and the media, will inevitably use unpleasant performance information in unpleasant ways. No matter what the program does, with or without performance measurement, opponents will find ways to criticize. Because of the major benefits it can confer in the context of managing for results, performance measurement should not be made the scapegoat.

## Participation by Other Levels of Government and the Private Sector

Many program services, especially at the federal and state levels, are ultimately delivered or otherwise affected by agencies of other levels of government or by the private sector. Thus, much of the data for outcome measurement may need to be obtained from, or at least with the cooperation of, these other agencies. One problem that arises is that the amount of detail needed by the different levels is likely to be different. For example, local governments and private, nonprofit service agencies are likely to need data on outcomes broken out by neighborhood—information not likely to be needed by state or federal agencies. State agencies are likely to need data broken out by county or municipality. Federal agencies may need data broken out only by state or region of the country.

Data might be collected by the lower-level agencies and then aggregated by the higher level agency. Alternatively, the higher-level organization can choose to collect the outcome information itself (such as by contracting with a consulting firm to survey samples of customers from lower-level service agencies). This has the considerable advantage of ensuring that the data collection procedures are the same across sites, thus making the data more comparable, but the data will not be as useful to the lower-level agencies because not many of their own customers will have been included in the samples. (It is usually desirable that the lower-level service agencies be encouraged to track the outcomes of their own services so they can use that information to improve their programs.)

In any case, the upper-level organization will need the cooperation of the lower-level agencies in providing information on customers, such as names, addresses, and/or telephone numbers, so they can be surveyed. A classic example occurs in county human services agencies. A county may want outcome data from its contractors and grantees, which are likely to be quite numerous. It is much easier for the county to ask each contractor or grantee to collect outcome data than to collect this information itself. This procedure has the added advantages of encouraging each contractor or grantee to build outcome information into its own management system and, at least on the surface, of saving the county government money.

*Agencies with such outcome relationships should consider ways to develop data collection partnerships with other organizations, including agreement (to the extent possible) on common data collection procedures. Performance partnerships should be considered.* Such partnerships can substantially increase the logistics and time required for outcome measurement development (to ensure that all interests are met). However, this joint effort is likely to pay off in the long run by yielding a smoothly running and more useful outcome measurement process.[1]

## Aggregation of Outcomes across Projects, Programs, or Sites

Aggregating outcomes is important to organizations that support a number of projects or programs from different sites that focus on similar objectives. Such organizations will likely want to assess the combined effects of groups of these projects, programs, or sites on key outcome indicators. For example, a local, state, federal, or private agency may be supporting a number of projects aimed at reducing juvenile delinquency. It would like to add up the outcomes of each project, program, or site to assess what total outcomes the total resources had achieved.

Aggregation can be messy. As a first step, the agency may need to separate its programs into groupings with similar objectives. For example, Ramsey County's (MN) Department of Community Human Services and United Way of Minneapolis Area (UWMA) have each been experimenting with identifying clusters of services and then synthesizing outcome findings across projects within each cluster. In 1998, UWMA had 14 clusters. About 19 service agencies were included in its Strengthening Families Cluster, 21 in its Youth Development Cluster, and about 23 in its Parenting/Teen Pregnancy Cluster. (UWMA also used subclusters in some cases.)

Even when programs have like objectives, aggregating performance information can be a much tougher problem than it looks, particularly if the data collection procedures are not standardized. If possible, an organization should identify a set of key outcome indicators and compatible data collection procedures that all, or at least most, projects and programs in the group would agree (or be required) to use and report. This would enable the organization to aggregate the outcomes from all of the reporting projects and programs.

One example is the Department of Education's need to aggregate data from individual states on indicators of learning achievement, such as test scores. But each state, and sometimes each school district, uses somewhat different tests, and each tests different subject matter and children in different grades. For some purposes, the federal government can make use of aggregate data from the National Assessment of Educational Progress (NAEP). However, the NAEP testing process covers only samples of schools and students. Such data are not adequate for many programs. This problem faces not only Department of Education programs but also those of other agencies that want to use learning indicators, such as educational programs of the National Science Foundation. Another example is the Environmental Protection Agency's National Estuary Program, which wants to aggregate progress in improving water quality across all the estuaries in its program. However, each estuary uses its own indicators of water quality.

An option in all these cases is to *aggregate the percent improvements* from each project or organizational unit, with or without some system of weighting. For the estuary program, for example, an estimate of percent improvement might be used for particular bodies of water and particular types of pollution. Each estuary might be weighted equally. (Or the estuaries might be weighted by the size of the body of water, funding, population, and so on.) For test scores, the Department of Education might aggregate percent improvement weighted by number of students represented by each project or organizational unit.

The alternative to collecting data from each project, program, or site is for the agency to undertake its own data collection, using common procedures for all projects and organizational units. The NAEP tests identified above are an example of this. While this approach may seem highly desirable, it may not be feasible because of the many measurements the agency needs. Even if feasible, cost control considerations will likely necessitate the use of sampling. This may be adequate for some uses of the data but not for all, especially if more detailed breakouts are sought.

This dilemma has not been resolved in any general sense, and it is likely to become increasingly challenging for agencies that need aggregate performance information. For agencies with mandating power, uniform reporting procedures can be required from lower levels. In other cases, one option for encouraging individual projects, programs, or sites to provide standardized performance data themselves is to offer incentives, such as partial subsidies.

## Communitywide versus Program-Specific Outcomes

A concern related to aggregation is the relationship of agency program outcomes to communitywide outcomes. Agencies may have severely limited resources and be able to help only a small number of persons in the community. Thus, no matter how good they are at achieving desired outcomes for their customers, they may not be able to significantly affect communitywide outcomes. For example, if a program only has resources to serve 100 persons in a community with 10,000 in need of help, even if it succeeded in helping all 100, it would still affect only 1 percent of the total population in need.

A program's scale needs to be considered when assessing its performance. If an organization has resources that enable it to serve only a small portion of the potential customers, it should be held accountable for only those customers its resources permit it to serve. An exception here is a particular government's responsibility to its whole jurisdiction. Even though the responsible public agency may only have sufficient resources to meet the needs of a portion of those in the jurisdiction, it should track, and be considered responsible for, the magnitude of unmet need as an overall performance indicator for the government as a whole. Government does, after all, have some responsibility for seeking to meet the full need.

Nevertheless, government officials and the public should distinguish between two public responsibilities: (1) the outcomes for those customers the program is able to serve and (2) the extent to which the program is able to meet the overall need in the jurisdiction. Clearly, the program's influence over this first outcome is considerably greater than its influence over the second, which is likely to be constrained by the program's resources. As discussed in previous chapters, we recommend that agencies categorize each outcome indicator as to the level of influence the agency and its programs have over the outcome and provide this information to users of their performance reports. This will enable users to make fairer interpretations of program performance.

The above issues and approaches also apply to nongovernmental community organizations such as United Way programs. These programs may also want to track and work to improve at least some communitywide outcomes. Usually, their resources will be too limited to have significant effects alone. However, such organizations can join in performance partnerships with other organizations in the community to undertake actions that can lead to significant communitywide effects.

## Legislative Support

As discussed in chapter 11, major incentives for agencies to produce sound, supportable performance information are reviewed by the legislature of outcomes related to budget submissions and agency proposals for program and policy changes. A number of concerns surround the role of legislatures, however, in helping or impeding the achievement of a successful performance measurement process:

1. The legislature's support for the performance measurement process is vital. While many performance measurement efforts in the United States have been solely executive branch efforts, it is clear that legislatures can undermine a particular effort if they have not been adequately involved in establishing the process, including deleting funding for data collection.

2. Legislators and their staffs need to be adequately educated about what outcome information can tell them and what it cannot tell them. A crucial need is for legislators to understand that outcomes only tell *what* progress is being made, *not why*. This is to reduce the potential for having the performance information used inappropriately and unfairly to agencies and their programs. Preferably, the legislature would provide its own training programs for its personnel. The executive branch should help provide such education informally whenever it briefs legislators or their staffs on executive branch proposals.

3. Legislators have an important role in ensuring the validity of performance data. Inevitably, legislators will be concerned about the quality of the data they are given. As discussed in chapter 13, data quality control is an important legislative concern. In judging the merits of the system, it is legitimate for the legislature to call for its own audits of the data and place requirements on the executive branch for quality control efforts.

For a legislature to perform these roles constructively, *the executive branch must provide data on important outcomes of interest to the legislature in a clear, easily accessible form.* Too often legislatures have been blamed for not being interested in or not using performance information when in fact they were given great volumes of data that were difficult to interpret and heavily weighted with process and output information—with the important outcome data buried in backup volumes (if there at all).

## Politics

Political concerns will at times have considerable effects on the results-based information that is developed and reported. This applies to annual performance reporting, to strategic plans, and to information provided as justification for budgets, especially projected performance targets.

A mayor of a city in Eastern Europe was recently asked about his interest in performance measurement. He responded that his current process of getting information at open hearings and through complaints to him personally was adequate. Performance information would be useful to him to the extent that he could use it to persuade members of the city council to support his programs. He worried that performance measurement might be an attempt to replace political decisionmaking, and he felt that it would hamper his ability to use his judgment—equating performance measurement to running the city by computer.

Such views are not unlike those of elected officials in other countries, including the United States. A strong case must be made that *having performance information <u>before</u> elected officials make decisions can help them improve their decisions to the benefit of their citizens and their own reputations.*

Even after reasonable support has been obtained from elected officials, problems can arise, particularly if the support has been primarily passive. For example:

- Political officials in both the executive and legislative branches may believe that spelling out the expected consequences—negative as well as positive—in budget proposals will cause resistance to the proposals from groups that feel they will not benefit sufficiently. This may lead to the suppression of particular performance indicators and particular break-out information.
- Political officials may insist in some situations on more optimistic targets than analysis has found to be feasible given the budgeted resources.
- Political officials may fear that targets will be perceived by some groups as quotas that will lead to harassment of their constituents; politicians may therefore discourage agencies from including important performance information in their systems. Such harassment is of particular concern in police (arrests and traffic citations), litigation, child support enforcement, and tax collection programs. As noted in earlier chapters, the way to alleviate the problem of considering certain outcomes as quotas is to also include performance indicators reflecting undesirable unintended consequences of excessive zeal, such as complaints of harassment.
- Political officials may believe that being very explicit about objectives in strategic plans and annual performance plans will raise the resistance of groups that do not agree with the way the program purposes are specified in those plans.

These are all real-life situations. Inevitably, the people implementing results-based performance measurement will need to make some compromises.

Preferably, those compromises will be made after everyone has fully considered the possible consequences of not being as clear and accurate as possible.

Educating elected officials on the benefits of results-based measurement should help to overcome their doubts. Results-based performance measurement cannot, and should not, replace political decisionmaking—but it should help to make the decisionmaking process better informed.

---

### Note

1. Ideally, private sector *customers* should be included in these performance partnerships. Private citizens and businesses that receive services from agencies almost always have important responsibilities that contribute significantly to service outcomes. For example, citizens need to put their garbage out in the right containers, at the right locations, at the right times, and, where required, with the right waste sorting. Parents are responsible for encouraging students to attend classes and complete their homework. Such responsibilities might be spelled out along with the responsibilities of the various public and private agencies.

# Part

# V

---

# Summary

# A Wrap-up of Key Performance Measurement Elements

T his chapter highlights key elements of an ongoing, results-based performance measurement system.

1. **Public services are for the benefit of the public,** the customers of those services—not for the benefit of the service providers (though providers need to be treated fairly).

2. **There are a number of prerequisites for a successful performance measurement system:**
   - *Data processing support.* Data processing personnel should be brought into the planning stages early.
   - *Analytic support.* Persons who know data and how to analyze it are needed to ensure reasonably reliable data collection procedures and proper interpretation of trade-offs.
   - *Upper-level support.* As with any ongoing process, support from upper management and legislators is crucial to providing needed resources and using the information generated.
   - *Patience and time.* Implementing a full performance measurement process is probably impossible in less than a year and will take several years for most programs. Agencies should expect many iterations before a stable set of performance indications is implemented.

3. **Outcomes and outcome indicators to be tracked should be developed primarily by the program,**

with input from upper-level management to make sure the indicators are appropriate for the agency. Input from the legislature (or the board of private, nonprofit organizations) is also highly desirable to reduce problems later. Outcomes tracked should include negative side effects (see chapters 3–5).

4. **Agencies and their programs need to distinguish between outputs and outcomes and between intermediate and end outcomes.** Outputs are products and services delivered by the program. Outcomes are events, actions, or behaviors that occur outside the program and in ways that the program is attempting to affect. Customer satisfaction with the helpfulness and quality of services should be considered important outcomes, but they are usually intermediate rather than end outcomes. Considerable effort should be made to ensure that agency programs understand the distinctions among these indicator categories.

   End outcomes should be included even though the program does not completely control them. Intermediate outcomes usually occur earlier, and programs usually have greater influence over them than end outcomes, providing program managers with important, timely information on which to act. Managers should be able to take credit for successful intermediate outcomes but should recognize that achieving end outcomes is the ultimate goal (see chapter 2).

5. **The limitations of performance measurement information should be made clear to all personnel and users of the information.** Everyone involved with preparing and using performance measurement information should recognize that outcomes only tell what happened, not why. Thus, outcome data should not be used to blame or praise a program in isolation from additional material explaining those outcomes. Because there has been considerable misunderstanding on this point, agencies should consider including in performance reports flags that indicate the extent to which the outcome values can be influenced by the agency (a simple scale such as *little influence, some influence,* and *considerable influence* may be sufficient).

6. **In order to track outcomes, most agency programs need to go beyond their currently available data,** using such major data collection procedures as customer surveys and trained observer ratings. Customer surveys, in particular, can be a very important tool for performance measurement. They can provide not only customer satisfaction information, but often—and usually more important—a variety of factual information on outcomes. Examples include changes in employment and earning status, the use of different services (such

as recreation, park, and library services) by households, and changes in behavior (such as fewer risky behaviors by clients).

A major gap in performance measurement systems has been the lack of follow-up of events *after* the service has been provided. Major outcomes of human services, education, health, environmental protection, economic development, and international relations programs cannot be assessed until some time has elapsed after the service was provided, such as one or two years. At that time, important indicators of success should be measurable. (Longer-term follow-up can become quite difficult and expensive; it is the province of special studies, not performance measurement systems, which seek more timely information for managing programs.)

New procedures require additional funds and efforts. Bargain-basement procedures are often available for programs that do not require much precision in measured values. However, organizations that are really serious about results-based performance measurement will probably need added resources to collect the new data. It can be argued that feedback on results is a basic element of program management. Any added expenditures should pay off in improved outcomes over the long run. If it becomes clear that this is not happening, the new data collection procedures should be dropped (see chapter 7).

7. **For budgeting purposes, reporting data only once a year may be sufficient; for management purposes, performance data need to be available more frequently.** Data should be collected, analyzed, and reported internally at least on a quarterly basis.

8. **Performance information, particularly on outcomes, will be considerably more useful to all users if the data are broken out by key characteristics.** Breakouts—by geography, by customer demographic characteristics, by organizational units providing the same service, by difficulty of the incoming workload, and by type and magnitude of service—enable users to identify where and under what conditions outcomes appear to be more or less successful. Such breakouts can provide major clues to program personnel about where problems exist; occasionally, they can even indicate particular actions that might be taken. Breakouts by customer characteristics also provide basic information on service equity—often extremely important for service agencies.

Breakouts add considerably to the amount of data generated by the outcome measurement process, so transmitting all of them to higher levels can overload users' capacity (and willingness) to examine the information. Therefore, program reports should highlight key breakout findings, which can be of considerable interest to even the highest levels of government (see chapter 8).

9. **To provide a sense of whether the performance information is good or bad, and to help guide adjustments, outcome information needs to be compared to other data.** Traditionally, the primary benchmark has been the previous year's performance. Other benchmarks should also be used. Comparisons can be made among breakout categories, for example. A government agency or a professional organization might establish a relevant standard, such as on air and water quality, that can be used by other agencies.

   In addition, comparisons can sometimes be made with similar organizations, such as other agencies in other jurisdictions delivering the same service, or in some cases private business organizations. However, comparisons with other organizations are fraught with problems and need to be carefully made to ensure reasonable comparabilty.

   The regular availability of performance information can encourage staff to try out new procedures, by enabling them to obtain information comparing the outcomes of old versus new program approaches.

   A major and increasingly frequent option is to compare actual performance against targets (goals) set by the program at the beginning of each year. It must be kept in mind, however, that selecting such targets is often more of an art than a science and that interpreting comparisons between targets and actual performance takes judgment (see chapter 9).

10. **Programs should be encouraged to provide appropriate explanatory information along with the performance data.** Explanations should be provided when performance on an indicator fell significantly short of or far exceeded a program's expectation. Explanations can be quantitative or qualitative. Elements affecting a program's performance level might be external (for instance, national economic changes or unusual weather conditions) or internal (such as major cutbacks in funding and staff that were not expected at the time targets were established). A classic example of internal factors is adding more responsibilities to a program without providing needed additional resources. Such situations can be alleviated somewhat if the performance measurement process allows programs to adjust their projections of outcomes as well as to provide explanations (see chapters 10 and 12).

11. **Performance information can be of substantial use for budget formulation and justification and for strategic planning**, as well as for ongoing program or policy analysis. Performance measurement infor-

mation provides baseline information and can be used, up to a point, to help project future performance. However, projecting into the future involves a number of quite difficult analytical issues that make it more difficult and uncertain than measuring past performance (see chapters 11 and 12).

12. **A results-based orientation should penetrate to all levels of agency personnel, not just upper level officials and not just managers.** Performance measurement data can and should play a major role in many key management activities, such as employee motivation and performance contracting. Incentives for managers and groups of employees can also be based, at least in part, on performance, as measured by efficiency and outcome indicators. In addition, the performance of contractors and grantees that provide services to customers can and should be assessed to some extent on outcome indicators. Outcome indicators and target values can be included in a variety of ways in performance (incentive) agreements and contracts.

    Basing incentives, especially monetary incentives, on outcome measurement needs to be done with caution. Agencies should recognize that employees will be highly sensitive about the fairness of the process of judging who receives rewards. Pay for performance, if used, should be linked to objective outcomes. Also, as highlighted above, achievement of outcomes should not be used alone to place blame (or credit) on a manager or group. The reasons for good or poor outcomes must also be explored. Employees and public officials need to accept the fact that such compensation schemes will yield rewards that are affected by external factors. If external factors are favorable, employees will receive windfall gains; if external developments are adverse, they will receive windfall losses (see chapter 11).

13. **Program managers should consider using performance reports as a basis for regular "How Are We Doing?" sessions with their personnel.** Such sessions seek to identify where things are going well and should be continued (and possibly expanded elsewhere) and where the program is doing not so well, so that the group can identify actions that might improve outcomes. Any actions taken can be followed up in later reporting periods by an assessment of whether and by how much outcomes have improved (see chapter 11).

14. **In-depth program evaluation and performance measurement should be considered complementary activities.** Program evaluations can likely use data from the performance measurement system as part of formal evaluations. Performance measurement data are useful in selecting the future program evaluation agenda because they identify

areas with outcome problems. Relevant information from completed program evaluations should be included in performance measurement reports. In some instances, it will supersede that obtained from the performance measurement system (see chapter 11).

15. **Few outcomes are affected only by one program, or even by a single agency.** Federal, state, and local governments and private, non-profit agencies often have joint influence over outcomes and have joint roles in service delivery. Each shares responsibility for the outcomes. Some form of performance partnership is highly desirable to determine what performance information should be collected by whom, how it should be analyzed and reported, and who needs to do what to improve the service. Such performance partnerships, while usually difficult and time-consuming, are likely to be a major future direction for public administration.

16. **Training is needed for all involved—program managers, their personnel, and users at all levels, including legislators.** Some training will need to be technical, but most should focus on providing an overall understanding of performance information, its limitations, and its uses. Refresher training and training for new employees should be routine. Training need not be lengthy. Technical assistance is likely to be needed in the early stages of performance measurement system development and in implementing later modifications (see chapter 14).

17. **It is incumbent on the agency and its programs to ensure that the data are of reasonable quality.** Information is power. The right type of information, reasonably accurate, needs to be provided. To ensure that the performance indicators, procedures, and data are reasonably valid and useful, agencies need to establish quality control steps, including periodic audits of the performance measurement system.

    Periodic audits should also be made of the usefulness of the performance measurement process. If not found to be useful, the process should be modified or dropped (see chapter 13).

18. **Agencies need to pay full attention to their performance report presentations.** Presentation can be half the battle! Attractive, clear, user-friendly reports are a necessity for agencies and their programs wanting to encourage interest in performance data. Poorly presented information, no matter how good its quality, will lose much of its power. Do not overwhelm readers with voluminous data. Be selective but in a balanced way. Highlight findings that deviate substantially from expectations (see chapter 10).

19. **Work with the news media to help them understand the data—and what the data tell and do not tell.**

**Steps to Promote the Use of Performance Information**

- Require that outcome information be included as part of *budget proposal justifications*.
- Require *new* programs to identify their objectives, outcomes, indicators, data collection procedures, and breakouts before full implementation.
- Use in training programs. Require each training program to contain at least a brief module on outcomes—not only management training but also training on specific operational topics.
- Require that *contracts* for services include outcome indicators and that appropriate procedures for data collection be established.
- Include a component related to progress on organizational outcomes in annual *performance appraisals of managers*.
- Give managers the positive incentive of more flexibility in the use of funds, contracting authority, and/or personnel authority if they achieve or exceed desired outcomes. Adjust flexibility periodically, based on recent performance (say, over the past two years).
- Use performance measurement findings to help establish the organization's annual program evaluation plan.
- Identify key outcomes and outcome indicators in strategic planning. Provide long-range targets for the key indicators. Use annual performance data to provide the baseline for plans and to assess progress on meeting the targets.
- Translate the performance findings, especially on outcomes, into attractive, readable, and substantive annual reports for the public—the customers of the services provided.

20. **A performance measurement system can be said to be fully implemented when it is taken for granted and its data are used regularly to help make program and policy changes—and to help improve the quality and outcomes of services.** Exhibit 15-1 summarizes a number of key steps to promote the use of results-based performance measurement information.

21. **Finally, it cannot be emphasized enough that the performance measurement process is only one source of information for government managers,** though it is a very important one. All performance information will have uncertainties, in some cases considerable uncertainties. Bad data are worse than no data. However, it is better to be roughly right than precisely ignorant.

When you get right down to it, much of performance measurement is just good old common sense. Its basic principles are hardly rocket science. Doing it right, however, can be a major challenge.

*A millionaire threw a lavish party in a hotel for his business associates and friends. After dinner he took them out to the hotel's swimming pool. Inside the pool was an enormous crocodile. The millionaire said, "I will* *give $1 million to anyone who jumps into this pool and swims to the other end." No one moved. They started walking back into the hotel dining room. They heard a splash. They turned around. There was Joe in the pool, swimming like crazy to the other side. They pulled him out. He was battered and bleeding but in surprisingly good shape. The millionaire ran up to Joe and gave him a check for $1 million. The millionaire said to Joe, "That was the bravest act I have ever seen. Is there anything else I can do for you?" Joe thought for a moment and then said, "Yes, tell me who pushed me."*

Don't blame the author for pushing you into performance measurement. The route to successful measurement is strewn with perils. However, for those who get to the other side with implementation of a good results-based measurement system, the rewards should be great.

# Appendix

# A

# Selected Readings

The list is grouped into four categories: general U.S. literature, basic international works, reprints produced by government agencies (federal, state, or local), and publications relating specifically to the private, nonprofit sector.

## General U.S. Materials

Ammons, David N. 1996. *Municipal Benchmarks: Assessing Local Performance and Establishing Community Standards*. Thousand Oaks, Calif.: Sage Publications.

_____, ed. 1995. *Accountability for Performance: Measurement and Monitoring in Local Government*. Washington, D.C.: International City/County Management Association.

Aristigueta, Maria. 1998. *Managing for Results in State Government*. Westport, Conn.: Quorum Books.

Brizius, Jack A., and Michael D. Campbell. 1991. *Getting Results: A Guide for Government Accountability*. Washington, D.C.: Council of Governors' Policy Advisors.

Carter, Reginald K. 1983. *The Accountable Agency*. Beverly Hills, Calif.: Sage Publications.

Chelimsky, Eleanor. 1997. "The Coming Transformations in Evaluation." *Evaluation for the 21st Century*, edited by Eleanor Chelimsky and William R. Shadish. Thousand Oaks, Calif.: Sage Publications, 1–26.

Epstein, Paul D. 1984. *Using Performance Measurement in Local Government: A Guide to Improving Decisions, Performance, and Accountability*. New York: Van Nostrand Reinhold Company, Inc.

Folz, David H. *Survey for Public Administration*. 1996. Thousand Oaks, Calif.: Sage Publications.

Friedman, Mark. 1997. *A Guide to Developing and Using Performance Measures in Results-Based Budgeting*. Washington, D.C.: The Finance Project.

Fund for the City of New York, Center on Municipal Government Performance. *How Smooth Are New York City's Streets?* 1998. New York: Fund for the City of New York, Center on Municipal Government Performance.

Gormley, William T., and David L. Weimer. 1999. *Organizational Report Cards*. Cambridge, Mass. and London: Harvard University Press.

Greenberg, David H., and Ute Appenzeller. 1998. *Cost Analysis Step by Step: A How to Guide for Planners and Providers of Welfare-to-Work and Other Employment and Training Programs*. New York: Manpower Demonstration Research Corporation.

Greiner, John M., Harry P. Hatry, Margo P. Koss, Annie P. Millar, and Jane P. Woodward. 1981. *Productivity and Motivation: A Review of State and Local Government Initiatives*. Washington, D.C.: Urban Institute Press.

Halachmi, Arie, ed. 1999. *Performance and Quality Measurement in Government*. Burke, Va.: Chatelaine Press.

Halachmi, Arie, and Geert Bouckaert, eds. 1996. *Organizational Performance and Measurement in the Public Sector: Toward Service, Effort and Accomplishment Reporting*. Westport, Conn.: Quorum Books.

Hatry, Harry P., Donald M. Fisk, and Richard E. Winnie. 1981. *Practical Program Evaluation for State and Local Government*, 2nd ed. Washington, D.C.: Urban Institute Press.

Hatry, Harry P., Craig Gerhart, and Martha Marshall. 1994. "Eleven Ways to Make Performance Measurement More Useful to Public Managers." *Public Management* (September).

Hatry, Harry P., Louis Blair, Donald Fisk, and Wayne Kimmel. 1987. *Program Analysis for State and Local Governments*, 2nd ed. Washington, D.C.: Urban Institute Press.

Hatry, Harry P., John E. Marcotte, Thérèse van Houten, and Carol H. Weiss. 1998. *Customer Surveys for Agency Managers: What Managers Need to Know*. Washington, D.C.: Urban Institute Press.

Hatry, Harry P., Louis Blair, Donald M. Fisk, John M. Greiner, John R. Hall, Jr., and Philip S. Schaenman. 1992. *How Effective Are Your Community Services? Procedures for Measuring Their Quality*, 2nd ed. Washington, D.C.: ICMA and the Urban Institute.

Hauser, Robert M., Brett V. Brown, and William R. Prosser, eds. 1997. *Indicators of Children's Well-Being*. New York: Russell Sage Foundation.

International City/County Management Association. *Comparative Performance Measurement: FY 1996 Data Report*. 1997. Washington, D.C.: International City/Council Management Association.

Leithe, Joni L. 1997. *Implementing Performance Measurement in Government: Illustrations and Resources*. Chicago, Ill.: Government Finance Officers Association.

Lichiello, Patricia, Bobbie Berkowitz, Jack Thompson, Aaron Katz, and Edward B. Perrin. 1998. *Enabling Performance Measurement Activities in the States and Communities*. Seattle: Northwest Prevention Effectiveness Center and the Health Policy Analysis Program, University of Washington.

Liner, E. Blaine, Harry P. Hatry, and Shelli Rossman. 1994. *Measuring Progress of Estuary Programs*. Washington, D.C.: U.S. Environmental Protection Agency, Office of Water, EPA 842-B-94-008 and 94-009.

Lipsey, Mark W. 1993. "Theory as Method." In *New Directions for Program Evaluation*, no. 57. San Francisco: Jossey-Bass Publishers, 5–38.

_____. 1998. "Unsolved Mysteries and Methodological Quandaries." Paper prepared for the Washington Evaluators Conference, George Washington University, Washington, D.C., March 7.

Magura, Steven, and Beth Silverman Moses. 1986. *Outcome Measures of Child Welfare Services: Theory and Applications*. Washington, D.C.: Child Welfare League of America, Inc.

Martin, Lawrence L., and Peter M. Kettner. 1996. *Measuring the Performance of Human Service Programs*. Thousand Oaks, Calif.: Sage Publications.

Millar, Rhona, and Annie Millar, eds. 1981. *Developing Client Outcome Monitoring Systems: A Guide for State and Local Social Services Agencies*. Washington, D.C.: Urban Institute Press.

Mullen, Edward J., and Jennifer L. Magnabosco, eds. 1997. *Outcomes Measurement in the Human Services*. Washington, D.C.: National Association of Social Workers.

National Academy of Public Administration. *Effective Implementation of the Government Performance and Results Act: A Study by the Panel on Improving Government Performance*. 1998. Washington, D.C.: National Academy of Public Administration.

National Advisory Council on State and Local Budgeting. 1998. *Recommended Budget Practices: A Framework for Improved State and Local Government Budgeting*. Chicago, Ill.: Government Finance Officers Association.

Naumann, Earl, and Kathleen Giel. 1995. *Customer Satisfaction Measurement and Management*. Cincinnati, Ohio: Thomson Executive Press.

Norquist, John O. 1998. *The Wealth of Cities: Revitalizing the Centers of American Life*. Reading, Mass.: Addison-Wesley.

Phillips, William R., Bonnie L. Brown, C. Morgan Kinghorn, and Andrew C. West. 1997. *Public Dollars, Common Sense: New Roles for Financial Managers*. Washington, D.C.: Coopers and Lybrand.

Rossi, Peter H., and Howard E. Freeman. 1993. *Evaluation: A Systematic Approach*, 5th ed. Newbury Park, Calif.: Sage Publications, Inc.

Stokey, Edith, and Richard Zeckhauser. 1978. *A Primer for Policy Analysis*. New York and London: Kennedy School of Government, Harvard University.

Tigue, Patricia, and Dennis Strachota. 1994. *The Use of Performance Measures in City and County Budgets, Research Report*. Chicago, Ill.: Government Finance Officers Association.

Walters, Jonathan. 1998. *Measuring Up: Governing's Guide to Performance Measurement for Geniuses and Other Public Managers*. Washington, D.C.: Governing Books.

Wholey, Joseph S. 1979. *Evaluation: Promise and Performance*. Washington, D.C.: Urban Institute.

_____. 1983. *Evaluation and Effective Public Management*. Boston: Little, Brown.

Wholey, Joseph S., Harry P. Hatry, and Kathryn Newcomer, eds. 1994. *Handbook of Practical Program Evaluation*. San Francisco, Calif.: Jossey-Bass Publishers.

Wye, Christopher G., and Harry P. Hatry, eds. 1988. *Timely, Low-Cost Evaluation in the Public Sector*. New Directions for Program Evaluation Series, no. 38. San Francisco, Calif.: Jossey-Bass Publishers.

# Government Materials

Austin, Texas, City of. 1999. *Citizens Prioritizing City Services: 1999 Citizen Survey Results.* Austin, April.

Centers for Disease Control and Prevention. 1998. "Youth Risk Behavior Surveillance—United States, 1997." *Morbidity and Mortality Weekly Report,* 14 August.

Hatry, Harry P., and Mary Kopczynski. 1998. *Guide to Program Outcome Measurement for the U.S. Department of Education.* Washington, D.C.: U.S. Department of Education, Planning and Evaluation Service.

Hawaii, State of. Auditor. 1994. *Sunset Evaluation Update: Nurses—A Report to the Governor and the Legislature of the State of Hawaii.* Honolulu, October 13.

Kowalewski, Rick. 1996. *Using Outcome Information to Redirect Programs: A Case of the Coast Guard's Pilot Project under the Government Performance and Results Act.* American Society for Public Administration Case Study F3. Washington, D.C.: American Society for Public Administration, April.

Legislative Budget Board, Texas Governor's Office of Budget and Planning. 1996. *Detailed Instructions for Preparing and Submitting Requests for Legislative Appropriations for the Biennium Beginning September 1, 1997—Executive and Administrative Agencies.* Austin, April.

_____. 1998. *Instructions for Preparing and Submitting Agency Strategic Plans: Fiscal Years 1999–2003.* Austin, January.

_____. 1998. *Planning for "Texas Tomorrow": Instructions for Preparing and Submitting Agency Strategic Plans for Fiscal Year 1999–2000.* Austin, January.

National Highway Traffic Safety Administration. 1995. *GPRA FY 1996 Performance Plan.* Washington, D.C.

_____. 1996. *Strategic Planning and Performance Measurement.* Washington, D.C.: American Society for Public Administration.

New York, City of. Office of Operations. *Mayor's Management Report,* for various fiscal years.

Office of National Drug Control Policy. 1998. *Performance Measures of Effectiveness: A System for Assessing the Performance of the National Drug Control Strategy.* Report no. NCJ 168953. Washington, D.C.

_____. 1999. *Performance Measures of Effectiveness: Implementation and Findings.* Report no. NCJ 174462. Washington, D.C.

Perrin, Edward B., and Jeffrey J. Koshel, eds. 1997. *Assessment of Performance Measures for Public Health, Substance Abuse, and Mental Health.* Washington, D.C.: National Research Council, National Academy Press.

Portland, Oregon, City of. Office of the City Auditor. 1998. *City of Portland Service Efforts and Accomplishments: 1996–97.* Portland, April.

Savannah, City of. 1996. *Neighborhood Quality Benchmarks: 1996 Report to the Community.* Savannah, Ga.

State of Minnesota Planning. 1999. *1999 Children's Report Card.* St. Paul, Minn.

Sustainable Seattle. 1998. *Indicators of Sustainable Community: A Status Report on Long-Term Cultural, Economic, and Environmental Health for Seattle/King County.* Seattle, Wash.: Sustainable Seattle.

U.S. Congress. Senate. Community on Governmental Affairs. 1993. *Government Performance and Results Act of 1993.* 103rd Cong., 1st sess. Report 103-58.

U.S. Department of Education. 1999. *FY 2000 Annual Plan.* Washington, D.C.

U.S. Department of Health and Human Services. Office of the Inspector General. 1994. *Practical Evaluation for Public Managers: Getting the Information You Need.* Washington, D.C.

_____. 1990. *Technical Assistance Guides for Conducting Program Evaluations and Inspections.* Office of the Inspector General. Office of Evaluation and Inspections. Washington, D.C., September.

U.S. Department of Housing and Urban Development. 1997. *Mapping Your Community: Using Geographic Information to Strengthen Community Initiatives.* Washington, D.C.

U.S. Department of Justice. Justice Management Division. 1995. *DOJ Manager's Handbook on Developing Useful Performance Indicators: Version 1.1, Managing for Results.* Washington, D.C., April.

U.S. Environmental Protection Agency. 1996. *Use of Performance Information in the Chesapeake Bay Program.* Washington, D.C.: American Society for Public Administration.

U.S. General Accounting Office. 1988. *Government Auditing Standards.* Washington, D.C.

_____. 1992. *Quantitative Data Analysis: An Introduction.* Washington, D.C.

_____. 1992. *Using Statistical Sampling.* Washington, D.C.

_____. 1993. *Developing and Using Questionnaires.* Washington, D.C.

_____. 1994. *Government Auditing Standards, 1994 Revision.* Washington, D.C.

_____. 1996. *Executive Guide: Effectively Implementing the Government Performance and Results Act.* Washington, D.C.

_____. 1996. *Motor Vehicle Safety: Comprehensive State Programs Offer Best Opportunity for Increasing Use of Safety Belts.* Washington, D.C.

_____. 1997. *The Government Performance and Results Act: 1997 Government-Wide Implementation Will Be Uneven.* Washington, D.C.

_____. 1998. *Agencies' Annual Performance Plans under the Results Act: An Assessment Guide to Facilitate Congressional Decision-Making, Version One.* Washington, D.C.

_____. 1998. *Managing for Results: Agencies' Annual Performance Plans Can Help Address Strategic Planning Challenges.* Washington, D.C.

_____. 1998. *Performance Budgeting: Past Initiatives Offer Insights for GPRA Implementation.* Washington, D.C.

_____. 1998. *Program Evaluation: Agencies Challenged by New Demand for Information on Program Results.* Washington, D.C.

_____. 1998. *The Results Act: An Evaluator's Guide to Assessing Agency Annual Performance Plans, Version One.* Washington, D.C.

Washington Suburban Sanitary Commission. 1999. *WSSC's Proposed FY '00 Budget: Performance and Outcome Measures.* Laurel, Md.

## International Materials

Auditor General of Canada. 1997. *Moving toward Managing for Results: Report of the Auditor General of Canada to the House of Commons.* Ottawa: Minister of Public Works and Services, chapter 11.

Canadian Comprehensive Auditing Foundation. 1987. *Effectiveness: Reporting and Auditing in the Public Sector.* Ottawa: Canadian Comprehensive Auditing Foundation.

Communications and Coordination Directorate, Treasury Board of Canada, Office of the Comptroller General, Evaluation and Audit Branch. *Your Guide to Measuring Client Satisfaction.* 1992. Ottawa.

Government of Costa Rica and the World Bank. 1996. *Guidelines for Drafting Compromiso de Resultados.* San Jose, Costa Rica: Government of Costa Rica and the Work Bank, February 2.

Mayne, John, and Eduardo Zapico-Goni, eds. 1997. *Monitoring Performance in the Public Sector: Future Directions from International Experience.* New Brunswick, N.J.: Transaction Publishers.

Organization for Economic Cooperation and Development. 1997. *In Search of Results: Performance Management Practices.* Paris: Organization for Economic Cooperation and Development.

Radin, Beryl A. 1997. "Performance-Based Management and Its Training Implications." Paper prepared for the International Symposium on Performance-Based Management and Its Training Implications, Caserta, Italy, September 24–26.

Schick, Allen. 1996. *The Spirit of Reform: Managing the New Zealand State Sector in a Time of Change.* Wellington: State Services Commission.

Trosa, Sylvie. 1997. "Public Sector Reform Strategy: A Giant Leap or a Small Step?" In *Monitoring Performance in the Public Sector: Future Directions for International Experience,* edited by John Mayne and Eduardo Zapico-Goni. New Burnswick, N.J.: Transaction Publishers.

The Treasury, Government of New Zealand. 1995. *Purchase Agreement Guidelines 1996/96: With Best Practices for Output Performance Measures.* Wellington: The Treasury, Government of New Zealand, April.

The World Bank, The International Bank for Reconstruction and Development. 1998. *Public Expenditure Management Handbook.* Washington, D.C.: The World Bank, The International Bank for Reconstruction and Development.

The World Bank Operations Policy Department. 1996. *Performance Monitoring Indicators: A Handbook for Task Managers.* Washington, D.C.: The World Bank Operations Policy Department.

## Private, Nonprofit Publications

American Nurses Association. 1996. *Nursing Quality Indicators: Definitions and Implications.* Washington, D.C.: American Nurses Association.

_____. 1996. *Nursing Quality Indicators: Guide for Implementation.* Washington, D.C.: American Nurses Association.

Greenway, Martha Taylor, and Harry P. Hatry. 1996. *Focusing on Program Outcomes: Summary Guide.* Alexandria, Va.: United Way of America.

Hatry, Harry P., Thérèse van Houten, Meg Plantz, and Martha Taylor Greenway. 1996. *Measuring Program Outcomes: A Practical Approach.* Alexandria, Va.: United Way of America.

United Way for the Greater New Orleans Area. 1995. *Service Effectiveness Assessment Manual.* New Orleans, La.: United Way of the Greater New Orleans Area.

United Way of America. 1997. *Workbook from United Way of America's Forum on Outcomes II*. Alexandria, Va.: United Way of America, December 3.

The United Way Outcomes Project. 1998. *Lessons Learned III: Using Outcome Data*. Milwaukee, Wis.: The United Way of Greater Milwaukee, December.

# Appendix B

# Sample Star Schools Teacher Survey*

1. How long have you been teaching? Please check one.
   ___ Less than 1 year
   ___ At least 1 year, but less than 2 years
   ___ At least 2 years, but less than 4 years
   ___ At least 4 years, but less than 6 years
   ___ More than 6 years

2. What subject areas did you teach this past school year in which you used or attempted to use distance learning? Please check all that apply.
   ___ English/language arts
   ___ Math
   ___ Science
   ___ Social Studies
   ___ History
   ___ Geography
   ___ Other (please specify) _____

3. What grade levels did you teach using distance learning this past school year? Please circle all that apply.
   Pre-K  K  1  2  3  4  5  6  7  8  9  10  11  12

*Many items in this instrument are based on a survey of classroom coordinators designed by the Pacific Star Schools Partnership/ESD 101-STEP Star Program of Educational Service District, Spokane, Washington.

4. How long have you been a [insert appropriate local name for distance learning effort] teacher? Please check one.

___ Less than 1 year

___ At least 1 year, but less than 2 years

___ At least 2 years, but less than 4 years

___ At least 4 years, but less than 6 years

___ More than 6 years

5. Approximately how many hours did you use [insert appropriate local name for distance learning effort] distance learning materials over this past year in your courses? Please check one.

___ 1 to 5 hours

___ 6 to 10 hours

___ 11 to 15 hours

___ 16 to 20 hours

___ 21 or more hours

6. How would you rate the effectiveness of the [insert appropriate local name for distance learning effort] learning materials (e.g., workbooks, hands-on kits, electronic field trips, videotapes, homework assignments) provided to students? Please circle a number on the following scale.

Very effective    5    4    3    2    1    Not effective

7. For the past school year, how satisfied were you with the *instructional support materials* which [insert appropriate local name for distance learning effort] provided to you. Please circle the number on the five-point scale that best applies for each of the dimensions shown below.

| | Very satisfied | | | | Not satisfied |
|---|---|---|---|---|---|
| a. Understandability | 5 | 4 | 3 | 2 | 1 |
| b. Helpfulness | 5 | 4 | 3 | 2 | 1 |
| c. Adequacy/Completeness | 5 | 4 | 3 | 2 | 1 |

8. Was the distance learning *equipment* provided to your school (please check one for each item):

a. Made available in a timely manner? ___ Yes ___ No ___ Not sure

b. Working properly? ___ Yes ___ No ___ Not sure

c. Adequate for its purposes? ___ Yes ___ No ___ Not sure

If you checked "no" to any of the above, please describe the problem.

9. During the past school year, have you made any significant improvements in your teaching practices because of the [insert appropriate local name for distance learning effort] program?
\_\_\_ Yes     \_\_\_ No

If "yes," please briefly describe the improvement practice(s) below.

10. Overall, how would you rate the helpfulness of [insert appropriate local name of distance learning effort] to you in your teaching? Please check one.
\_\_\_ Not at all helpful
\_\_\_ A little helpful
\_\_\_ Somewhat helpful
\_\_\_ Considerably helpful

11. To what extent do you believe your students were able to improve their learning because of the use of [insert appropriate local name for distance learning effort]? Please check one.
\_\_\_ Not at all
\_\_\_ A little
\_\_\_ Somewhat
\_\_\_ Considerably

12. To what extent do you believe that at least in part because of distance learning activities your students (Circle the appropriate number for each response):

|  | Not at all | A little | Some-what | Consid-erably |
|---|---|---|---|---|
| a. Had increased interest in the subject area | 1 | 2 | 3 | 4 |
| b. Increased their attendance | 1 | 2 | 3 | 4 |
| c. Improved critical thinking and problem solving | 1 | 2 | 3 | 4 |

13. a. During the past school year, did you participate in any professional development activities?

    ___ Yes    ___ No

b. If "yes," were any of the professional development activities conducted by distance delivery media (e.g., telecast, teleconference, the Internet)?

    ___ Yes    ___ No

c. If "yes," how would you rate the following characteristics of the distance learning media used in these professional development activities? Please circle a number on the following scale.

|  | Very good |  |  |  | Very poor |
|---|---|---|---|---|---|
| a. Understandability | 5 | 4 | 3 | 2 | 1 |
| b. Relevance | 5 | 4 | 3 | 2 | 1 |
| c. Overall effectiveness | 5 | 4 | 3 | 2 | 1 |

If you circled "1" or "2" for any characteristic, please describe the problems you saw.

14. What suggestions do you have for improving the [insert appropriate name for local distance learning effort] in the future?

**THANK YOU!**

# Appendix C

# Sample Star Schools Student Survey*

## I. Background Information

1. What is your current grade?

2. In what subject areas during the past school year did you have the opportunity to use distance learning materials and equipment? (Please check all that apply.)
   ___ English/language arts
   ___ Math
   ___ Science
   ___ Social studies
   ___ History
   ___ Geography
   ___ Other (please specify) _____

3. Was this your first experience with distance learning?     ___ Yes     ___ No

   If "no," how many previous classes have you taken in which distance learning was used?

4. Which of the following best describes the type of distance learning activity in which you participated during the past school year?
   a. Full course
   b. Curriculum module
   c. Field trip or teleconference (single event)
   d. Computer networking
   e. Did not participate in distance learning this year

*In these questions, substitute for "distance learning" any terms that you believe to be clearer to students in the school.

## II. Distance Learning Courses and Activities

5. Approximately how many hours per week did you spend on distance learning activities for each of the following items:
   a. Classroom activities? _____hours per week
   b. Homework assignments? _____hours per week

6. To what extent do you think that the Star Schools activities added significantly to the quality of the course?
   ___ Not at all
   ___ A little
   ___ Somewhat
   ___ Considerably

7. To what extent were you able to apply the information learned or acquired through distance learning to your other courses, activities, or interests?
   ___ Not at all
   ___ A little
   ___ Somewhat
   ___ Considerably

8. Do you think distance learning courses (or courses that use distance learning activities) are better than courses not using distance learning methods?
   ___ They were considerably worse
   ___ They were somewhat worse
   ___ They were somewhat better
   ___ They were considerably better
   ___ Not sure

   Please tell us why.

9. Do you feel that your participation in distance learning courses or activities affected your interest in the subjects where the technology was used?
   ___ Increased my interest considerably
   ___ Increased my interest somewhat
   ___ No effect

___ Decreased my interest somewhat
___ Decreased my interest considerably

Please tell us why.

10. Would you take another distance learning class or participate in future distance learning activities?
___ Yes   ___ No   ___ Not sure

Why or why not?

## III. Distance Learning Equipment and Media

11. To what extent was the distance learning equipment *available* in your school?
___ Always or almost always available
___ Usually available
___ Usually unavailable
___ Always or almost always unavailable

12. To what extent was the distance learning equipment *working properly* in your school?
___ Always or almost always working properly
___ Usually working properly
___ Usually not working properly
___ Always or almost always not working properly

13. Was assistance made available on how to use the equipment?
___ Yes   ___ No

14. How would you rate the usefulness of the distance learning materials (e.g., workbooks, hands-on kits, electronic field trips, videotapes, homework assignments) used in your course or distance learning activity?
   a. No materials used
   b. Not at all useful
   c. A little useful
   d. Somewhat useful
   e. Very useful

**THANK YOU!**

# Index

## A

accountability, 5, 225
  elected officials' and public's demands for, 158, 159
  of managers, 164–165
activities, 13–14. *See also* workload
  determining which to include, 28–29
agency employees, role of, 9
agency priorities, changes in, 243
agency records, as data source, 73–75
aggregate targets, 129, 193–194
aggregation, 144–145
  need for, 247–248
allocative efficiency, 19
"archival data," 99n.2
attendance counts, 99n.5
auditing, performance, xiii–xiv, 174, 229
  performance measurement and, 8
auditors, 237–238

## B

bar charts, 148–152
baselines, 9, 158, 167, 175, 212, 259, 261. *See also* benchmarks/comparisons
benchmarks/comparisons, types of
  different service delivery practices, 124–127
  outcomes for different workload or customer groups, 121–122
  performance in previous period, 120–121
  performance of other jurisdictions or private sector, 123–125, 129
  performance of similar organizational units or geographical areas, 121
  recognized general standard, 122–123
  targets established at start of performance period, 128–130
bias, 221
breakout characteristics, special, 116
breakout data, reporting, 154
breakouts/disaggregation, 257
  by individual staff members, 116
  need for, 103–105
  procedures for choosing, 117–118
  types/categories of, 104, 116
    by difficulty of workload, 109, 111–113
    by geographical location, 108–111
    by organizational unit or project, 105–107, 135–136

by reason for outcome or rating, 115–116
by type and amount of service, 113–115
by workload or customer characteristics, 106–108
budget allocation decisions, 212
budget proposals, justifying, 3–4
budget requests, steps for examining performance information in, 197–207
budgeting, 179, 208, 258
based on outcomes *vs.* outputs, 183–184
performance measurement and, 8–9
"budgeting-by-objectives," 209

## C

comparative outcome indicator data, 123–124, 126–127
comparison-group design, 144
comparison period, 120–121
complaint data, 75–76
compliance outcomes, 203
compliance perspective, 16
comprehensiveness of indicators, 58
condition rating, 89
confidentiality, 67, 75, 97
contractors. *See* performance contracting
control. *See* influence/control
control limits, 137
cost-benefit analysis, 210–211
cost-effectiveness analysis, 209–210
costs, 6
assessing, 6
of data collection, 58, 84–86, 96, 98, 105
of performance measurement systems, 218, 242–243
credibility, 96
customer complaint data, 75–76

customer feedback, 98, 176. *See also* customer surveys
customer participation, 22–23, 141
customer satisfaction, 23, 75, 79
customer survey questionnaires, examples of, 78–82
customer surveys, 75–76, 105, 140–141
advantages and disadvantages, 76, 256
content, 77, 140
design and administration, 84
administration methods, 81–84
trained observer procedures, 86–90, 92–93
ways to reduce costs, 84–86
elements to include in contracts for, 84, 85
household *vs.* user surveys, 77–78
information obtainable from, 76
multiple uses, 80
seeking information on citizen participation rates, 141
customers, 41n.3, 106. *See also* difficulty; focus groups
identifying categories of, 38–40
programs with anonymous, 67
who are businesses, 107

## D

data, missing, 97
data collection
frequency, 97–98
potential problems in, 97
data collection procedures, 64. *See also specific procedures*
pilot testing, 96–97
selecting appropriate, 96
data quality control, 137, 260
data reporting. *See* reporting
data sources, 64. *See also specific sources*

selecting appropriate, 96
demand, 20
demographics, 20–21, 148, 149
difficulty, workload/customer/ client, 109, 111–113, 121–122, 128
reporting outcomes by, 148
disaggregation. *See* breakouts/ disaggregation

## E

effectiveness, meaning of, 24n.2
efficiency, 19–20, 60
defined, 6, 13, 18
measurement
outcome-based, 6, 190–191
output-based, 6, 190
efficiency indicators, 60, 190–191
efficiency ratios, 20
eligibility determinations, procedures for processing, 126–127
emergency response programs, 68
end-outcome-based focus, 16
end outcomes, 18, 19, 200–202
defined, 13, 18
intermediate outcomes and, 15–17, 19, 80, 140, 256
in sample programs, 48–52, 61–63, 66, 235
linking inputs to, 188–189
short- and long-term, 18
equity, 4
evaluability assessment, xiv
exception reporting, 137–138
experimentation, 127
explanatory information, 21, 138–139, 152–153, 196–197, 202, 258

## F

family services program, 105, 107
focus group steps, 46
focus groups, 45

## G

gaming targets, 194–195
geographical breakouts, 108–111
geographical location, reporting outcomes by, 146–147, 152
goals, 227–229, 231. *See also* targets
government, participation by various levels of, 246–247
government managers, sources of information for, 261
Government Performance and Results Act (GRPA), xv, 182, 218
grantees. *See* performance contracting

## H

household surveys, 77–78
human services program, logic model for, 23, 24

## I

impact, 24n.6
improvements. *See* program improvements
incentives, 41, 161–162, 259
monetary, 161, 165–169, 259
negative, 168, 169
nonmonetary, 161–165
"incubator" approach, 243
indicator breakouts. *See* breakouts
indicator data, comparative outcome, 123–124, 126–127
indicator definitions, 55
indicator specification sheet, 244–245
indicator stability over time, maintaining, 243–244
indicators, 24n.1, 55–58, 197
consistency of data across, 139–140, 143
constructing, to help identify causes, 69–70
defined, 13

examining a set of, 142–143
identifying overarching, 207
need to be clear about time covered by, 57
numerical forms, 60, 63–64
providing for qualitative outcomes, 69–70
reliability and validity, 223
selection of
criteria for, 58
factors affecting, 64–65
use of special equipment to collect data for, 94–95
using outcome-sequence charts to identify, 58–63
influence/control, level of, 19, 58, 70, 137, 197
information. *See* performance information
innovation, type and amount of service used to encourage, 114–115
input information, 12–13
inputs, 12–13, 45–47
defined, 12, 13
linking to expected future results, 186–190
intermediate outcomes, 15–17, 19, 22, 23, 200–202
defined, 13, 19
linking inputs to, 187–188
internal support activities and services, 79
applying results-based budgeting to, 207–208

## J

Job Training Partnership Act (JTPA), 122–123

## L

legislating performance measurement, 179
legislation, 41, 134, 139, 152
legislative priorities, changes in, 243

legislative support, 249–250
legislators, need for training, 260
line graphs, 148, 150
logic models/outcome sequence charts, 23, 24, 48–53
used to identify outcomes and indicators, 58–63

## M

mail surveys, 81–82
ways to increase response to, 83
management practices, performance-based, 225
managers
fear and resistance from, 245–246
flexibility and accountability given to, 164–165
guidelines for, 7, 237–238
importance of performance information for, 3–4
managing-for-results, 6–7, 225, 242
manipulability of indicators, 58
maps, 152
measure, meaning of, 24n.1
measurement. *See also specific types of measurement*
taken at different points in time, 64
media, 167–168, 260
meetings, 45
mission/objectives statement, 35–38, 40. *See also* program mission(s)/objectives
sources of information on, 38
suggestions for developing a, 36–37
motivational programs, interagency model for, 169–171

## N

negative/side/unintended effects, 15

normalization procedures, 123

## O

objectives. *See* program mission(s)/objectives

organizational units
  breakouts and, 105–107, 135–136
  reporting outcomes by, 148

outcome-based performance contracting, 171–174

outcome-focused efficiency measurement, 6

outcome-focused measurement systems, xiv

outcome indicators. *See* indicators

outcome information, need for comparison to other data, 258

outcome measurement process, documentation of, 244–245

outcome tracking, 4, 6, 255–257

outcome values, normalizing, 123

outcome(s), 14–15. *See also* end outcomes; intermediate outcomes
  accountability for, 5, 158, 159, 164–165, 225
  aggregation across projects, programs, or sites, 247–248
  applying to a small number of events, 67–68
  assessing a program's influence on individual, 70
  categories of, 44
  combining candidate, 53
  communitywide vs. program-specific, 247–248
  compliance, 203
  defined, 13, 15

difficult-to-measure, 65–69
distinguishing between outputs and, 256
early occurrence, 19
focusing on types of workload, 107
information sources for, 44
linking outputs to, 189–190
presence of different aspects of an, 64
procedure for identifying, 47
responsibility for, 5
societal, 24n.6
that cannot be measured (directly), 5, 53
types of, 13, 15–18

outputs, 14–15
  defined, 13–15
  linking inputs to, 186–187. *See also* efficiency

## P

participation, customer/citizen, 22–23, 141

"partners," input from, 45–47

pass-through programs, problem for, 41

pay, linked to performance, 165. *See also* incentives, monetary

payment schedules, performance, 173

performance
  incentives for improving. *See* incentives
  monetary sanctions for prolonged low, 168
  past
    considered when determining targets, 129, 163, 171
    data on, 120–121, 143–144, 184
    explanatory information on, 196–197

performance agreements, between central officials and agency heads, 165

performance contracting, 170–172
  examples of, 172–173
  issues in considering, 173–174

performance data
  avoiding misunderstanding of, 158, 159
  limitations, 132, 177
  *vs.* outcome, 5
  procedures for analyzing, 132–133, 139–140, 145
    comparing outcomes to similar programs' outcomes, 137
    examining changes over time, 133–134
    examining multiple outcomes together, 142–143
    examining outcome breakouts, 135–137
    focusing individual outcome indicators, 140–142
    obtaining and explaining explanatory information, 138–139
    using exception reporting, 137–138
    using past data to trigger trials of new procedures, 143–144
    when outcome data comes from many sources, 144–145
  reporting of. *See* reporting
  uses, 131–132

performance data strategies, strengthening the quality of, 224

performance indicators. *See* indicators

program records, as data source, 73–74

program stability, 28

programs. *See also specific topics*
  assessing the fairness of, 4
  broader impact of circumscribed, 68
  improving public confidence in, 176–177

## Q

quality, criteria for assessing, 218–226

quality control, 217–239, 260
  statistical, 137

questionnaires. *See* customer survey questionnaires

## R

rating scales, 88–90

ratings, asking for explanations of positive, 99n.4

recognition awards, 162–163

regulatory programs, 67, 203

reporting, 145–146
  content, 152–153, 258
    providing highlights, 152–153
  formats, 146–152
  frequency, 97–98, 120
  suggestions for external, 153–155
  when performance news is bad, 153

requests for proposals (RFPs), 170

research activities, 67

resource allocation decisions, 159–160, 212, 225–226

response times for service requests, 23

responsibility, shared, 5

results-based budgeting, 179–181
  history regarding, 181–183
  key issues in, 183–184, 197–207, 209
    applications, 197, 207–208

linking inputs to outputs and outcomes, 186–190

program influence over future outcomes, 197

role of efficiency indicators, 190–191

setting performance targets, 192–196

time frame to be covered, 184–185

use of explanatory information, 196–197

use of special analytical techniques, 209–211

value of performance measurement, 184

relationship between performance measurement and, 212–213

results-based orientation, 259

results-based performance measurement, xv, 180

results-oriented organizations, 220

risk factors, 67

role-playing by program staff, 47

## S

service quality characteristics, 17, 141–142

side effects. *See* negative/side/ unintended effects

strategic planning, 8–9, 175–176, 258–259

support services, internal, 68–69

surveys. *See* customer surveys

## T

target range option, 194

target ranges, 137

targets. *See also* goals
  vs. actual outcomes, 146
  vs. actual values, 146, 147
  aggregate, 129, 193–194
  in contracts and grant agreements, 170–171
  numerical, 41n.2

reporting, and liability for failing to achieve, 196

target setting, 128–130, 163, 192–196

technical efficiency, 19

telephone surveys, 82

tracking expenditures and outputs, 4

trained observer procedures, 86–90, 92–93

trained observer process, implementing, 90, 93

trained observer ratings
  advantages and disadvantages, 87–88
  automating, 93

trained observers, types of rating systems used by, 88–90

training needs, 241–242, 260

## U

uncertainties, 135–136, 184, 186, 259

unit-cost ratio. *See* efficiency

unit-costs, 191

Urban Institute, xiv–xvi, 28

user surveys, 77–78

## V

value-for-money auditing, xiv

variable target option, 192–193

visual rating scales, 90, 93

## W

working group meetings, sample agendas for, 31

working groups, 29–30, 33
  key steps for, 30

workload, 13–14, 114, 115, 200–202, 207. *See also* activities

workload characteristics, 20–21

workload difficulty breakouts, 106–109, 111–113. *See also* difficulty

# About the Author

Harry Hatry is a principal research associate at the Urban Institute in Washington, D.C., where he is the director of the Institute's Public Management Program. Since the early 1970s, he has been a leader in developing procedures that allow nonprofit organizations and federal, state, and local government agencies to track how well they are performing their services—including social, education, mental health, economic development, sanitation, parks and recreation, transportation, police, fire, corrections, and environmental protection services. In recent years, he has also worked to improve performance measurement and management in other countries, including Thailand and Hungary.

He has authored or co-authored numerous books, reports, and articles describing performance measurement procedures, including publications for the U.S. Departments of Education and Justice, the International City/County Management Association, and United Way of America. Key works in which he has been an author include *How Effective Are Your Community Services? Procedures for Measuring Their Quality*; *The Guide to Program Outcome Monitoring for the U.S. Department of Education*; *Measuring Program Outcomes: A Practical Approach* (for United Way of America); *Service Efforts and Accomplishment Reporting: Its Time Has Come—An Overview* (for the Governmental Accounting Standards

Board); *Practical Program Evaluation for State and Local Governments*; and *Program Analysis for State and Local Governments.*

He has received awards relating to his work in performance measurement and evaluation from a number of organizations, including the American Society for Public Administration and the National Academy of Public Administration.